GAME DEVELOPMENT ESSENTIALS

GAME SIMULATION DEVELOPMENT

William Muehl

Jeannie Novak

THOMSON

DELMAR LEARNING

Australia   Canada   Mexico   Singapore   Spain   United Kingdom   United St

THOMSON

DELMAR LEARNING

Game Development Essentials: Game Simulation Development

William Muehl & Jeannie Novak

Vice President, Technology and Trades ABU:
David Garza

Director of Learning Solutions:
Sandy Clark

Managing Editor:
Larry Main

Acquisitions Editor:
James Gish

Product Manager:
Sharon Chambliss

Marketing Director
Deborah Yarnell

Marketing Specialist:
Victoria Ortiz

Director of Production:
Patty Stephan

Production Manager:
Stacy Masucci

Content Project Manager:
Michael Tubbert

Technology Project Manager:
Kevin Smith

Editorial Assistant:
Sarah Timm

Cover: *Spore* courtesy of Electronic Arts, Inc.

Library of Congress Cataloging-in-Publication Data has been applied for.

ISBN-13: 978-1-4180-3857-1
ISBN-10: 1-4180-3857-1

NOTICE TO THE READER

CONTENTS

Chapter 5   Military:
virtual soldiers on a simulated battlefield 97

Part III: Entertainment & the Future 131

Chapter 6   Sports: bringing the action into the living room 133

Chapter 7 Creative Arts: tools that challenge and inspire 163

Introduction

Game Simulation Development:
re-creating reality

Although electronic games have traditionally been associated with entertainment applications, simulation elements have always been present. (Consider the first blocky representations of tennis balls and rackets in *Pong!*) In the years since the first rudimentary graphics appeared onscreen, advances in hardware, software, design, and development techniques have made games a powerful avenue for the development of simulations for industries that would otherwise seem far removed from an entertainment-based medium.

Attendance at conferences dedicated to game-based simulations, such as the Serious Games Summit, is increasing—and both funding and media attention continue to grow in this segment of the industry, as companies and government agencies learn to leverage the tools and techniques honed over the years by game developers. Opportunities for careers in game simulation development in business, government, healthcare, and education are expanding rapidly—and many colleges and universities are starting to offer concentrations and degree programs in game simulation development in response to the demand.

Simulation innovation in the game industry continues to evolve rapidly. In 2007, Sony and Nintendo announced new products (PlayStation Home and the Wii Fit board, respectively) that expand the reach of virtual environments and simulation input devices. As the industry continues its relentless push forward, the relationship between entertainment and simulation aspects of game development will remain symbiotic; each needs the other to become more effective at drawing players in to engaging virtual experiences.

William Muehl   Jeannie Novak
Chicago, IL   Santa Monica, CA

About the *Game Development Essentials* Series

The *Game Development Essentials* series was created to fulfill a need: to provide students and creative professionals alike with a complete education in all aspects of the game industry. As more creative professionals migrate to the game industry, and as more game degree and certificate programs are launched, the books in this series will become even more essential to game education and career development.

Not limited to the education market, this series is also appropriate for the trade market and for those who have a general interest in the game industry. Books in the series contain several unique features. All are in full-color and contain hundreds of images—including original illustrations, diagrams, game screenshots, and photos of industry professionals. They also contain a great deal of profiles, tips and case studies from professionals in the industry who are actively developing games. Starting with an overview of all aspects of the industry—*Game Development Essentials: An Introduction*—this series focuses on topics as varied as story & character development, interface design, artificial intelligence, gameplay mechanics, level design, online game development, simulation development, and audio.

Jeannie Novak
Lead Author & Series Editor

About *Game Development Essentials: Game Simulation Development*

This book provides an overview of game simulation development—complete with historical background, audience, applications, and future predictions.

This book contains the following unique features:

- Key chapter questions that are clearly stated at the beginning of each chapter
- Coverage that surveys the topics of simulation development concepts, techniques, market, serious games, and entertainment applications
- Thought-provoking review and study questions at the end of each chapter that are suitable for students and professionals alike to help promote critical thinking and problem-solving skills
- Case studies, quotations from leading professionals, and profiles of game developers that feature concise tips and problem-solving exercises to help readers focus in on issues specific to game simulation development
- An abundance of full-color images throughout that help illustrate the concepts and techniques discussed in the book

There are several general themes associated with this book that are emphasized throughout, including:

- Distinguishing between "serious games" and simulations developed strictly for entertainment purposes
- Creating a balance between accuracy and gameplay
- Design considerations for peripheral devices used in simulation games
- Relating concepts such as emergence, realism, and storytelling to both market and game structure
- Online factors affecting simulation development—including issues specific to massively multiplayer online games and online distance learning

Who Should Read This Book?

This book is not limited to the education market. If you found this book on a shelf at the bookstore and picked it up out of curiosity, this book is for you, too! The audience for this book includes students, industry professionals, and the general interest consumer market. The style is informal and accessible with a concentration on theory and practice—geared toward both students and professionals.

Students that might benefit from this book include:

- College students in game development, interactive design, entertainment studies, communication, and emerging technologies programs
- Art, design, and programming students who are taking game development courses
- Professional students in college-level programs who are taking game development courses
- First-year game development students at universities

The audience of industry professionals for this book include:

- Graphic designers, animators, and Web developers who are interested in becoming game artists
- Programmers and Web developers who are interested in becoming game programmers
- Professionals in other arts and entertainment media—including film, television, and music—who are interested in transferring their skills to the game development industry. These professionals might include writers, producers, artists, and designers.

How Is This Book Organized?

This book consists of three parts—focusing on industry background, serious games, and entertainment applications.

Part I Background & Market—Focuses on providing a historical and structural context to game simulation development. Chapters in this section include:

- **Chapter 1 History: how did we get here?**—discusses the history of game simulation development, the role of hardware/software technology, and the evolution of associated production methods
- **Chapter 2 Audience: who uses simulations & why?**—explores the elements of realism, storytelling, and emergence as they relate to consumer and professional markets

Part II Serious Games—Focuses on how game simulations are used for institutions such as business, education, and the government. Chapters in this section include:

- **Chapter 3 Education: game simulations for learning & instruction**—reviews how educational simulations are used to foster competition, encourage responsibility, and enhance online distance learning
- **Chapter 4 Business: simulating the workplace**—focuses on how business simulations translate to the consumer market, incorporate fuzzy logic, and may increase both safety and profits
- **Chapter 5 Military: virtual soldiers on a simulated battlefield**—explores how military simulations utilize reward and penalty systems, balance accuracy and gameplay, and incorporate team-based cooperation online

Part III: Entertainment & the Future—Focuses on how simulations are used for entertainment purposes (such as sports, creative arts, and sandbox games), along with thoughts on the future of game simulation development. Chapters in this section include:

- **Chapter 6 Sports: bringing the action into the living room**—discusses the distinction between simulation- and arcade-style sports games, the challenge of modeling professional athletes, and the effect of complexity on sports simulations
- **Chapter 7 Creative Arts: tools that challenge and inspire**—highlights design considerations for custom and motion-sensing peripherals, components of rhythm-based music games, and techniques for simulating theoretical worlds and altered states of mind

- **Chapter 8** **Sandboxes: open-ended simulations**—outlines how emergence, socioeconomic factors, and the inclusion of procedurally generated content affect sandbox simulations
- **Chapter 9** **The Future: where we're going**—predicts future developments in graphics, audio, design, interfaces, career paths, and education related to game simulation development

The book also contains a **Resources** section, which includes a list of game development news sources, guides, directories, conferences, articles, and books related to topics discussed in this text.

How to Use This Text

The sections that follow describe text elements found throughout the book and how they are intended to be used.

key chapter questions

Key chapter questions are learning objectives in the form of overview questions that start off each chapter. Readers should be able to answer the questions upon understanding the chapter material.

quotes

Quotes contain short, insightful thoughts from players, students, and industry observers.

sidebars

Sidebars offer in-depth information from the authors on specific topics—accompanied by associated images.

tips

Tips provide advice and inspiration from industry professionals and educators, as well as practical techniques and tips of the trade.

notes

Notes contain thought-provoking ideas provided by the authors that are intended to help the readers think critically about the book's topics.

case studies

Case studies contain anecdotes from industry professionals (accompanied by game screenshots) on their experiences developing specific game titles.

profiles

Profiles provide bios, photos and in-depth commentary from industry professionals and educators.

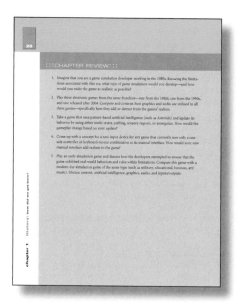

chapter review

A *chapter review* section at the end of each chapter contains a combination of questions and exercises, which allow readers to apply what they've learned. Annotations and answers are included in the instructor's guide, available separately (see next page).

About the Companion DVD

The companion DVD contains the following media:

- Game engines: *Torque* (Windows and Mac versions 1.5.1) and *Game Maker* (version 7)

- 3D modeling and animation software: *3ds Max* (version 9) and *Maya* (version 8.5 PLE)

- Game design documentation: GDD template (Chris Taylor/Gas Powered Games), *Sub Hunter* GDD (Michael Black/Torn Space), and *Uncivilized: The Goblin Game* [code name: Salmon] call for game design/submission (Wizards of the Coast)

- Game design articles: Harvey Smith/Witchboy's Cauldron and Barrie Ellis/One-Switch Games

- Game concept art: *Half-Life 2*, *Viewtiful Joe 2*, *Resident Evil 4*, *Devil May Cry 3*

- Game demos/trial versions: 2K Games (*Prey*), Blizzard (*Diablo II*), Firaxis (*Civilization IV, Sid Meier's Railroads!*), Stardock (*Galactic Civilizations II: Dread Lords*), THQ (*Company of Heroes*), Enemy Technology (*I of the Enemy: Ril'Cerat*), Star Mountain Studios (*Bergman, Weird Helmet, Frozen, Findolla*), GarageGames (*Dark Horizons: Lore Invasion, Gish, Marble Blast: Gold, Rocket Bowl Plus, Zap!, Tube Twist, Orbz, Think Tanks*), CDV (*City Life, Glory of the Roman Empire, War Front: Turning Point*), Last Day of Work (*Virtual Villagers, Fish Tycoon*), Hanako Games (*Cute Knight*), Microsoft (*Zoo Tycoon 2: Marine Mania*), and U.S. Army (*America's Army*).

About the Instructor's Guide

The instructor's guide (e-resource, available separately on DVD) was developed to assist instructors in planning and implementing their instructional programs. It includes sample syllabi, test questions, assignments, projects, PowerPoint files, and other valuable instructional resources.

Order Number: 1-4180-4209-9

About the Authors

William Muehl is Senior Producer at Midway's headquarters in Chicago, IL—where he facilitates the development of globally shared technology, art, and design initiatives across six studios and multiple game teams. He was also Development Director for the central animation, cinema, audio, character, environment, concept, and user interface departments for Midway—titles including *John Woo Presents: Stranglehold, Mortal Kombat: Armageddon*, and *NBA Ballers*. Prior to joining Midway, William was a producer at High Voltage Software and an online analyst at Sony Computer Entertainment America. He has also written and performed voiceover roles for several published titles and volunteers as Business Committee Coordinator for the Game Audio Network Guild to promote excellence in interactive audio. William received a BA in English from the University of Wisconsin. When he's not doing something game-related, William dabbles in music, filmmaking, cars, and scotch. He generally avoids dabbling in the last two simultaneously.

Photo credit: Luis Levy

Jeannie Novak is the founder of Indiespace—one of the first companies to promote and distribute interactive entertainment online—where she consults with creative professionals in the music, film, and television industries to help them migrate to the game industry. In addition to being lead author and series editor of the *Game Development Essentials* series, Jeannie is the co-author of three pioneering books on the interactive entertainment industry—including *Creating Internet Entertainment.* Jeannie is the Academic Program Director for the Game Art & Design and Media Arts & Animation programs at the Art Institute Online, where she is also producer and lead designer on a educational business simulation game that is being built within the *Second Life* environment. She has also been a game instructor and curriculum development expert at UCLA Extension, Art Center College of Design, Academy of Entertainment and Technology at Santa Monica College, DeVry University, Westwood College, and ITT Technical Institute—and she has consulted for the UC Berkeley Center for New Media. Jeannie has developed or participated in game workshops and panels in association with the British Academy of Television Arts & Sciences (BAFTA), Macworld, Digital Hollywood, and iHollywood Forum. She is a member of the International Game Developers Association (IGDA) and has served on selection committees for the Academy of Interactive Arts & Sciences (AIAS). Jeannie was chosen as one of the 100 most influential people in high-technology by *MicroTimes* magazine—and she has been profiled by CNN, *Billboard Magazine,* Sundance Channel, *Daily Variety,* and the *Los Angeles Times.* She received an M.A. in Communication Management from the University of Southern California (USC), where she focused on games in online distance learning. She received a B.A. in Mass Communication from the University of California, Los Angeles (UCLA)—graduating summa cum laude and Phi Beta Kappa. When she isn't writing and teaching, Jeannie spends most of her time recording, performing, and composing music. More information on the author can be found at *http://jeannie.com* and *http://indiespace.com.*

Acknowledgements

The authors would like to thank the following people for their hard work and dedication to this project:

Jim Gish (Acquisitions Editor, Thomson/Delmar), for making this series happen.

Sharon Chambliss (Product Manager, Thomson/Delmar), for moving this project along and always maintaining a professional demeanor.

Michael Tubbert (Content Project Manager, Thomson/Delmar), for his helpful pair of eyes and consistent responsiveness during production crunch time.

David Ladyman (Image Research & Permissions Specialists), for his superhuman efforts in clearing the many images in this book.

Jason Bramble, for his efforts in tracking, capturing and researching the many images for this book.

Sarah Timm (Editorial Assistant, Thomson/Delmar), for her ongoing assistance throughout the series.

Gina Dishman (Project Manager, GEX Publishing Services), for her diligent work and prompt response during the layout and compositing phase.

Per Olin, for his organized and aesthetically pleasing diagrams.

David Koontz (Publisher, Chilton), for starting it all by introducing Jeannie Novak to Jim Gish.

A big thanks also goes out to the people who contributed their thoughts and ideas to this book:

Aaron Marks (On Your Mark Music)

Barrie Ellis (One-Switch Games)

Chad Haddal (Congressional Research Service)

Chris Rohde (Art Institute of Portland)

Chris Taylor (Gas Powered Games)

Frank T. Gilson (Wizards of the Coast)

Greg Costikyan (Manifesto Games)

Harvey Smith (Midway Games)

Jason Mallios (BreakAway, Ltd.)

Jeremy McCarron (Art Institute of Vancouver)

Joel Rogness (Simley High School)

John Comes (Gas Powered Games)

Josh Bear (Twisted Pixel Games)

Kraig Kujawa (Midway Games)

Mark Skaggs (Funstar Ventures, LLC)

Martin Murphy (Midway Games)

Michael Black (Torn Space)

Milan Petrovich (Art Institute of San Francisco)

Roby Gilbert (Art Institute of Seattle)

Starr Long (NCsoft Corporation)

Titus Levi

Travis Castillo (InXile Entertainment)

Thanks to the following people and companies for their tremendous help with referrals and in securing permissions, images, and demos:

Adam Houston (University of Nebraska, Lincoln)

Adam Pasick (Reuters)

Adrian Wright (Max Gaming Technologies)

Ai Hasegawa, Hideki Yoshimoto (Namco Bandai)

Alexandra Miseta (Stardock)

Anne-Marie Schleiner & Velvet-Strike Team (Open Sorcery)

Aram Jabbari (Atlus USA)

Brian Hupp (Electronic Arts)

Brianna Messina (Blizzard Entertainment)

Briar Lee Mitchell (Star Mountain Studios)

Bryan Lam (RedOctane)

Chris Glover (Eidos Interactive)

Chris Mihos (Case Western Reserve University)

Chu Tim Kin (Enlight Software)

Claudia Northrup (Applied Research Associates)

Daniel Wood (responDesign)

David Greenspan (THQ)

David Swofford (NCsoft)

Dennis Shirk (Firaxis)

Derek Lane (Dassault Systémes)

Diane Theiss (ITS Corporation, in support of the National Coordination Office for Information Technology Research & Development)

Don McGowan (Microsoft Corporation)

Dr. Brian Beckman (Software Architect, Microsoft Corporation)

Dr. Frank Biocca (Michigan State University / M.I.N.D. Labs)

Dr. Mariano Alcañiz (Technical University of Valencia / M.I.N.D. Labs)

Eric Fritz (GarageGames)

Estela Lemus (Capcom)

Frank Gilson & Greg Yahn (Wizards of the Coast)

Gena Feist (Take-Two Games)

Georgina Okerson (Hanako Games)

Grace Huang (Shapiro Institute for Education & Research)

Jana Rubenstein, Makiko Nakamura & Eijirou Yoshida (Sega of America)

Janice White (The CAD Zone)

Jason Holtman (Valve)

Jennifer Pool (Banner Good Samaritan Medical Center)

Joan Kowalski (Bob Ross Co.)

Jo-Ann Bryden & Helen Van Tassel (Hasbro)

Jonna Chokas (MPRI Simulations Group)

Jordan Wong (Controllica Technologies)

Joseph Donaldson & Josh Resnick (Pandemic Studios)

Josh Johns (BreakAway)

Josiah Pisciotta (Chronic Logic)

Kathryn Butters (Atari Interactive)

Kelly Conway, Steve Weiss & Olivia Malstrom (Sony Online Entertainment)

Kelvin Liu & Mike Mantarro (Activision)

Kevin DeVito (CyberCity 3D)

Kirsten Mellor (Riverdeep)

Kristen Keller (Atari)

Kristin Kwasek, John Golden (Turbine)

Lori Mezoff (U.S. Army)

Mario Kroll (CDV Software)

Mark Morrison, Chari Ong & Reilly Brennan (Midway Games)

Mark Overmars, Sandy Duncan & Sophie Russell (YoYo Games)

Mark Rein & Kelly Farrow (Epic Games)

Mark Temple (Enemy Technology)

Michael Goldstein (Actuality Systems)

National Aeronautics & Space Administration

National Highway Traffic Safety Administration

Nintendo

Noriko Kato (Taito Corporation)

Oliver Wächter (.theprodukkt)

Olivier Morisot (ESI Group)

Peter Salfinger (Immersive Technologies)

Piers Sutton (HopeLab)

Rebecca Nesson (Berkman Center for Internet & Society at Harvard Law)

Rob Noble (Empire Interactive)

Robert Wilhelmson (National Center for Supercomputing Applications)

Ryan & Justin Mette (21-6 Productions)

Scott Gagain (House of Moves)

Sony Computer Entertainment America

Sophie Jakubowicz (Ubisoft)

Steven Kendrick (Cybershooters)

Susanna Hughes (Lewis PR for Emotiv)

Ted Brockwood (Calico Media)

Terri Perkins (Funcom)

Terry Day (Engineering Dynamics Corporation)

Therese Gregorio (Fakespace Systems)

Therese Snow (Delmia Corp.)

TSgt Rebecca Danét, MSgt Deshan Woods (U.S. Air Force)

Wade Tinney (Large Animal Games)

Yoh Watanabe (Tecmo)

Questions and Feedback

We welcome your questions and feedback. If you have suggestions that you think others would benefit from, please let us know and we will try to include them in the next edition.

To send us your questions and/or feedback, you can contact the publisher at:

Delmar Learning
Executive Woods
5 Maxwell Drive
Clifton Park, NY 12065
Attn: Graphic Arts Team
(800) 998-7498

Or the series editor at:

Jeannie Novak
Founder & CEO
INDIESPACE
P.O. Box 5458
Santa Monica, CA 90409
jeannie@indiespace.com

DEDICATION

To my wife Alex, who supports me always and keeps me sane when I'm writing—and to my parents Jim and Jackie, and my sisters Sarah and Kristina, for encouraging me in all my pursuits.

—William

To Luis, who is sharing the real thing with me—and to the "Godzilla" *Second Life* development team for pushing the envelope!

—Jeannie

Part I:
Background
& Market

History

how did we get here?

Key Chapter Questions

- How did developers simulate real worlds with severely limited graphics hardware?

- How has audio technology evolved to immerse players in the simulated experience?

- What are some ways developers scale artificial intelligence with hardware capabilities?

- What role does input and output hardware play in facilitating user control and feedback?

- How have production methods changed as simulations grow more complex?

Game simulations have grown from rudimentary abstractions into dynamic, increasingly realistic representations of reality. What used to be defined by a few crude pixels and repetitive, low-fidelity audio is now brought to life by millions of polygons, three-dimensional sound effects, and musical scores generated in real time. The time span between both extremes is full of experimental technologies and techniques; some proved revolutionary, advancing the possibilities of game simulations—while some proved ineffective and fell by the wayside. Other failed technologies were ahead of their time and deemed too cumbersome in their earliest forms. Subsequent, refined versions built on the existing technology and eventually became incorporated in highly effective simulations. Incremental progress has brought the industry to its present form and made game simulations accessible and relevant to an enormous and diverse audience.

Virtual Worlds

What does a virtual world look, sound, or feel like? Our minds are capable of re-creating the experiences of our past in vivid detail. The sights, sounds, and smells of a distant vacation to Fiji can come rolling back by recalling memories. We can also mentally construct an experience from secondary information. A friend might describe a trip to Antarctica in great detail—transporting you to the cold, desolate location. The mind can push further and imagine scenarios no human has ever experienced. We can even imagine hopping from star to star at the speed of light to discover and colonize new lands.

We may also participate in real-life simulations. A street court basketball player can become fully immersed in the final seconds of an imaginary NBA Finals game, down by one as the player squares up to take the shot that gives the team the championship. Soldiers run through a mocked-up urban environment to train before being dropped into a similar live combat zone. Game simulations can trigger many of the same sensory responses that result from imagined or participated scenarios; these virtual representations of reality can effectively teach, train, and entertain users.

Photos.com

A playground basketball court can host an imaginary buzzer-beating shot to win the NBA Finals.

Graphics

Realistic imagery is a significant factor in transporting players to a virtual world. Whether the simulation is intended for education, training, or entertainment, it is the graphics that initially hook an audience. Game simulation developers are constantly pushing the boundaries of graphics hardware to eke out the last drop of performance that might make their simulation more convincing.

Laying the Foundation

When graphics technology was relatively rudimentary, simulation developers had a limited range of colors and objects to work with. White pixels were clustered together to create a raster image on a black background to represent soldiers, athletes, or race cars. White lines were drawn with individual pixels in a similar fashion to mark the perimeter of the respective battlefield, court, or road. The resolution was usually so low that curved objects were drawn with horribly jagged edges and in-game text required a large portion of the screen to be legible. Furthermore, early hardware was incapable of animating more than a few objects at a time. When developers pushed hardware beyond its limits, the resulting simulation often became frustrating or unplayable.

Simulating real-life scenarios that involved many moving people or objects was simplified during development when necessary. Simulating the movements of 22 football players simultaneously, for example, was far too demanding on early hardware—so developers scaled the game simulation back to include two or three players on each team. Without simplifications, animations bogged down and player input became sluggish. Excessive onscreen movement also generated distracting screen flicker and "warping" objects as the hardware tried to keep up with the overly ambitious demands of the software.

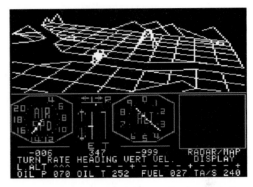

SubLOGIC used raster graphics to simulate flight in its 1980 release of *Flight Simulator 1*.

Even though graphics in early simulations did not come close to depicting real-life characters, objects, and environments, players became immersed in the experience. The relatively crude pixilated graphics were only capable of displaying rudimentary shapes. However, even with only two moving lines and a dot, *Pong* was identifiable as a tennis simulation. Developers pushed the hardware as far as they could and relied on players to use their imaginations to fill in the missing information.

Vector Graphics

In the late 1970s and early 1980s, many developers used vector graphics—an alternative to raster-based graphics. Vector graphics drawn with lines and polygons had several advantages over their pixilated counterparts. When rendering performance was at a premium, game simulations built with vector graphics could create more detailed objects and environments than could raster-based rendering techniques on comparable hardware. To display a vector, an electron beam is guided across the screen—drawing the visible objects and environments one line segment at a time against a static, black background.

With vector graphics, the hardware draws only the visible components of the simulation, so the memory requirements are only a fraction of the cost of raster-generated images. Raster-based images require that half of all the pixels on the screen be refreshed every cycle—whether they need to be updated or not. Vector images also scale without losing any definition, unlike raster images that become blurry and jagged when scaled. Vector techniques are still used in almost every modern game simulation. Developers leverage the efficiencies of vector operations to render a scene before it is stored in internal memory and translated to a raster image and drawn to the screen one pixel at a time.

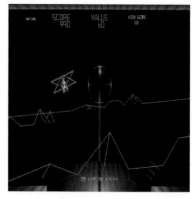

Vector graphics in games such as *Red Baron* were an appealing alternative to their pixelated counterparts.

Sprites and Scaling

Graphics hardware improvements in the late 1980s and early 1990s opened up many more options for developers. This period was the heyday for two-dimensional (2D) graphics. Color palette support exploded from the single digits into the millions, offering more realistic shading and color depth of in-game characters and environments. Dozens of sprites could be drawn onscreen simultaneously, allowing developers to populate their worlds with more characters and objects. Additional lines of screen resolution and buffering techniques made characters more defined and fonts more legible.

In this phase, hardware also began to offer support for scaling and rotation—techniques that allowed developers to alter the size and perspective of sprites without a drastic performance penalty. Developers became proficient with these techniques and used them to translate a 2D background texture into a flat plane that was perpendicular to the vertical axis. Textures could be drawn in this new perspective to simulate a floor or sky on which sprites could be rendered, cracking open the door to visuals that mimicked real-time, three-dimensional (3D) rendering.

Nintendo

Pilotwings 64 used scaling and rotation techniques to create a pseudo-3D flight simulation.

Entering the Third Dimension

In the early 1990s, consumer simulation hardware began supporting true 3D graphics. Prior hardware was capable of rendering rudimentary 3D objects, but it had limited use in interactive applications. In one sense, developers who created the first iterations of interactive 3D simulations took a few steps back before they could go forward. Game simulations in two dimensions were peaking after years of optimizations and could crank out bright, colorful graphics at smooth frame rates. Graphics in early 3D game simulations were plagued with jagged edges and muddy textures often rendered at poor frame rates. Since developers were cutting their teeth on new hardware and un-optimized libraries, most of the graphical horsepower was dedicated to simply drawing the polygons on the screen and there was little juice left to smooth them out.

©1995 NAMCO BANDAI Games Inc.

The move into the third dimension opened up new possibilities for realistic game simulations. After several iterations of hardware, tools, and techniques, 3D game simulations began to come into their own. Our physical world is, after all, in three dimensions—and developers could begin modeling more literal interpretations of the world around them. The additional axis allowed players to control characters and interact with objects in a virtual space instead of on a flat plane. Once acceptable rendering performance was achieved, developers could turn their attention to improving aesthetics and increasing realism.

In the late 1990s, game simulation developers began to hit their stride with 3D graphics (*Air Combat*, shown).

The High-Definition Era

There is a saying that usually comes up when discussing game simulation graphics. It is often a variation of something like, "Graphics do not matter; it is all about the gameplay." Well, gameplay is certainly important—but simulations rely on graphical accuracy to convey the visual component of real-world situations. A graphically superior simulation will blur the line between real and virtual worlds more effectively than an otherwise equal competitor with inferior visuals. Consumer-grade hardware capable of cranking out over two million pixels per frame is now par for the course. The high-definition equivalent has been available for several years for personal computer-based simulations, but the next-generation consoles from Microsoft and Sony (Xbox and PlayStation 3) have brought increased visual fidelity into the living room.

Reprinted with permission from Microsoft Corporation

Simulation graphics have advanced steadily in the 25 years between SubLOGIC *Flight Simulator 1* and *Microsoft Flight Simulator X* (pictured).

Do players need to see every facial expression on a virtual soldier's face or every bead of sweat running down a virtual athlete's neck? If the goal of a simulation is to create the most accurate representation of real life, then yes, developers should continue to incorporate even the slightest visual touches. The incredible detail of high-definition game simulations opens up new avenues of visual cues. A soldier's emotive facial expression can convey his morale or pain level without unrealistic meters cluttering the user interface. Similarly, sweat building on an athlete's neck and a slight change in his posture can give game simulation players a non-disruptive signal that the athlete may need a substitution.

Audio

Game simulation audio is frequently neglected in favor of graphics. Developers and publishers that fall into this trap usually realize late in production that their game simulation lacks the immersive qualities they hoped for. Unfortunately, for developers and publishers who don't give audio the attention it requires, poorly implemented audio can fatally damage an otherwise outstanding game simulation. Conversely, well-implemented audio can raise an otherwise serviceable simulation to new heights of immersion and effect. Game simulation audio is so critical that audio designers, composers, and engineers should be hooked in at every stage of planning and production to maximize the likelihood of success.

Blips and Bleeps

Early game simulation audio was restricted by rudimentary or nonexistent audio processing power, constrained memory space, and tiny speakers with limited range. Developers made the most of the technology by looping phrases of notes to create the musical score, and adjusting the pitch or tempo to influence the mood. In-game sound effects were limited because the hardware could not support concurrent audio channels. Imagine playing a keyboard with one finger versus using all your fingers on both hands. A single finger can play only one note at a time and a keyboardist using that one finger cannot play chords or drop notes on top of a background melody. Pioneering audio designers had to work within these limitations and focus their efforts on the most significant events of the simulation.

Digitized Samples

In the late 1980s and early 1990s, dedicated audio processors began appearing in game simulation hardware—opening up new possibilities for interactive audio. Developers could use the new power to implement samples of digitized instruments and voices to create more complex music and more realistic speech. The hardware also enabled programmers and audio designers to loop soundtracks in the background while multiple sound effects played simultaneously. Suddenly, players could hear an announcer call the on-field action while the sound effects of colliding players and piercing whistles battled through the digitized roar of the crowd. The fidelity may not have been exceptional, but digitized multi-channel audio was a significant step toward bringing players deeper into game simulations.

High-Fidelity Immersive Audio

When optical storage arrived, it brought an incredible leap in game simulation audio. The massive increase in storage capacity enables composers and audio designers to create soundtracks and voices at resolutions close to the limits of human perception. Increasing system memory also allows developers to use sound effects sampled at much higher rates, making them nearly indistinguishable from the real thing.

Diagram by Per Olin

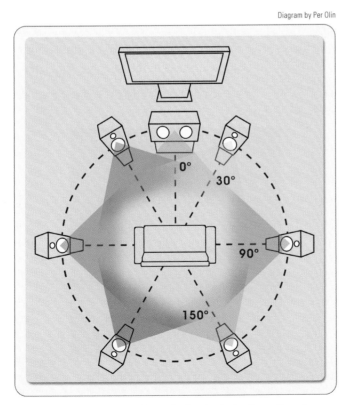

Surround sound immerses players in the simulation from all angles.

During development, sound effects can be designed and tested using real-time 3D audio tools and processing. When game simulations designed with these tools are matched with common amplifiers capable of driving up to seven surround sound speakers, the soundscape of a player's living room can be transformed into the virtual world of the onscreen character. Hardware is becoming less of a limitation to re-creating real-life aural experiences. For all intents and purposes, the audio a player hears in a modern football simulation could be indistinguishable from the sounds hitting the eardrums of players standing in the middle of the field on game day.

Artificial Intelligence

Simulating intelligent behavior is a daunting task. In a game simulation designed to be as realistic as possible, the ultimate goal is to create virtual beings that behave indistinguishably from their real living counterparts. Tools and technology haven't reached this goal yet, but significant advancements have been made in artificial intelligence over several decades.

Patterns

Early game developers pushed the limits of hardware and software to simply get graphics drawn on the screen, leaving precious few processing cycles for artificial intelligence. Developers often worked within the hardware limitations by implementing pattern-based artificial intelligence. In this strategy, simulated characters follow a predetermined path that loops or reverses sequence.

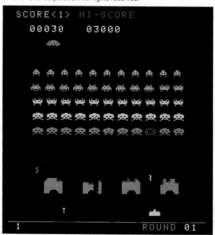

If Earth is attacked by aliens, we should hope they're as predictable as the *Space Invaders* attackers: left, left, left, down, right, right, right, down, left, left, left, down....

Pattern-based artificial intelligence is "cheap" in terms of performance and memory because there are few, if any, calculations. As game simulation hardware improved, pattern-based artificial intelligence became more robust as developers increased pattern complexity and injected randomized variables.

Multi-States, Pathing & Sensory Regions

Pattern-based artificial intelligence techniques evolved to include branching patterns and multiple states for in-game characters. Stylized military espionage simulations like *Metal Gear* include enemies with multiple states like alert, patrol, and idle. Characters transition among states based on randomized or user-triggered inputs. An enemy in *Metal Gear* might simulate the behavior of a real-life night security guard by walking along the exterior perimeter of a building, pausing at the corner to make a 270-degree visual sweep, and continue walking down the adjacent wall.

Characters that follow patrol-based artificial intelligence algorithms usually obey set paths and sensory regions. A virtual security guard's visual detection capabilities may be limited to the line of sight represented by a cone extending from his or her eyes. Aural detection may be represented by a large circle surrounding his or her current location. The guard might also be programmed to only detect characters that are moving, within a certain range, or lacking aural or visual camouflage.

Reprinted with permission from Microsoft Corporation

Zoo Tycoon 2: Marine Mania uses pedestrian pathing to simulate intelligence.

Setting the Stage for Behaviors to Emerge

As hardware capabilities continue to advance, it becomes increasingly difficult for developers to hide behind the excuse of limited resources forcing them to cripple artificial intelligence. Granted, the insatiable performance appetite of high-resolution graphics, dynamic audio, and complex physics consume a significant portion of technological advances, but enough power remains in modern hardware for very robust artificial intelligence.

Electronic Arts, Inc.

Artificial intelligence in sandbox-style simulations such as *Spore* is influenced by so many variables that new behaviors and consequences can emerge.

This power is being used in a couple ways. Developers can leverage traditional artificial intelligence algorithms and extend them to dozens or even hundreds of characters onscreen simultaneously. This approach can yield impressive results, especially in genres like military simulations that might control the behavior of massive numbers of soldiers on a virtual battlefield. Developers can also use this growing power to increase the depth and scope of artificial intelligence in sandbox-type simulations. Games such as *Black & White* and *Spore* allow players to start from a clean slate, molding their own virtual creatures and environments. By giving players a toolbox and a loose set of guidelines, sandbox simulation developers create artificial intelligence that must learn and adapt to millions of potential outcomes. In such complex, open-ended scenarios, advancements in artificial intelligence enable new behaviors and consequences to emerge.

Inputs & Outputs

In many pre-digital era game simulations, the input and output mechanisms were one and the same. When plotting a military invasion on a tabletop map, for example, the input of moving military pieces representing battalions, weapons, or equipment on a map also changes the output; the status of the simulation is updated in real time. As simulations started incorporating digital elements, the distinction between inputs and outputs grew.

Simulations on a Game Board

Digital simulations existed before anyone thought it necessary to connect a screen or a joystick. The creatively titled *Computer Football* was an early entry in digital simulations that preceded monitor-based output. Released in the late 1960s, *Computer Football* simulated a football game on a wooden board with plastic game pieces. The game had digital features, including several buttons, a timer, and a row of lightbulbs along one border of the "field" painted on the playing surface. A rudimentary circuit board inside the case coordinated which lights were illuminated to communicate offensive and defensive plays on the board matrix. Players manually moved their plastic game pieces forward or backward according to the outcome of the computer-generated plays. *Computer Football* merged traditional tabletop board games with rudimentary but functional digital features to create a new gameplay experience.

Computer Football simulated the sport using an array of lightbulbs and buttons to generate the outcome of offensive and defensive plays.

The Gradual Evolution of Display Technology

Once hardware was capable of rendering images of virtual worlds, developers needed a way to present them to their audience. Computer monitors were an obvious choice because they were used to develop the simulations and their capabilities were already widely known. The first game simulations were viewed on monitors in corporate and academic laboratories because the hardware was prohibitively expensive for consumers. Lower-cost game consoles brought simulations into homes by interfacing with one of the most ubiquitous output mechanisms: televisions.

Photos.com

Big Stock Photo

This is how far we've come in 30 years. Are these two output devices really that different from each other?

The technology behind monitors and televisions has improved steadily since the first simulation was rendered—making characters, objects, and environments appear more realistic than ever before. Developers can utilize more pixels, higher contrast ratios, faster refresh rates, and more vibrant colors—but players are still viewing images drawn pixel by pixel on a 2D surface.

Not Quite Ready for Prime Time

In 1995, Nintendo decided to break away from conventional 2D displays and wade into the commercial virtual reality waters when it launched the Virtual Boy game system. Virtual Boy hardware included dual displays (one for each eye) built into goggles mounted on a tripod. Light-emitting diodes in each display generated separate images for each eye. Software for the system was programmed using parallax techniques to draw slightly offset images in each display, giving the illusion of 3D worlds.

Nintendo

Nintendo

Nintendo's Virtual Boy (*Golf*, shown) was hampered by cumbersome hardware and technical limitations. Pick any color you want, as long as it's red.

Unfortunately, the anticipated benefits of 3D output were outweighed by negative factors that ultimately doomed the system. Hardware costs forced Nintendo to incorporate display technology incapable of generating more than one color: red. The limitation essentially sent developers back to the era of monochrome displays, eliminating features they had grown to take for granted with broad color palettes. The bulky hardware also made transporting the Virtual Boy system awkward. Furthermore, the direct-view nature of the goggles caused eye fatigue and prevented non-participants from observing or joining the onscreen action. Although the concept was ahead of its time, technology and consumers were not ready for hardware dedicated to 3D output.

The Ubiquitous Input Device

Displaying a virtual world on a screen was a significant accomplishment, but developers needed to implement an intuitive means for players to provide input. The keyboard, an input mechanism that remains relatively unchanged since the first game simulations, is still the controller of choice for computer-based game simulations. When the keyboard is paired with a mouse, the combination offers unparalleled customizability and control for almost any type of simulation. Nearly all potential simulation users are familiar with the functionality of the keyboard and mouse from years of typing and moving a cursor in applications such as word processors and spreadsheets. Although the physical hardware may be familiar, the transition to using the keyboard-mouse combination for less conventional input such as moving a virtual character on the screen or swinging a simulated object can be confusing due to the sheer number of keys.

Joysticks & Buttons

To streamline and simplify input for game simulations, some manufacturers created custom controllers for game consoles and computers. Early versions usually included a joystick and one or more buttons. The joystick was a breakthrough device that translated physical movement into onscreen movement. A four-way joystick could detect up, down, left, and right. If the joystick hardware was capable of detecting and transmitting simultaneous signals, such as up + left, the simulation software could interpret diagonal inputs. The more directions a digital joystick was capable of detecting, the more precise the movement.

Early controller buttons were also digital, meaning they could detect two states: on or off. In this binary configuration, the only variable that players and developers could control was the duration of button presses. The design of most early joysticks favored function over form; the hard edges and non-ergonomic button layout on controllers in this era made extended sessions uncomfortable or even painful.

Courtesy of Atari Interactive, Inc.

The Atari 2600 joystick detected five digital inputs: up, down, left, right, and button press.

Inputs Doubling as Outputs

In the late 1990s, hardware manufacturers introduced controllers capable of generating tactile feedback. Nintendo's "Rumble Pak" plugged into the Nintendo 64 controller—and Sony followed suit, launching its Dual Analog Controller. Both technologies housed motors that spun offset weights to generate vibrations when triggered by software commands. The vibrations corresponded to onscreen actions, simulating the tactile output of real-life events such as hitting rumble strips when veering off the road or the recoil of a firearm.

Analog Buttons & Sticks

Digital controllers were limited by binary button states and the number of directions their joysticks could detect. When hardware began to include analog buttons and sticks, game simulations achieved a new level of input precision. Analog controllers can detect from dozens up to thousands of degrees of input. With digital controls, simulated cars were limited to discrete states such as "accelerate" and "brake." A car simulation built with analog controls can detect a much wider range of states—allowing developers to mimic the smooth, gradual response of an accelerator pedal on an analog stick or custom peripheral. The clear benefit to analog input technology has made it standard on all modern game simulation console hardware. As internal functionality of controllers has advanced, manufacturers have also made gradual improvements to controller ergonomics, reducing the risk of premature fatigue and injury.

Reprinted with permission from Microsoft Corporation   Reprinted with permission from Microsoft Corporation

Microsoft's analog steering wheel and pedals for the Xbox 360 immerse players in driving simulations by modeling the real-life input hardware.

A More Natural Method of Input

Several motion-sensing peripherals have been released over the years for personal computers. None was able to get significant traction because the technology was not particularly precise and game simulation developers did not want to develop titles for such a limited market. When the Nintendo Wii and Sony PlayStation3 were released in 2006, both obstacles were removed—paving the way for mainstream motion-sensing simulation input. Motion-sensing controllers open the door to new techniques for simulating real-world actions. Natural gestures that translate to onscreen movement are more intuitive than pressing a key or tilting an analog stick.

How Production Has Evolved

Continued advances in all facets of technology have increased the complexity of producing modern game simulations. As expectations, scope, and budgets rise, production methods have evolved to support the changing development landscape.

Budget & Resources

Most game simulations are for-profit endeavors, requiring developers and publishers to work within a budget. Budgets were easier to track and manage before game simulations became multi-million dollar projects. Early game simulations could be developed by a single person or a small team of talented individuals. The demand for increased realism and scope has pushed development out of basements and garages and into huge corporations. The cost of software and hardware has increased steadily over the years, but the single largest contributor to ballooning budgets for nearly every simulation is the number of people on the team. Game developers that can maintain the optimal amount of employees will have a lower likelihood of blowing their production budgets.

Expertise & Specialization

Increased realism has also put higher demands on developers to build their teams with highly specialized personnel. Small teams in the past could get away with individuals handling tasks from multiple disciplines. A programmer was often tasked with writing the artificial intelligence code and maintaining the project schedule while an artist built all the levels and wrote the musical score.

Modern development teams have members who specialize in specific elements of development. A character artist may focus solely on facial animations for months to make them as realistic as possible. An audio designer might spend several weeks on location to capture sounds in the field so the simulation accurately represents the soundscape of the real aural environment. Programmers may have an advanced degree in hydrodynamics and apply their expertise to create in-game water that looks and behaves incredibly realistically. Online distribution may revive the possibility for a small team to deliver simulations to a wide audience, but the most accurate simulations still require a large team of people who specialize in making their component of the overall experience as realistic as possible.

If a development team is not forced to operate within a well-defined schedule, a simulation risks losing its window of opportunity due to competition, audience disinterest, or outdated functionality. A competitive market does not allow developers the luxury of open-ended production schedules. Similar game simulations may be in development at competing studios, especially if the market for the simulation is large or has significant growth potential. A chronically slipping schedule can also damage a game simulation's perception in the target audience. The market segment that eagerly anticipated a release can turn against the product if they are burned too many times with pushed launch dates.

Some teams get so wrapped up in polishing every last detail that they lose sight of the bigger picture: delivering the product to the end user. When people work so closely toward a goal, they often obsess over minutia that the vast majority of end users will never notice. Tweaking animations or artificial intelligence to the nth degree usually results in rapidly diminishing returns with each iteration. Successful developers get the simulation out the door, on time, and generate a list of improvements to make for the sequel.

Technology

Even if a development team is given an unlimited budget and hundreds of top-tier artists, designers, producers, and programmers, it is still bound by limitations of technology. Just as game simulation developers in the 1970s were forced to work with single-channel audio systems and 2D monochrome graphics, today's developers must make compromises in the realism of their simulations. Hardware performance is not boundless, and software algorithms have a long way to go before they can exhibit fully realistic behavior.

When breakthroughs are made in areas such as immersive audio, animation, and artificial intelligence, it can take many generations of hardware improvements before they can be implemented in real-world development pipelines. A cluster of the most powerful computers can render a photorealistic human, but once developers begin adding components like real-time advanced lighting, procedural animation, artificial intelligence, and an environment with long draw distances, the simulation becomes too complex for the hardware to handle. Researchers, students, employees, and consumers will not tolerate an unstable or sluggish simulation; poor performance will destroy a simulation's credibility more than any visual, aural, or tactical imperfection.

Developers & Collaboration

The rapid growth of the mass market game simulation industry has accelerated the technology used to develop and play games. Game simulation developers have also grown very agile as the six-year console hardware cycle forces them to create and utilize new tools and techniques with each new generation. These developments have not gone unnoticed by government and academic institutions. Some government and academic researchers use retail mass market game simulations, while others have teamed up with developers to create simulations tailored to their research or training objective. Commercial organizations, like professional sports teams, also utilize game simulations for training or to analyze the competition.

Whether virtual environments, objects, and characters are built with white dots emitting monotone beeps or built using millions of polygons with high-fidelity voices and sound, game simulation developers have always worked within the tools and technologies available. Hardware, software, and development techniques have advanced through the years, but the goal of game simulations remains the same: create a model that accurately represents a real-life experience or scenario. The industry is still relatively young and poised for continued growth as new audiences discover how game simulations can improve fields of research, training, education, and entertainment.

chapter 1

:::CHAPTER REVIEW:::

1. Imagine that you are a game simulation developer working in the 1980s. Knowing the limitations associated with this era, what type of game simulation would you develop—and how would you make the game as realistic as possible?

2. Play three electronic games from the same franchise—one from the 1980s, one from the 1990s, and one released after 2004. Compare and contrast how graphics and audio are utilized in all three games—specifically how they add or detract from the games' realism.

3. Take a game that uses pattern-based artificial intelligence (such as *Asteroids*) and update its behavior by using either multi-states, pathing, sensory regions, or emergence. How would the gameplay change based on your update?

4. Come up with a concept for a new input device for any game that currently uses only a console controller or keyboard-mouse combination as its manual interface. How would your new manual interface add realism to the game?

5. Play an early simulation game and discuss how the developers attempted to ensure that the game exhibited real-world behaviors and rules within limitations. Compare this game with a modern day simulation game of the same type (such as military, educational, business, art/music). Discuss content, artificial intelligence, graphics, audio, and inputs/outputs.

CHAPTER

Audience

who uses simulations & why?

Key Chapter Questions

- What strategies can developers use to increase the realism of a simulation?
- How can simulations affect business decisions?
- What makes a simulation a candidate for emergent gameplay?
- How can simulations be used to tell a story?
- Why are some simulations controversial?

Simulations play a role in the development and production of things you see and use every day. Your car was modeled virtually before the first pieces of metal were welded together. The materials in the tires on your car and the shoes on your feet probably endured extended tests that simulated wear over many miles. Your favorite sports team designs and tests its plays against a simulated opponent on real and virtual fields before each game. Simulations are an integral part of these and many other aspects of our social and commercial culture. Over the past two decades, game developers have expanded their influence beyond entertainment to contribute to a much broader spectrum of influence in the simulation market. The line between game and non-game simulations continues to blur as technology advances. Methodologies used to develop game simulations for entertainment have found new life in fields such as education, training, and manufacturing. Advances historically driven solely by game developers are now expanding to conferences and research on game simulation tools and technologies and how they can be applied to non-game situations. With such a broad scope of influence, the value of game simulations beyond entertainment cannot be ignored.

Variety as a Virtue

Game simulations are used by an incredibly diverse audience. Academic and commercial researchers, corporate trainers, politicians, and consumers of entertainment are just a few of the groups using game simulations on a regular basis. The broad reach of game simulations illustrates how flexible and adaptable they can be. The variety also demonstrates the range of knowledge and professional talent required of game developers who must become intimately familiar with the subject matter.

Developers of games such as *Gran Turismo* and *Call of Duty* make a conscious effort to build their respective models of car racing and World War II as close to the real thing as possible. In these types of game simulations, developers set out to create games that simulate real-world models. The commitment to accuracy via research and planning must permeate the entire development cycle. During preproduction, research must focus on re-creating the real-world experience— favoring authenticity over creativity. Developers of racing simulations like *Gran Turismo* de-emphasize crash sequences and physics-defying, rocket-like acceleration commonly found in arcade-style racing games in favor of precise controls and highly accurate models of real sports cars. Research saves time, money, and headaches during the course of development. A thorough development plan also forces the team to focus on the aspects of simulation that the target audience will expect from the game.

Activision

Reprinted with permission from Microsoft Corporation

Getting sidetracked on a plasma rifle discussion in a WWII game (*Call of Duty 3* and *Halo 2*, pictured) can be a waste of time.

As production gets rolling, the development plan must strip away all issues that interfere with the objective: to build a model of the real-world situation. When leading a team of developers on a World War II simulation, a producer employs this focused strategy when reigning in programmers and designers to avoid wasting time on anachronistic elements. If the codebase or design documents veer off into the realm of plasma rifles and supersonic fighter jets, the team is wasting its time.

The Onus on Developers

Consumers of game simulations can spot a fraud a mile away. Those who use simulations for business and entertainment are very familiar with the subject matter and have preconceived notions about how the simulation should behave. Game developers use two strategies to increase the likelihood of an accurate simulation: consulting and research.

Consulting

Game developers must bridge the gap between the experience of consultants and the creative and technical challenges of game simulation development. Contracted consultants are often unfamiliar with the complexities of game development. Developers can use the earliest phase of preproduction to encourage consultants to disregard limitations and describe the ideal simulation rather than becoming bogged down in technicalities. Developers use this information to build a framework and forecast what will be possible considering the constraints of time, resources, and technology. After the initial pass, developers bring back the consultant to evaluate how they might work within the new constraints. The goal is to achieve maximum effectiveness of the simulation, while accounting for the constraints on the project. Frequent communication between consultant and developer early in the design phase of development can save enormous amounts of time, money, and frustration later in the schedule. Even when production is fully ramped up, periodic communications with consultants ensure that the simulation is on the correct course to create the most authentic experience possible.

Martin Murphy
(Director of Art,
Midway Games)

Martin Murphy, a graduate of Ringling School of Art and Design, has worked in entertainment for 15 years. He is contributed to feature films, theme parks, cartoons, commercials, broadcast graphics and games. In 1997, Marty joined Midway Games where he has held various roles including Artist, Animator, Cinematic Manager, Technical Art Director, and Studio Art Director. In his current position as Director of Art, he is responsible for the art efforts on all of Midway's projects. He has led company-wide efforts to improve the quality of game artists' lives and the visual impact they make on Midway's games.

When deciding what experiences you want to present, whittle your goals to 2-3 memorable moments that will resonate with the audience and build from there. I would far rather leave an audience wanting more than give them a watered down experience. Start by analyzing other games or interactive applications and distilling the gameplay experience into the 2-3 most memorable moments. Marketing uses the term "USP (unique selling proposition)" when describing these moments. Picture these moments as if they were bullet points on the back of the box of your favorite game. Did the moments live up to the hype? Was it really a unique experience? The games I have enjoyed the most have typically had a dead-on relationship with these USPs. If the game or application you are analyzing does not live up to its own hype, ask yourself how these interactive experiences fell short.

It is important to determine if your memorable moments will resonate with your audience before you commit a large amount of resources to them. Test them. Through inexpensive means create pre-visualizations of these moments and then solicit feedback from relevant sources on the experience. Ask "Was it compelling? Was it memorable? What could have been better?" Once you are confident that your memorable moments will, in fact, be memorable; make sure your project schedule has plenty of built-in iteration time for these moments. Do not wait for a bunch of new code to be written to begin your early prototypes—use existing tech available to you for mock up and/or create animatics to visualize the intended results. You want to create an experience that your average audience member can interact with in a flawless manner. If done right, you will see the users get hooked to the mechanic and start to grind on it trying to either break it or see what dynamic experience they can have with the mechanic. A few memorable hooks are all you need.

Most of what we do in games comes down to execution. Knowing what to do is the first step and doing it well is the labor intensive, time consuming second step. In other words, form follows function. As the visual designer, you should go to great conceptual lengths to potently support intended expression of functionality. Look for every nook and cranny of form that can support function and cut out any superfluous decorations that can distract the viewer. Just because you can make the text on screen bold, italicized and glowing does not mean you should. Think about an actor who tries to perform a play after reading only his lines beforehand, think about a cheesy TV show where the set should be an old warehouse but there is no grime or wear to the place. Uncoordinated efforts do not hold up. Give each pixel, poly, and frame of animation history and purpose. Every visual decision you make should be justified by how well it supports the key functionality (memorable moments).

Again, this investigation into the best expression of functionality can be done in an inexpensive manner. Before assigning engineering or 3D modelers resources, brainstorm with word choices that match the feeling you want to evoke; sketch out how these word choices would be visually represented; create a large array of different expressive takes to choose from and definitely be sure to get outside opinions. After you have chosen your concept, frame out the production of this vision with gross movements first. Do not start by painting in details or animating the finger tips…paint with a big brush, animate props or actors as if they were stick puppets. Make sure you are using lighting, time of day, and atmosphere to evoke expression before noodling out the cracks in the sidewalks. Then try to touch-up all of the graphics to some state of shippable quality before noodling as quickly as possible. Finally, level up the graphics and support for functionality with the remaining time and resources that you have available.

Remember, if the required technology for the content creation pipeline is not available (or not a slam dunk to be developed), punt and use brute force to achieve your visual goals. Do not plan on wishful thinking. If the tech required to achieve your visual (form) goals is not available, find another way. Trust me, there is plenty of other work that can be done to make the experience you are creating higher quality and more memorable.

The goal with an interactive application is to make the experience compelling enough for the user to want to continue the interaction. A few key moments can make that happen. If you focus on those moments in how you plan and use your resources, you will make a compelling experience no matter what segment of the interactive media industry you are in.

Research

Consultants are very useful resources, but the value of firsthand experience cannot be overstated. If a development team has the time and means to research the field they are simulating, they should take advantage of that opportunity. In an ideal situation, everyone on the team, including the producers, artists, designers, and programmers, immerse themselves in the subject. If time and resources are at a premium, the team directors and leads go on-site and relay the information back to the rest of the team through extensive notes and recorded materials.

Here are a few suggested research techniques for different types of simulation games:

Simulating a movie or television show
- Visit the set and meet with the directors, actors, set designers, and writers.
- Keep abreast of changes to the script and art direction.
- Request access to dailies and voice talent.

Sports simulations
- Join a league, gym, or association so the team can physically play the sport.
- Review team playbooks and archival footage.
- Visit several of the sport's stadiums, tracks, or arenas.

Military simulations
- Visit a firing range to use and record real firearms.
- Visit a military base to observe training and tactics.
- Employ military tactics in real scenarios such as paintball or reenactments.

Education simulations
- Shadow teachers in their class environment.
- Observe students interacting with a variety of instructional mediums.
- Observe and participate in educational psychology studies.

Authenticity

If a simulation is developed for training purposes, the model should reflect reality as much as possible. Military, medical, sport, and educational fields rely heavily on accuracy in all forms of training, and simulations must be faithful to the demands of the discipline. The most effective simulation closes the gap between the end of the simulation and the start of the real-world scenario. As this gap narrows, the transition from simulation to reality becomes more efficient.

Authenticity can also enhance less mission-critical scenarios and draw the player into the virtual world. Game simulations like *Blitz the League* authentically re-create some of the seedier sides of professional football, including performance-enhancing drugs and off-the-field antics routinely covered up by public relations officials in professional sports.

Simulated medical procedures such as *GeRTiSS Surgery Simulator* prepare medical students for real-world operations.

The depth and credibility of a simulation can be increased by including aspects that are rarely talked about but are known to occur in real life. When realities are omitted, the missing material can, at best, be overlooked and, at worst, prevent trainees from being adequately prepared when facing the real experience. No one will get hurt because they didn't see the full range of life as a professional football player in an NFL-licensed game, but a medical simulation that omits a technique or procedure due to the existence of trade secrets or value judgments could put lives at risk.

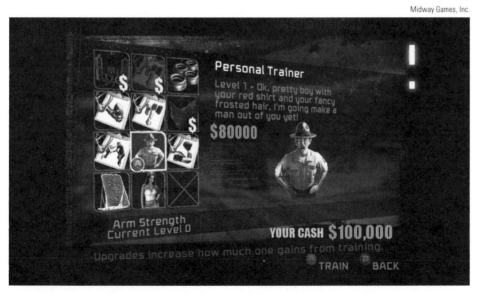

Blitz: the League goes beyond the standard gridiron simulation to include aspects hidden by the professional footbal leagues.

Jason Mallios on the Importance of Immersion :::::

Jason Mallios
(Programmer,
BreakAway Ltd.)

Jason Mallios has a Masters in Computer Science from Brown University, where he studied graphics and motion synthesis. His research involved blending motion capture and rag doll physics through the use of joint torques and a probabilistically–organized motion database. He is currently a programmer for BreakAway Ltd. working on graphics and effects for the *Pulse!!* research project at Texas A&M University - Corpus Christi.

The primary measure of a simulation's success is the level of immersion the end user experiences. Does the player perform in-game identically to how they perform in a real situation on which the simulation is based? If they are successful in-game, would they have been in real life, and would a proven expert in real-life perform equally well in-game?

Hardware and software UI can be a significant source of immersive "breaks" in a simulation. It is important for the UI not to limit or distract the end user from immersing themselves. That being said, such things as peripheral vision, stereoscopy, voice recognition and force feedback are only as important as they are in performing the real-world tasks. I think one of the biggest challenges to serious games is to explore and enhance UI keeping in mind that it is the task we are trying to mimic, not just the available options.

Traditional entertainment games are based on rules and states, often encapsulated by a point system. Real-world tasks can rarely be constrained to this structure. I believe there is a bias in the game industry to use a traditional RTS-style point system when grading sophisticated tasks that emulate real life. It is often better instead to store the user's actions and have a human expert evaluate performance.

End users determine the validity of a simulation, and this adds an extra layer to quality assurance in the form of user studies. Meaningful user studies are paramount to a successful simulation and should involve a subset of end users of the same specialization as, but not part of, the design consultancy. Entertainment games are typically designed for a large audience, albeit one extremely familiar with the gamer paradigm. Serious games are often designed for specialists, and it is helpful to talk through immersive breaks with subjects, particularly when they know what they should do in the real-world but are unable to actualize it in-game.

Theoretical Research

Many simulations represent scenarios we see or read about in everyday real-life. *NBA Ballers* simulates the life of an NBA player, *Call of Duty* simulates soldiers fighting in World War II, *Spore* simulates a range of life from cells to solar systems, and a virtual medical procedure can simulate bypass surgery for medical students. These are tangible representations of real life—but simulations can also validate theoretical results, optimize existing models, or allow entirely new outcomes to emerge. Simulations leveraged at solving theoretical problems go beyond the traditional definition of simulations as a representation of real-life.

> Despite occasional harsh criticism that their work amounts to little more than "Nintendo" astronomy, astronomical modelers have long insisted that they're not simply playing games when it comes to simulating the universe and its evolution. Finally, new observational data from one of the world's largest ground-based telescopes confirms that these terabyte theorists have been on the right track all along.
>
> —*William Schomaker ("Cosmic models match reality." Astronomy. Milwaukee: September 2001.Volume 29, Issue 9; p. 22–23)*

In one example, astronomers rely heavily on theoretical models as they wait for improvements in optical and sensor technology to enable them to look deeper into the universe. In 2001, results from an enormous telescope in Chile were compiled by an international team of astronomers—validating the predictions of theoretical computer-based simulations about the earliest formation of our universe. A summary in the scientific journal *Astronomy* observed the crossover functionality of simulations with a reference to the maturing game industry.

Chris Mihos (Case Western Reserve University)

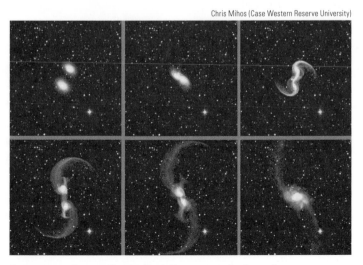

Astronomers frequently use simulations on a galactic scale.

Modeling Return on Investment

Corporations use simulations to maximize *return on investment (ROI)*. Rolling out new products or modifying existing lines introduces risk, and managers usually want to see data to back up proposals before moving forward. Imagine you are a safety engineer at an automotive manufacturer. Your job is to ensure that the vehicles your plant produces meet federal safety guidelines to protect passengers when a crash occurs. Experience tells you that the amount of aluminum allocated to the passenger cage is too light; erring on the safe side, you decide to double the thickness of the tubes that make up the passenger cage of the car. Your decision eventually makes it to the desks of the accountants, performance engineers, and fuel efficiency engineers. They are livid.

The accountants might bark down your neck that doubling the amount of aluminum in the frame will add $500 of raw material cost to the vehicle. They also determine that the additional welds will add five minutes to the build time of the vehicle. The performance engineers accuse you of making their job difficult because doubling the aluminum has doubled the weight, and the engine class allocated to the car is already straining to deliver the power necessary to push the projected vehicle weight. The fuel efficiency engineers latch on to the performance engineers' information and cry foul because the increased weight matched with available engines will push the vehicle out of a tax-favorable EPA miles-per-gallon bracket. As if they needed more ammunition, this point also infuriates the accountants. With the heat heading in your direction, it is clear you need some evidence to back up your case.

Applied Research Associates, Inc.

National Highway Traffic Safety Administration

Simulated crash tests provide massive amounts of data before costly real-life crash tests are necessary.

Rather than use precious time and money to build and crash test several functional prototypes, you approach your research and development lab to simulate the tests. You collaborate with the team to model many test cases with varying amounts of aluminum in the passenger cage. In one week, you have the data equivalent of 20 performance and crash-test scenarios. It turns out that your hunch about the aluminum specification being too low was correct, but doubling the amount of aluminum is not necessary. The simulation data shows that 1.7 times the amount of aluminum will provide adequate protection for passengers in all government safety tests. And look at that; the marketing department caught wind of your work and wants to use your simulation in their upcoming PR campaign to promote the safety of the new vehicle.

The Controversy of Simulating 9/11 Victims

9-11 Survivor is a controversial game simulation based on the aftermath of the September 11, 2001 World Trade Center attack. When the simulation begins, the player is on the 87th floor of the World Trade Center moments after the plane hits the first building. The player sees gaping holes in the floor, and smoke and debris begin to fill the room. Non-player characters (NPCs) appear disoriented and jump out of broken windows or holes in the walls. As the situation deteriorates around the player character (PC), the player has two options: attempt to descend down a seemingly infinite stairwell, or jump out of one of the windows and fall to her death.

9-11 Survivor simulates the moments after the 2001 terrorist attack on the World Trade Center.

When *9-11 Survivor* was presented at the Game Developers Conference in 2004, the audience's discomfort was palpable. The range of emotions included outrage, disgust, disbelief, curiosity, and intrigue. The developers preemptively answered the question on everyone's mind: How do the relatives of those who died in the World Trade Center feel about the simulation? According to the developers, when relatives of the deceased saw the simulation, many expressed appreciation and felt that it contributed to their ability to have closure on the tragic event.

John Comes on Real-World Knowledge vs. Realism : : : : :

John Comes
(Lead Game Designer,
Gas Powered Games)

John started in the game industry in 2001 at Westwood Studios, where he was Senior Level Designer on the MMOG, *Earth & Beyond*. He next worked on the *Command & Conquer* series. In 2003, John moved to Electronic Arts -Los Angeles, where he did design and artificial intelligence (AI) work on *Command & Conquer: Generals - Zero Hour* and *The Lord of the Rings: The Battle for Middle Earth*. In 2005, he began working with Gas Powered Games in Redmond, WA and shipped *Supreme Commander* as Lead Content Engineer before becoming Lead Game Designer.

Players' real-world knowledge plays a huge role in designing a simulation game. Keeping a short learning curve is important for your game to be adopted by the masses. The easiest way to do this is to make your gameplay intuitive by relating it to the real world. I do not believe we should get to realism completely in simulation games. "Hollywood" realism is usually more entertaining than "real" realism. Reality is not normally fun—but with a few tweaks, it can be a riot!

"Design Things that Make Sense"

Don't design a game for someone to play and have it follow rules that a player might never have any idea about. And you don't want to have to explain everything in the game. Making controls feel intuitive and designing challenges that use the abilities given to them will allow players to feel accomplishment and enjoyment with what they are playing. What they thought they could do works because it makes sense in the real world.

—*Josh Bear (Co-Owner & Creative Director, Twisted Pixel Games)*

Accidental & Sandbox Simulations

Developers like to think that they know what their audience wants. They spend countless hours tweaking parameters, adjusting positive and negative reinforcement, planning scripted events, and balancing gameplay—all in the name of giving players the best possible experience. When developers finally hand over their labor of love and the game hits the store shelves, it is completely out of their control. Once out in the wild, most games are used as intended—but once in awhile, players will use a game in a completely unintended way, sometimes discovering a new tool for simulation.

Creative players have used traditional action games such as *Halo* and *Counter-Strike* to create short films and elaborate physics demonstrations, and to make social and political statements. When games are used in an unintended manner to simulate an entirely different genre, developers may learn that their creation is far more versatile than they thought.

Red vs. Blue, produced with the *Halo* engine, is one of the most popular machinima series.

Storytellers & Directors

Technological advancements have made game simulation character models and animations more realistic. The increased realism captured the attention of storytellers and directors as a new medium to convey their ideas. This new medium, *machinima*, is another example of emergent gameplay unforeseen by developers when they originally designed and produced a game. Machinima directors use the characters and animations from mass-market games to create short movies without the immense cost and resources required to produce pre-rendered animated films such as those made by Pixar.

Simulations as Political Statements

Games released for personal computers are frequently modified (or "modded") by users who want to alter the intended game experience. Some mods, such as *Counter-Strike*—an online derivative of the *Half-Life* engine pitting terrorists against commandos—become so successful that they are released commercially. Other mods are used to broadcast social or political messages to all online players.

Velvet-Strike Team

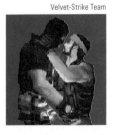

"Heart" spray (left) juxtaposes military and peace symbols; "MyBannerofGod" spray (middle) questions wars that are based on religious justifications; and "love1" spray (right) suggests eroticism in traditionally masculine characters.

One modder infiltrates online matches of the popular *Counter-Strike* military simulation, and flashes the names of real soldiers killed in wars waged by the United States. Another group created *Velvet-Strike*, a mod that plugs into the existing *Counter-Strike* game engine. Players using *Velvet-Strike* can access a variety of user-created spray paints to "shoot" graffiti onto in-game walls, ceilings, and floors. Many of the graffiti sprays carry religious, social, and political statements to share with the other online players.

Mark Skaggs on "Hollywood Realism" :::::

Mark Skaggs
(CEO & Executive
Producer, Funstar
Ventures, LLC)

Mark is best known for his work in the real-time strategy (RTS) genre, leading award-winning products such as *Command & Conquer: Red Alert 2*, *Command & Conquer: Generals*, *The Lord of the Rings: The Battle for Middle-Earth*, and more. With a game career spanning over 13 years, Mark has been responsible for production, game design, technical direction, and art direction on hit products that have sold over 10 million units of PC games since 2000.

I like creating what people call "Hollywood realism" for my games. This is the level of realism or expectation of realism that people have learned from Hollywood movies. For example, if there is a car crash in a movie, one of the cars usually explodes into a fireball moments later. This is not real, but it is the expectation of realism that many players have built up in their heads after watching lots of action movies. As game makers, I think our jobs partly come down to satisfying players' expectations while giving them lots of fun. This "Hollywood" style gives enough realism to engage the player, but not so much that it is starts to feel like work for the player. I like it when a player looks at a game element and says, "I think it should do and act like this" and then when they try it, they are right. Following this same style of realism, I like to think of the units in an RTS game as interesting and realistic looking "toys," while remembering that they are "toys" for the player to have fun with. From the look of the toy (i.e., helicopter or "laser tank"), players will have expectations on how it should act and maybe even a very thin layer of knowledge on how to control the real-world equivalent of that toy (i.e., helicopter controls)—playing into these expectations and even giving the player opportunities to make the "toy" do new fun things (i.e., barrel roll for a helicopter) through simple controls. With respect to graphics, sound, and other elements of the game, I like to use the same philosophy. Some people call this type of simulation a "light" simulation because it does not get into all the nitty-gritty of how things work in the real world and instead plays on players' expectations of how things work in the real world while focusing on fun for the player.

Experimenters & the Curious

When *sandbox* (or open-ended) game simulations began allowing players to explore worlds at their leisure and experiment with multiple levels of object interaction, new strategies and gameplay options emerged. Sandbox game simulations provide players with a vast array of tools and options. To facilitate experimentation in sandbox titles, developers remove time restraints and provide a loose, if any, framework for goals.

Even games that are not commonly classified as sandbox titles have developed a dedicated base of users who enjoy experimenting in the game world. *Halo* is wildly successful because the developers implemented an intuitive control scheme, well-designed maps, effective artificial intelligence, and a compelling story. These aspects captivated 99.9% of the *Halo*-playing population, but a minority became fascinated with the physics system in *Halo* and spent countless hours experimenting with vehicles, characters, and explosives to create elaborate stunts and chain reactions. The physics model in *Half Life 2* is even more advanced than *Halo* and, as such, has become a virtual playground for users creating elaborate Rube Goldberg-esque sequences. Players use a mod to manipulate objects and place triggered events. The chain of events may be set off by a crane catapulting a box into the air that knocks over a wall which trips a zip line pulley that runs into a switch opening a tank of compressed air that pushes a cart of virtual characters down a track into a pool. *Halo* and *Half Life 2* were not designed to reward this behavior with traditional points, unlockable content, or weapon upgrades. The reward comes from the satisfaction of accomplishing a rare feat and the drive that comes from competition with fellow experimenters.

A *Half-Life 2* mod enables players to experiment with the game's robust physics engine.

Politicians & Constituents

The popularity of social simulations utilizing *Second Life* and *The Sims Online* has caught the attention of several technology-aware politicians. In 2006, former Virginia governor Mark Warner held a virtual town hall meeting in *Second Life* where constituents gathered to hear him answer a moderated list of questions. At the meeting, Warner covered topics including the Iraq war, his political action committee, and reproductive rights. Attendance at virtual political events in *Second Life* has not broken the thousand mark yet—but, if virtual town hall meetings begin reaching a larger audience, politicians are bound to utilize them as inexpensive forums to communicate with their constituents. In July 2007, volunteer Jeremee Richir set up an "in-world campaign" for presidential candidate John Edwards in *Second Life*— with the full support of Edwards' team.

Frank Gilson on the Role of Realism :::::

Frank T. Gilson
(Senior Producer,
Wizards of the Coast)

At Wizards of the Coast, Frank Gilson manages game design and development in the R&D department. Frank was a producer at Atari's Santa Monica, CA office—managing aspects of third-party development, contracting with talent (such as composers and writers), and overseeing external development. Prior to Atari, Frank was Associate Producer at Blizzard for *Warcraft III: Reign of Chaos* and the *Frozen Throne* expansion. He also worked in quality assurance as QA Technical Engineer (*Diablo 2*), QA Lead Analyst (*StarCraft: Brood War*), and QA Analyst (*StarCraft* and *Mac Diablo*). Prior to joining the game industry, Frank was a graduate student at UC Irvine in Mathematical Behavioral Sciences, studying formal models for economics, voter choice, and psychology.

You can balance the pursuit of realism while maintaining intuitive gameplay by allowing the game software to track and manage a lot of the "realism" without requiring player attention. You can also permit players to select varying detail levels and be exposed to more and more of the "guts" of the simulation as they desire. You also have to make sure that your simulation game does not strongly conflict with players' real-world knowledge. Your fan community will notice every little thing and tear you apart on the forums. When you do vary from reality, it needs to be consistent, justified, and well presented.

Athletes

Coaches and managers know that simulating an upcoming game or race is one of the best ways to prepare for the real thing. Athletes have analyzed footage of their competition for decades on film reels and video tape. Sports simulations take research to the next level by enabling coaches and managers to test and demonstrate new strategies against a simulated opponent. If developed properly, sports simulations help players and teams prepare for game day. Race car drivers and golfers can use simulations to visit virtual versions of the respective tracks and courses they encounter. Basketball and football coaches can use simulations to test offensive plays against a variety of simulated defenses.

Starr Long on Realistic Characters & Environments :::::

Starr Long has been in the business of making games for over 12 years. Along with Richard Garriott, he was the original project director for the commercially successful *Ultima Online*. Starr worked his way up through the ranks of Origin Systems, starting in quality assurance on *Wing Commander*, *Ultima*, and many other titles. He was Producer on *Ultima Online 2*. He also worked with Richard Garriott on *Tabula Rasa* for the Korean online game giant NCsoft—creator of *Lineage*, the world's largest online game.

Starr Long
(Producer, NCsoft
Corporation)

My experience is mainly in online games where we do not have very much control of the environment. The number of players and corresponding enemies must fluctuate to make the game fun. Increases in hardware and software allow us to put more players and NPCs in the environment and we can have them make many more decisions per unit of time than ever before. That is how we can make an enemy you have riled up follow you around the corner and kick you in the face, versus just standing around stupidly while you heal up. It also allows us to give the players much greater variety of visual feedback. Every single kind of damage type in the game, for instance, can look completely unique. I think consistency is actually more important than realism. In games I think all that realism means is that things "make sense as long as they are fun."

News Consumers

Reuters recently set up shop in the *Second Life* world to dispatch news. The international news and financial information provider's presence includes a virtual news bureau and Adam Reuters, an in-game reporter representing real-life reporter Adam Pasick. Reuters saw an opportunity to explore the uncharted waters of reporting news about the social, political, and financial elements of a virtual world and *Second Life* had become robust enough to warrant coverage. The foray into virtual reporting could give Reuters a critical foothold as more companies and users leap into sandboxes and world simulations such as *Second Life*.

Reuters

News and financial corporation Reuters opened a virtual news bureau in *Second Life*.

Marketing, Consumers & In-Game Advertising

Credibility is a significant component of gaining consumer trust. Therefore, public relations and marketing firms have incorporated simulations into their messages. In medical marketing, for example, simulations are usually a drastic oversimplification of the effect a product has on patients. How many times have you seen an ad use a simulated human body with the advertiser's product flowing through it? Orally ingested pain relievers magically float from the mouth to the brain, neutralizing the migraine; "soothing" pink liquids flow down the virtual trachea to calm the upset, bright-red virtual stomach—which, upon the liquid's contact, turns a healthier shade of pink; a circle of lightning bolts flash around a virtual ankle and dissipate when the treatment cream is applied.

Simulations are convenient mechanisms for marketing many products' effects that would otherwise be too complex or disturbing to show in real detail. Without simulations, the health product marketing examples would be less effective. Consumers are unlikely to respond positively to a dry, technical lecture about how the product functions. Similarly, they do not need literal proof via demonstrations on a cadaver or a camera snaking through a live human. Instead, clean and tidy simplified versions of the human form stand in to market the goods.

Big Stock Photo

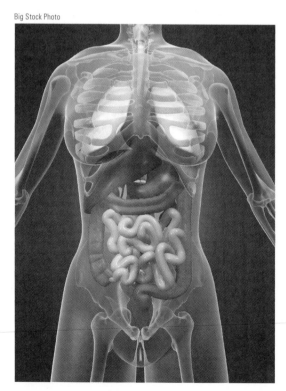

Marketing uses simulations when the real content might be too hard to swallow.

:::::When In-Game Advertising Adds Legitimacy

Professional sports organizations have capitalized on advertising dollars for decades. Sports associations like NASCAR, FIFA, and the NHL have embraced advertising so thoroughly that consumers balk at simulations of these sports unless it includes heavy branding. NASCAR cars are plastered with logos, and players in FIFA and NHL games are surrounded by ads on the boards enclosing the action. ESPN has become so intertwined with professional sports that its logo, music, personalities, and user interface themes add legitimacy to sports simulations.

Game simulations that focus on social interaction, such as *Second Life*, are also hotbeds for product placement. Brands like Adidas and Reebok have already opened virtual stores in the popular open-world simulation where players can view and customize shoes. Advertising in multi-user virtual environments such as *Second Life* is not necessarily more effective—but it certainly makes it look more like a trip to the shopping mall, if that is what players are seeking.

Sony Computer Entertainment America

Advertising legitimizes sports simulations such as *Gran Turismo* that rely heavily on sponsors.

In 2005, the in-game advertising market totaled approximately $56 million. According to Yankee Group, a technology research and consulting firm, the in-game advertising market will grow to $733 million by 2010. For better or worse, in-game advertising is here to stay. Companies cannot resist the game-playing demographic, heralded as brand-savvy consumers with disposable income, also known as the holy grail for marketing departments. On the other side of the coin, developers and publishers cannot resist the lure of advertising cash to offset some of the ballooning development costs. Early implementations of in-game advertising were clumsy, obnoxious implementations of static logos or other branding on low-resolution textures plastered throughout a game environment. New dynamic ads are far more flexible and enable developers to incorporate them much more efficiently and effectively without completely destroying the artistic vision of the product. Dynamic advertising also gives marketing and PR departments the capability to update in-game ads and harvest valuable metrics about how frequently their ads are being viewed. Although adding in-game advertising introduces legal hoops and artistic compromises, the costs offset by accepting a marketing deal can make the difference when trying to hit a production budget.

The audience for game simulations is growing rapidly. Hardware continues its relentless push forward and software tools and techniques are maturing, enabling more realistic simulations to be developed more efficiently. Traditional game developers are finding new markets by collaborating with corporations, which in turn are discovering how simulations can benefit their workers, clients, and market share. As the push for realism continues, game simulations will reach a broader audience and reduce the separation between real and virtual experiences.

:::CHAPTER REVIEW:::

1. Come up with a concept for a simulation that is intended to persuade an audience—whether political, social, economic, or commercial (such as in a marketing campaign). How would you tie in the simulation with your real-world campaign?

2. Why are multi-user virtual environments such as *Second Life* being used to create simulation games? How does the online multiplayer component and lack of non-player characters affect the development of simulation games created in these environments? If you were to create a simulation using *Second Life*, what topic(s) would you explore?

3. Simulation games such as *9-11 Survivor* are considered highly controversial. Choose a sensitive topic, and then create a concept for an associated simulation game. How would you handle the topic so that it was beneficial to the players?

Part II:
Serious Games

Education

game simulations for learning and instruction

Key Chapter Questions

■ What prevents custom educational game simulations from reaching the immersive level of mass market games?

■ How are mass market games utilized in classrooms?

■ Why is competition healthy, and how do educational game simulations foster competition?

■ What are some strategies used to prevent students from becoming frustrated or confused by game simulations?

■ How are educational game simulations changing distance learning?

A sector of the game industry has emerged to research and develop games that have value in the classroom. The "serious games" sector leverages proven techniques from entertainment development and merges them with proven educational methods. Design considerations are based on the premise that engaged students are more likely to retain information and participate for longer periods of time. Advancements in simulations do not signal the demise of the classroom teacher or professor. On the contrary, new simulation tools have enabled instructors to increase their influence through efficient, interactive learning. Consumers also have access to a wave of new titles incorporating educational elements. Game publishers have noticed the relative success of mass-market educational game simulations, and are busy filling their development pipelines with additional titles in the genre. Developers understand that the challenges associated with instruction and learning can be some of the most compelling aspects of game design, subtly tricking players into an education whether they know it or not.

An Uphill Battle

The public perception of the game industry has been shaped by several factors. Unfortunately, the majority of these factors have not helped game simulations earn legitimacy in educational environments. The legitimacy of games as educational tools is hampered by several stubborn factors: money, marketing, politics, and stigma.

1. *Money*: Budgets for blockbuster retail games are reaching Hollywood film proportions. The $20 million game is not unheard of, and $50 million games are around the corner. Budgets this high preclude educational games from competing with their flashier retail counterparts: the rich, complex games kids now expect. Anything less can be a let-down.

2. *Marketing*: Massive marketing efforts for blockbuster game releases are targeted at the game-playing demographic. Such promotions highlight the advanced graphics or controversial aspects to hook the audience, factors that push the entertainment potential over the educational value. Marketing and PR departments do not create the wedge, but they drive it deeper because the money flows much faster into the private sector. (See first point.)

3. *Politics*: Legislative posturing and high-profile lawsuits (no matter how baseless) have cast a negative light on the game industry. Unfortunately, for educational game simulations, the media frequently lump all games together—even though the legislative bills and lawsuits are targeted at only a sliver of the thousands of games on the market.

4. *Stigma*: For a significant number of people outside the target audience for blockbuster retail games, the game industry might as well have been in stasis for the past 15 years. To them, games still mean *Pac-Man* or *Super Mario Brothers* and are played by antisocial teenagers in their parents' basement. This segment of the population is usually shocked to hear that the average age of the video game player is 33 years old and 69% of American heads of households play computer and video games (Entertainment Software Association).

Investors are also weary of the educational sector of game development. According to *Education Week,* Executives of game and educational technology companies admit that learning games are frequently regarded as risky, money-losing propositions. While the potential upside of scoring a contract to roll out software to a state-wide school system may seem appealing, the bureaucratic nature of the educational system, combined with the lack of direct-marketing options, can make success very difficult to achieve. The limited likelihood of profitability also has kept the talented developers out of the market, which, in turn, has stunted the potential of the software as educational tools. This "catch-22" has limited the overall growth and capabilities of the educational game simulation market.

An Emphasis on Quality

Quality is the big driver in educational simulations. Just like any other material brought into a classroom, it needs to be good stuff. So it needs to be appropriate, it needs to address skills and information that students want/need, and it needs to really engage the minds of students *and* the teacher. (The same is true for books, case studies, lecture notes, and the rest of it.)

—*Titus Levi (Media & Arts Consultant)*

Joel Rogness on Issues Facing the K-12 Market :::::

Besides all the technical design hurdles, the real difficulty with incorporating technology into the classroom is financial; since compelling educational games are relatively expensive to create and operate—and there are few, if any, agreed upon standards by which to objectively measure student learning—schools often find technology purchases difficult to justify. Once game developers can demonstrate that their products do a more efficient job of teaching than traditional classroom environments alone, and can demonstrate in real dollars that the cost-to-student-learning-ratio is low enough, schools will get on board. If traditional public schools don't get on board, the endlessly more flexible private and charter programs will inevitably spring up to do so.

Joel Rogness
(English Teacher,
Simley High School)

It seems to me that this price point will be demonstrably reached, and that when it does simulations will become increasingly incorporated into classrooms. I envision adult literacy programs that feature virtual tutors who do strip-teases; I see open world environments in which, rather than control the physical movements of the characters, students tweak their personalities and priorities in order to produce different outcomes; I can see a day when math teachers no longer exist and have been replaced by virtual math tutors that quickly target curriculum to the strengths and weaknesses of each student; I can envision the widespread incorporation of games and simulations within schools, as soon as they are shown to have tangible results regarding student learning.

Mass Market Games in the Classroom

Education game simulations are built from the ground up, since classroom tools require significant planning and resources. Custom simulations also take time to design, develop, test, and publish before they can be integrated into a curriculum. Some educators bypass these hurdles by bringing traditional mass-market games into the classroom.

> Educational games are a viable supplement to the classroom as well as any other training environments. However, they are in no way a replacement for the hands-on interpersonal communication a student may find in the classroom or learning environment.
>
> —Roby Gilbert
> (Academic Department Director, Art Institute of Seattle)

Mayor of a Virtual City

One of the most successful commercial games, *SimCity*, has been widely heralded by teachers for its educational value. In the game, players create their own cities—complete with urban and residential zones, public transportation, utility infrastructure, government services, public spaces, and entertainment venues. *SimCity* illustrates the impact of the planning and administration of a city's economic, social, environmental, and political consequences.

Electronic Arts, Inc.

Students use games such as *SimCity 4* to learn about city planning, economics, and resource management.

A game such as *SimCity* is very useful when discussing how city management affects students' real lives. As students play, they can identify and experiment with how their virtual decisions might impact the real-world city they know. Students are continuously monitoring the cause and effect of in-game actions and judging how "realistically" the simulation portrays the result. According to Marc Prensky, author of *Digital Game-Based Learning*, if *SimCity* permitted players to build a modern virtual city without electricity, no one would play it. Developers will continue to build on the educational aspects of games such as *SimCity*, expanding the potential of game simulations as classroom tools for students to learn more about the world around them.

Life as a Pioneer on the Trail

Oregon Trail is an educational game that was very popular in schools in the 1980s. The game was designed to teach students about life on the historic cross-country route during the 19th century. *Oregon Trail* simulates life on the trail as the player leads a group of pioneers to the West coast. Each player can choose to start the game as a banker, carpenter, or farmer—a decision that determines the amount of money players are allocated at the beginning of the journey. Before getting underway, the player stocks up on supplies—including food, clothing, oxen, ammunition, and spare parts for the wagon.

The game simulates many situations that real pioneers faced while on the Trail. When players encounter a river, for example, they must decide whether to use some of their funds for a ferry, delay their trip by waiting for the low tide, or use the free and fast method of attempting to cross and risk injuring their oxen or damaging their wagon. Some events such as fires, food spoilage, disease, and severe weather occur randomly, altering the conditions and forcing players to make calculated decisions on how to proceed.

Oregon Trail also teaches players about pacing and strategy. The game requires players to set the pace of their trip and offers incentives for reaching the end of the trail as fast as possible. Players might decide to push the oxen as hard as possible in an attempt to reap the rewards—but the harder they push, the greater the risk of wagon damage or oxen death. A slower pace might reduce the likelihood of wagon and oxen problems due to exertion, but it increases the chances that the group will experience the devastating effects of the winter. The player must also decide how to allocate food to the group. A well-nourished crew is more likely to stay healthy, but there is a greater risk of depleting supplies before they can be replenished, either by hunting or being purchased at the next outpost. On the other hand, a player who is too conservative with food allocations is more likely to experience death and disease among the group. Teachers used the variables and tradeoffs to teach students about the consequences of their actions in a historical setting. *Oregon Trail* was successful because it offered an entertaining and challenging premise that required planning, risk mitigation, and a bit of luck.

©2000-2007 Riverdeep Interactive Learning Limited

```
A fire in the wagon
results in loss of:
        455 bullets
        57 pounds of food
Press RETURN to size up the situation
              Date: April 14, 1848
           Weather: cool
            Health: good
              Food: 1005 pounds
     Next landmark: 119 miles
    Miles traveled: 185 miles
    Press SPACE BAR to continue
```

Life was not easy for pioneers as they headed west. *The Oregon Trail* game simulates the challenges faced during the cross-country trip.

Detectives in the Classroom

Where in the World is Carmen Sandiego? covers a broad range of educational subjects under the guise of a detective hot on the trail of a villain, the titular Sandiego, and her gang of thieves who have stolen some of the world's great treasures. Players are given a limited amount of time to investigate the crimes in cities across the world.

Each city holds clues to the crimes—and players must track down evidence, obtain warrants, and arrest the criminals before the trail goes cold. The clues are based on real-world historical and geographical information that players must interpret based on their knowledge of the world.

©2000-2007 Riverdeep Interactive Learning Limited

Where in the World is Carmen Sandiego? is one of a series of detective games that tricked millions of kids into learning about geography and world history.

Where in the World is Carmen Sandiego? was widely used in classrooms across the country, compelling many teachers to build it into their curricula. An article in *Social Education*, the official journal of the National Council for Social Studies, outlined three instructional approaches to using the game in the classroom:

1. *Teacher-Directed Grouping*: An intensive approach over two weeks that encourages teacher-directed instruction concerning game logistics, group dynamics for tracking criminals, and a wrap-up discussion focused on concepts learned and skills attempted. Groups of students create maps, dossier images, and database charts, and the finished materials are posted on classroom walls. The teacher uses the game software and student-created materials to guide players in cooperative and competitive play, blending the game-based and classroom environments. The duration of the Teacher-Directed Grouping method could be expanded to cover the entire school year, providing the opportunity for investigation of additional topics in social studies and other disciplines.

2. *Curriculum Integration*: A one-week lesson involving diverse curriculum areas. The game can be incorporated into many areas, including math, language arts, art, music, values, teaching, research skills, data gathering, and group dynamics. Students might:
   - Create a timeline of the game's progress
   - Discuss the concept of values
   - Analyze careers, hobbies, and interests of gang members and crime witnesses
   - Plan, prepare, and consume the foods of countries and regions involved

3. *Isolated Lessons*: Avoid using *Where in the World is Carmen Sandiego?* as a game; do not use the software for its intended purpose. Instead, use the map screens, pictures, city departures, or clues to generate isolated instruction in geography, problem solving, decision making, and analysis of data. The value of the game as a geography tool alone can be used to teach about:

- continents and other land forms
- oceans and other water forms
- cities, counties, and political divisions
- directions, both cardinal and intermediate
- scale
- hemispheres
- latitude and longitude
- time zones

> *Europa Universalis* has amazing depth of research and variety of play. You could teach a course in Early Modern History with this game.
>
> —*Greg Costikyan*
> *(Chief Executive Officer, Manifesto Games)*

Chris Rohde on Educational Simulation Opportunities:::::

Chris Rohde has several years of professional experience as a 3D modeler for virtual simulators and as a character modeler, rigger, and animator for online children's games. In addition to being Assistant Director, Chris teaches various game courses at The Art Institute of Portland.

Educational games that simulate classroom activities could be a viable supplement to traditional education, but not a viable alternative. For a number of reasons which I will not go into, games could never successfully replace traditional education; however, I could think of a number of areas where educational simulation games could be great supplements as course activities. Imagine students experimenting in virtual chemistry or physics labs, or interacting with a music simulation game that allows them to apply music theory. Simulations that cover the fields of business, sports, music, medicine, art, science, etc., could give additional experience and alternative ways for students to apply the theories that they've learned through simulation games. It is important in the field of education to try to accommodate to as many students as possible to give everyone the same opportunity to learn, and simulation games provide one more avenue for this to occur.

Chris Rohde
(Assistant Director,
Game Art & Design /
Visual & Game
Programming, The Art
Institute of Portland)

Travis Castillo
(Level Designer &
Environmental Artist,
InXile Entertainment;
Professor, Art Center
College of Design)

Travis Castillo began his career in the game industry in 2002 by landing an internship at Activision's Central Technology, working under the art team. He then landed a job with Paramount Studios creating top secret military simulations in the Unreal engine in partnership with the Army and USC. After graduating in 2004 with a BA in Game Art and Design, Travis was offered a job teaching level design at Santa Monica College, where he helped form the game curriculum for the school's blossoming program. Since then, he has taught and helped form curricula for the Art Institute Online and Westwood College—and he is currently teaching Unreal level design at Art Center College of Design. Travis was the lead level designer and consultant on the highly acclaimed *Tactical Language* games: *Tactical Iraqi* and *Tactical Pashto*. At InXile Entertainment, he creates games on the Unreal 3 engine for the Xbox 360 and PlayStation 3.

Education is a branch that probably has the most to gain from games and simulations out of all the categories. In recent years, we have seen a significant drop in the quality of public education. There is nothing like a teacher who brings true experience and wisdom to a lecture to spark the brain of a child. But unfortunately, in my experiences of public education, these people are a rarity in the system. For the most part, teachers in front of a class of students will spout out facts that the student will need to memorize for a test to be held at the end of the week. The best students are those who can memorize these facts and can recall them the best come test time. The problem with this is, of course, that these facts are stored only in the short-term memory banks of the brain and most of this information is purged and replaced by new short-term info that needs to be memorized. Education is a complicated subject and everyone has strengths and weakness when it comes to learning, but one thing is certain. When a person is engaged directly with the learning, they will retain that data more readily, and nothing can engage a child like a good game!

User Interface Considerations

Developers collaborating on educational simulations must employ many of the same user interface considerations from retail games. Teachers have enough to juggle during their day-to-day responsibilities, and a well-designed layout can make the difference between a classroom of frustrated kids who want to give up and a group of students eager to jump into the game.

1. *Reduce screen clutter.* A clean, simple layout is critical to an intuitive end-user experience. If there are any icons or designs in the user interface that are not relevant to the purpose of the screen, get rid of them.
2. *Call attention to important areas of the screen using visual or aural cues.* This generally does not mean obnoxious flashing images or blaring noises. Slight motion, glow effects, and angles and lines that guide the eye toward the most important screen elements are key. Subtlety goes a long way.
3. *Concise messages.* Well-written text and dialogue adds credibility to the experience. Remember, the language and sentence structure you use has an impact on how students perceive the simulation. If done properly, the simulation could be a model for how to communicate effectively.
4. *Start with the basics.* Do not overwhelm students with a ton of information right off the bat. If there is a lot of information to convey, consider breaking it up into smaller chunks across several screens. Let the user get acquainted at a reasonable pace. Remember, even if you think something is obvious or can be taken for granted, most users are starting from square one and they probably prefer the obvious over being confused.
5. *Select clear, readable fonts.* Highly stylized fonts generally look unprofessional and become dated quickly. Test text readability on a wide variety of displays, including inexpensive and older-model televisions and monitors.
6. *Once fonts are selected, stick with them.* Do not start throwing in new fonts half-way through the simulation. Inconsistency is annoying.

Competition

There is a movement in the United States school system away from games that incorporate overt competition. Schools in states across the country—including Massachusetts, Wyoming, Washington, and California—have banned tag and other "chase" games because they believed it puts children at risk of being injured physically and psychologically. The principal of one school wanted to do away with competition altogether. "I discourage competitive games at school," he told the Associated Press. "They just don't fit my worldview of what a school should be."

Getty Images

We can only hope dodgeball during recess did not scar these children for life.

Parents do not want their child to feel inferior—and, yes, we want all students to succeed. School is a time to nurture confidence, but the educational setting is also a place to expose students to the reality that they need to function independently and prepare for times where they will not always come out on top. Students sheltered from the realities of a competitive market may be in for a rude awakening. Should employers hire every person from a pool of candidates so no one's feelings are hurt? Should anyone who can hold a microphone get the same access to an audience as those who have practiced their craft for years? The real world is competitive. Overly protected students could be at a disadvantage when they eventually need to compete for jobs and deal with rejection.

Competitive Learning in Game Simulations

Teachers can frame classroom competitions as a specific challenge for a single student or groups. Individual challenges may involve asking a student to simply complete a task or achieve a personal best score or completion speed. Group challenges take competition to an interpersonal level where students vie for position with classmates.

1. Traditional individual challenges
   - Fill out a multiplication table with less than three errors.
   - Find all the words in a puzzle in sixty seconds.
   - Write a short play in iambic pentameter.
   - Play the first thirty-two bars of a snare drum piece from memory.

2. Traditional group challenges
   - Place in the top three in the spelling bee.
   - Be the last student standing in a flash card showdown.
   - Take the top spot in a science fair.
   - Defend a position in a structured debate.

Educational game simulations can build on these long-standing competitive scenarios. Game simulations such as *Brain Age* excel at taking traditional classroom-based activities like flashcards and making the tests approachable and challenging. Like their real-world counterparts, the *Brain Age* games score players on speed and accuracy as they complete basic arithmetic and solve simple puzzles like counting syllables or number progressions.

Getty Images

Nintendo

Voice Calculation | Back | More

Please try to do this training in a quiet place.

Quit

Nine!

54÷6=

8−8=   L   R

Answer out loud.

Traditional classroom challenges such as flash cards (left) translate well to competitive game simulations (*Brain Age*, right).

Developers designing games for group competitions may incorporate "community" components. Teachers can configure the virtual public areas for students to collaborate on solving a problem or to post their progress. The community forum may also be used to foster competition through leaderboards and statistics.

Big Stock Photo

Games designed for group competitions are built for simultaneous participation from multiple students. The quantity of simultaneous users is limited by budgets during the development phase and in the classroom. Basic multiplayer educational simulations, such as those involving networked flashcards, have very little development cost overhead. However, when developers embark on creating a robust multiplayer educational game simulation, such as the latest iteration of *SimCity*, supporting additional users increases costs significantly. Even if the software scales to an infinite number of players, the number of simultaneous users is still limited by classroom resources. Each

Shared computer labs help defray costs, but limit teachers' ability to fully integrate game simulations into their curricula.

student requires a workstation—including screen, computer, and interface equipment. Shared central locations such a computer lab or library can spread costs across departments—but without dedicated workstations in their classrooms, teachers cannot build extended simulation exposure into their curricula.

Monitoring Progress

Educational game simulations can also help teachers track progress by maintaining a record of students' scores over time. The results are superior to manual records because they can be sorted by a multitude of variables—including score, time, student, and date. Teachers also benefit from the wide range of filtered views afforded by simulations—from a holistic view covering all students over the entire year, all the way down to an individual student on a specific day. These metrics can illustrate trends in performance, enabling teachers to proactively address each student's situation.

1. *Upward trend*: Reward the student with praise and additional challenges.
2. *Downward trend*: Backtrack to the date and circumstances at the start of the downward trend and attempt to isolate the factors that caused the tipping point.
3. *Flat trend*: Investigate roadblocks the student is encountering and adjust the challenges appropriately.

Teachers face many challenges when instructing a group of students. Even if a teacher has a command over the classroom and a well-structured lesson plan, keeping students focused on the task at hand and monitoring their progress can be difficult. According to *Education Week,* educational game simulations facilitate both these issues by capturing and holding people's attention and constantly assessing players' progress.

Ramping Up Difficulty in Games

A smooth ramp-up of difficulty in games mirrors the natural progression of learning in an educational setting: Start with the basics and build complexity along the way. Children cannot be expected to master calculus before learning arithmetic, geometry, trigonometry, and algebra. Similarly, people who have never played video games—or have not played them in many years—lack the early and intermediate stages that prepare them for the complexity of modern, immersive game simulations.

Difficulty is also an issue in the more compressed learning timeframe of a single game. Developers need to consider the wide degrees of experience different users will have when the game is turned on. If the game detects it is running for the first time on the system, it should assume the player is unfamiliar with the game. Designers may include a training stage where onscreen dialogue and icons explicitly indicate how to operate the controls. The training stage may be a basic obstacle course or "island" environment free from the challenges or time constraints of the regular game so that player can take their time to become familiar with the game. Designers may alternatively choose to drop the player into an environment that resembles the real game experience, but include rudimentary non-player character (NPC) artificial intelligence, forgiving objective requirements, and simplified puzzles. If the training component of the artificial intelligences determines the player is having trouble, it can provide additional visual or aural advice, reduce the difficulty, or simply provide encouragement to keep the player engaged. Without the familiarity that comes with experiencing the growth along the way, jumping right in to the "live" action can be jarring and discouraging.

"Learning By Doing" & Trying Something New

Simulations can be very strong in their ability to teach. They can enliven an otherwise dense subject. The ability of electronics and software to keep track of things and present a good UI can truly facilitate "learning by doing" through simulation games. Game simulation software can let many more people experiment with subjects that they are unlikely to otherwise encounter. This is especially important to young students who are trying to understand what they enjoy doing. Educational games are a good supplement to traditional education.

—*Frank T. Gilson*
(Senior Producer, Wizards of the Coast)

Mainstream Educational Games

Do consumers really seek educational video games for recreation? Indeed, some of the top-selling titles on the market are thinly veiled educational games. The high sales suggest consumers gravitate to games that have traditional learning elements such as memorization, pattern recognition, and basic calculations. If growing sales are a sign of things to come, there might be hope for a large percentage of our population to learn in their spare time rather than absorbing the latest sitcom.

Brain Trainers

The portable game console market has grown steadily since Nintendo's Game Boy redefined its capabilities. Nintendo's latest portable system, the DS, has captured a massive portion of the market because of its touch screen, dual displays, and several games that are unabashedly education-oriented. *Brain Age* was one of the first games released for the DS. The title is a compilation of many basic lessons from grade school. Basic mathematics, syllable counting, reading aloud, and memory-based challenges are all included in the game. As players participate in the tests, the game records the results and players can track their progress over time. *Brain Age* takes a playful approach to charting a player's progress by calculating a "brain age" after each test sequence. A player who finishes tests rapidly and accurately will have a low brain age; a young brain age implies a healthier and sharper brain.

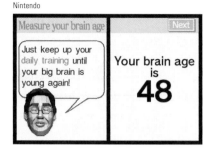

Nintendo

Fast completion times and accuracy equals a young "brain age." This player has some training to do!

A Virtual Interpreter

Talkman, a personal interpreter for the Sony PSP, includes a small microphone peripheral that plugs into the portable system. Players speak into the microphone and the software translates words between English, French, Italian, German, Spanish, and Japanese. If the user is not shy about using the technology in public, *Talkman* can be a convenient alternative to translation books when traveling through foreign countries. Users are also encouraged to bolster their fluency by playing games that test pronunciation and listening comprehension. The software also includes other helpful traveling tools such as a world clock and a conversion application covering currency, temperature, and distance. Although the speech recognition is not fool-proof, *Talkman* is a useful translation and educational tool. As technology marches forward, hardware and software improvements will make future *Talkman*-like applications indispensable for world travelers.

Measuring Zombies Slain Per Minute

Typing tutors are rarely heralded for brilliant design or entertaining software. The standard typing tutor experience requires users to copy passages of dry, uninspired text for several minutes. When complete, the software calculates the rate in words per minute and number of errors. Traditional typing tutors get the job done, but they do not exactly leave the user begging for more. *The Typing of the Dead* destroys all typing tutor conventions by replacing the traditional uninspired design with zombie-killing action.

The zombie-based typing tutor is built on the engine used for *The House of the Dead*, Sega's successful arcade light-gun franchise. In the adaptation, players use keyboards instead of guns to ward off the relentlessly advancing zombies. Words and phrases appear in front of every enemy and players must type the characters quickly and accurately to take the zombies out before they reach the screen and attack the player. The fast and furious action in *Typing of the Dead* does an excellent job of distracting players from consciously thinking about words per minute or typing conventions.

Sega did an admirable job of opening up the game to a wider audience when converting the original light-gun game. The brutal weapons such as axes and guns were replaced with comedic weapons such as rubber mallets, keyboards, and maracas. *The Typing of the Dead* also includes a mode for players who want to get back to typing tutor basics. The "drill mode" includes mini-games that measure players' speed, accuracy, and reflexes.

Standard typing tutors boring you to death? *The Typing of the Dead* gives players a better incentive to type words quickly and accurately.

Fitness

As United States obesity levels become increasingly worrisome, video games are frequently held as scapegoats for encouraging inactivity. Some schools hope to counter the trend by incorporating game simulations into their physical education programs. The most widespread form of fitness-related games was made popular by Konami's *Dance Dance Revolution (DDR)*—which promotes movement by eschewing the traditional handheld controller in favor of a floor mat lined with sensors. Players step on sections of the mat that correspond to onscreen symbols synchronized with the beat of the soundtrack. As players progress, the tempo increases and the patterns become more complex. The dancing simulation gives players an incentive to advance via high score challenges and unlockable content including new stages and songs.

::::: Dance Dance Revolution Roll-Out

Students in the West Virginia public school system have, or will soon have, access to *Dance Dance Revolution (DDR)* in their classrooms. West Virginians rank third in the nation for obesity, and public school officials believe *DDR* will help kick-start students into a more active lifestyle.

The dance simulation has been rolled out to over 100 junior and middle schools and the state spent half a million dollars to distribute the dance simulation to all 765 public schools in 2007. The ambitious collaboration between game publishers and public schools to combat obesity is the first of its kind.

Titus Levi on Experiential Learning :::::

Titus Levi
(Media & Arts
Consultant)

Titus Levi is an economist working as a consultant for individuals and organizations in the arts and media industries. His clients include Interep, Susquehanna, and the Durfee Foundation. Titus has been a faculty member at the University of Southern California's Annenberg School for Communication—where he taught classes in business strategies and conducted research on the economics of the radio industry. His work in radio has spanned more than a decade, including serving as program host and producer for KUSC-FM and KPFK-FM. Titus also worked as a freelance journalist, most significantly writing for *Keyboard Magazine*'s new talent column, "Discoveries." He has also been an arts administrator, organizing and producing concerts for the California Outside Music Association and the Los Angeles Festival.

For experiential learners, games offer the chance for a more direct kind of experience of information and knowledge. They can also get students/learners to "rehearse" situational intelligence. That is, one can be confronted by various scenarios and practice inside the simulated environment that allows students/ learners to make mistakes, learn from mistakes, and try different means for solving problems. The military has been working hard on this, but alas, they focus too much on the "hard" aspects of military work (killing people; destroying things) and not on the soft part (dealing with differences in language and culture in an urban low-level conflict situation; e.g., Iraq).

A Virtual Fitness Trainer

While *DDR* and similar rhythm games provide an alternate route to an active lifestyle, they are not a replacement for traditional means to get a workout. In 2005, developer responDesign, Inc. saw the void in the market for a more traditional fitness training simulation and released *Yourself!Fitness*—which includes Maya (a virtual fitness coach), multiple workout environments, and over 500 exercises. The simulation is superior to any workout DVD because it can dynamically adjust its difficulty. As players progress, the regimen adapts to match the proper workout to the condition of the user.

Boredom is the last thing someone needs when trying to muster the motivation to work out. *Yourself!Fitness* avoids this problem by randomly generating a workout plan every time it loads. Will fitness simulations like *Yourself!Fitness* catch on in the United States? If the installed base of computers and game systems continues to rise and simulations continue to reduce the barriers and excuses to working out at home, these simulations could play a larger role combating obesity.

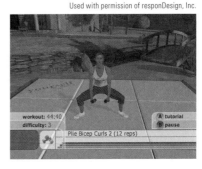

Used with permission of responDesign, Inc.

Yourself!Fitness is a virtual fitness package that adjusts difficulty dynamically.

Simulating Responsibility

The market for virtual pets is growing rapidly. Developers are responding by creating pet simulations that can bring some of the fun and responsibility of pet ownership into people's lives. Improvements in artificial intelligence enable game developers to design simulated pets that exhibit increasing realistic behavior. Graphical improvements are making headway at winning over the crowd that swoons when a certain threshold of digital pet cuteness is achieved. Online connectivity is opening up a new world of social interaction for virtual pets and their owners.

One of the best-selling games of all time is designed on a simple premise: model some of the most beloved breeds of dogs and put them in an environment where people can train, play with, and care for them. Nintendo ignited a virtual pet craze when they released *Nintendogs*, a dog simulator for the DS system. The cute graphical style of *Nintendogs* is what hooks many players right off the bat. The developer wisely chose to model the animals as playful companions, eager to please their masters.

Nintendo

In the game, players train their puppies using the DS microphone and stylus to respond to their name and perform over a dozen tricks, including sit, follow, and lay down. While interacting with their virtual dog, players must be conscious of their pet's stamina; too much training or playing will cause the pet to become tired, requiring dog and owner to take a break from the game. The dogs are not overly needy, but they are healthier virtual companions if players spend the time to periodically feed, wash, and play with them.

Millions of people were unable to resist the allure of the playful digital puppies of *Nintendogs*.

If *Nintendogs* is a cute and playful pet simulation, *Seaman* is its cold, obstinate distant cousin. The pet in the latter game starts as an egg and grows through several stages of development, becoming more advanced physically and mentally. During the tadpole-like stage, the creature listens for speech and sounds that the user delivers into the microphone. When it detects words, the pet mimics them in a vaguely infant-like babble-speak. After a period of time, the creature develops into an amphibious frog-like creature with a human-like face. When the odd creature reaches this Seaman stage of development, players converse with it by asking it questions and providing information for the game's advanced artificial intelligence to utilize for future exchanges. Conversations with the Seaman are full of trivia and historical information, usually guided at the whim of the creature. The pet is also prone to spells of disinterest during which it may simply turn away and ignore its owner. When the Seaman does feel like conversing, it may become agitated and insult the player—sometimes throwing personal barbs by drawing on knowledge gleaned from past conversations.

Players must monitor and adjust a few variables to keep their Seaman healthy—including his food, and his tank's cleanliness, oxygen supply, and temperature. Compared to *Nintendogs'* relatively modest requirements for caring for the virtual pet, *Seaman* is downright brutal and uncompromising. Forget to check on your Seaman in a 16-hour span? Too bad. It is dead.

How would Seaman have been different if the virtual creature were designed as a furry puppy-like animal always willing to please, rather than the pasty, scowling, bottom-dwelling animal the developers chose? The appearance would not have matched the snide, cynical wit of the Seaman, and the experience raising the vocal pet would not be nearly as entertaining.

The art style of *Seaman* matches the virtual pet's attitude. Neither are designed to cheer you up.

:::::: Darwinian Simulation

Natural selection takes center stage in the quirky GameCube game, *Cubivore: Survival of the Fittest.* As the game's subtitle implies, *Cubivore* pits players against creatures competing to survive in a kill-or-be-killed world. When the game begins, the player's cubivore is "born" as a cube with a single limb. Like most living things just arriving in the world, priority number one is to find something to eat. Players must guide their weak newborn in search of other cubivores to defeat and consume. Eating other cubivores mutates the main character, usually changing its color and moving its limb(s) to a more advanced location. For example, the horizontally oriented limb on the lowest level cubivore can only pull or push it around. As the animal consumes its competition, the limb may mutate lower on the body so it can begin hopping and attacking from above.

There are two primary goals in the game, both designed to evolve the main character into the most advanced creature.

- *Mutate*: The player must seek out an opponent and then weaken, kill, and eat it. Consuming the limbs of opponents mutates the cubivore, giving him more strength and evolves the orientation of his limbs into a more advanced state.

- *Breed*: As the player's cubivore mutates and becomes stronger, natural selection comes into play and female cubivores show an increased interest in breeding with him. After breeding with multiple females, the resulting offspring are born with an additional limb, and the player selects a new character from among the evolved children.

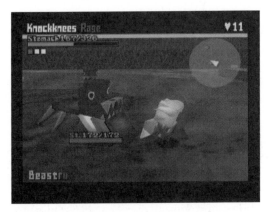

Cubivore is a lightweight simulation of species mutation and evolution.

Once the cubivore reaches a high enough state of evolution, the player can battle an advanced boss character for supremacy in the virtual kingdom. *Cubivore* is an effective demonstration of Darwinian evolution in an abstract environment. Although the game is built with rudimentary graphics and controls, players can use it to see the effects their actions have on their character and learn basic principles of mutation and evolution.

Educational Road Blocks

I think the biggest problem in the classroom these days is keeping the kids' interest level high in both the classroom and at home. Teachers can usually do their part—it's my opinion that the parents need more help getting their kids to do homework and engaged in the curriculum once they walk out of the school. Perhaps educational games can help in that regard—maybe school-issued homework programs would be the way to go. I don't really see educational games replacing one-on-one school time. It seems like mavericks who want to revolutionize educational software have walked into a bit of a road block. I was talking to one developer who wanted to teach more life skills in their product who said that it's hard to get into Walmart and other mass markets without getting educational board endorsements for your product. That makes a lot of sense, but the problem is that these education boards only want you to stick to the basics. And as anyone with any shred of creativity knows, sticking to the basics tends to bend opposite to innovation.

—Kraig Kujawa (Lead Designer, Midway Games)

Remote & Distance Learning

Internet connectivity has changed the way people work and study all over the world. The use of email, video conferencing, and online collaboration tools such as wikis and message boards is established throughout most professions. These tools revolutionize the way we share information, but they do not address the perception that participants are in different physical locations. Over the past several years, teachers and professors have been exploring technologies that bring people together in a virtual classroom.

Games created within an online multiplayer environment in particular contain three main features that contribute to education:

- *Constructivism*: learning by doing; customization of the learning experience. Users can customize their avatars and objects, and explore, modify (if allowed), and interact with the environment.
- *Social interaction*: learning through interacting with others; lateral learning. Online multi-user environments are often social communities—where users can easily form special interest groups and friendships inside the world.
- *Simulation*: The very definition of "simulation" implies *learning within a real-world context*—and situations and rules in an online multi-user environment could be virtually (if not completely) identical to those found in "real life." The capacity to present real-world situations to users is stronger in 3D rather than within 2D, primarily text-based platforms (such as Blackboard, Intralearn, WebCT, and eCollege) often used by the online distance learning segment.

Milan Petrovich on Educational Simulations in 3D Online Environments :::::

Milan Petrovich taught game design theory and development at the Art Institute of Las Vegas and was Academic Director for Game Art & Design. Prior to the Art Institute, Milan was Director of Production for the pioneering Internet television studio WireBreak Entertainment. He has over 17 years of professional experience in design and multimedia. Milan received his MFA from the USC School of Cinema-Television, where he studied the development of online games under the Sega Interactive Fellowship.

Educational simulations are an innovative way to deliver content in a form to which today's students have grown accustomed. Chat boxes and menu-driven systems are technologies that have been around for decades and seem tired in comparison to an avatar-based 3D environment. Given the number of hours the average student spends playing online games, educational simulations may prove to be a viable alternative to going to class. The military has already experienced success in using games to simulate combat. These games do a much better job of teaching students to deal with complex situations than any classroom experience could replicate. Adding elements of competition and fun further the learning objectives rather than subtracting from them.

Milan Petrovich
(Associate Dean
of Academic Affairs,
Art Institute
of California -
San Francisco)

The Virtual Campus

Some professors post their lecture notes online for students to access, but a virtual world called *Second Life* takes online collaboration to the next level by enabling professors to hold lectures for their students in a simulated classroom. *Second Life*, created by Linden Lab, is a diverse online world where users can create nearly every aspect of their environment. The open-ended nature of the virtual environment has caught the attention of academia and has led to a great deal of experimentation and participation from established academic institutions. A professor can model his lecture hall and mark his students' attendance by the avatars sitting in the seats. This literal transposition of a campus classroom into a virtual representation brings another dimension to remote learning and instruction. The professors and students can be physically located across the globe as their avatars gather in the virtual classroom.

Students and observers gather to listen to a professor speak in Harvard University's virtual classroom in *Second Life.*

In the fall semester of 2006, the Harvard Law School, via Harvard Extension, offered a class with mandatory weekly activities in *Second Life*. At that time, over sixty schools and educational organizations had already created a presence in the virtual world and were exploring ways it can be used to promote learning.

Players can join the *Second Life* community free of charge, but most virtual property comes at a real-world price to keep the servers running. Linden Lab offers discounts to verified real-world educators and academic institutions or non-profit organizations that use the virtual land to support their official work.

:::::: *Second Life* as an Educational Tool

Author Jeannie Novak is producer and lead designer on a project that utilizes the *Second Life* (*http://www.secondlife.com*) multi-user virtual environment as a learning system. (Although Second Life might be described more appropriately as a social network, it has the capacity to exhibit features of a massively multiplayer online game [MMOG].) The course, being developed for the Art Institute Online (a division of the Art Institute of Pittsburgh), is a Business Communications course that behaves like a process simulation game with some role-playing, adventure, and strategy elements. It is planned that students taking the course will log onto *Second Life* and "teleport" to Ai Pittsburgh Island, where they will find themselves as interns in a fictional cor-

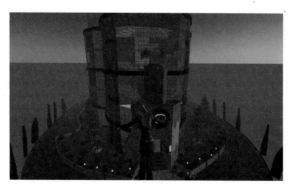
Surveying construction of the Business Communications educational simulation game being built in *Second Life.*

poration. During the 5-½ week course, students ("player characters") will learn the inner workings of the corporation through real-world scenarios. They will also discover how to communicate with other employees ("non-player characters") within the corporate environment. This is a big step forward in integrating games into education. Eventually, all courses may be taught as games. All games involve "covert learning"—often unintended by the developers. The reverse can also be true: All courses could conceivably involve "covert gaming"! This is just the beginning of an educational revolution. See *http://www.simteach.com* for forums discussing using *Second Life* as an educational environment.

With the seemingly limitless potential of education in a virtual world, real class-rooms are not going away anytime soon. Game developers are still laying the foundation for massively connected online environments in *Second Life* and in the massively multiplayer online role-playing game (MMORPG) *World of Warcraft*, which supports thousands of simultaneous users. As these games scale even higher, academic institutions will have more flexibility to grow into the new environment. Commercial game developers currently have the experience and technology to create compelling mass-market games, but the breakthrough that elevates educational game simulations to their potential will be driven by educators, not game designers (*Education Week*).

Schools & Degrees Built on Game Industry Demand

Given the rapid growth of the game industry, it is no surprise that secondary education institutions have scrambled to catch up to create curricula to match market demands. The Art Institute, Vancouver Film School, Savannah College of Art and Design, Full Sail, and Digipen are a few of the pioneers in the game industry education field—but it did not take long for long-established academic institutions to jump into the fray. Major universities, including the University of Southern California (USC), Georgia Tech, and Carnegie Mellon, now offer bachelors or masters degrees in game development.

Most developers prefer candidates trained in the rich, deep artistic or technical theory provided by universities even if it means a relatively long ramp-up to producing game-ready art or code. Regardless of the school, the academic environment is a unique opportunity to study game theory and develop games without the pressures of commercial game development. Students have access to many of the same tools and techniques while they can push the boundaries of game development and explore areas on which private companies cannot afford to spend time or resources.

Screening for Signs of Autism and Learning Disorders

Educational games can also be designed to screen children for early signs of autism and learning disorders. The computer-based tests are designed as entertaining games, so children are unaware they are being tested. Tests are built with colorful cartoon characters and simple puzzles based on words, sounds, and pictures. If children score in a specific range on one of these targeted tests, they can be referred to a specialist for professional diagnosis. One developer of these tests, Learning for Children, emphasizes that these simulations are not a replacement for professional in-person screening, diagnosis, or therapy, but they provide another means for early detection (*Newsweek*).

Simulations for Disabled Children

Because many games and tests are designed around precise timing and movement, they can be exceedingly difficult or impossible for disabled children to play. Daniel Bogen, an associate professor of bioengineering at the University of Pennsylvania, has developed instruments, interfaces, and error-correcting software to adapt to the less precise inputs from disabled children. He has also developed sensors that translate inputs like head movement or blowing into a tube to trigger percussive instruments that would otherwise be difficult or impossible for the child to play. Bogen also believes that toys and games "can act as a social lubricant for disabled kids who might otherwise sink into isolation" (*Newsweek*).

Established game developers have powerful tools and techniques to create engaging interactive educational simulations. Developers must use their experience to maintain focus on their expertise, while integrating proven and emerging instructional methods into the medium. Working directly with teachers in the community is still the best way to ensure that educational game simulations deliver the content needed to help students.

:::CHAPTER REVIEW:::

1. Why do you feel that the synthesis of entertainment and education (known as "edutainment") did not capture a wide market? How can games created for educational purposes maintain a high entertainment value? If you were to create a game intended for educational purposes, how would you balance education and entertainment?

2. Some of the simulations discussed in this chapter incorporate "covert" rather than "overt" learning. What are the benefits and disadvantages of each? Do you agree or disagree that most games are educational—even if they are not designed as such? Why or why not?

3. The multi-user virtual environment known as *Second Life* has been used by educational institutions for virtual classroom simulations and simulation games. What characteristics of this environment facilitate learning, and why?

4. Create a concept for an on-ground classroom simulation game. Discuss the genre, theme, market, and objectives of the game. Would you make the educational components of the game "overt" or lean more toward an "immersive," covert environment? If you were to create an online version of this simulation game, how would you modify it?

5. Play an existing educational simulation and discuss five features that distinguish the game from other types of simulations. How effective were the education and entertainment elements?

4

CHAPTER

Business

simulating the workplace

Key Chapter Questions

- What are some common misconceptions about business simulations?

- How do simulations incorporate fuzzy logic?

- What aspects of business simulations translate to the consumer market, and how do corporate simulations affect consumers?

- How do simulations developed for different industry segments address training needs associated with each segment?

- How can advances in simulation technology simultaneously increase safety and profits?

If you tried to start a conversation about corporate training during dinner, you might elicit a collective yawn from your guests. The words "corporate" and "training" sit on the lowest rungs of the ladder of socially appealing topics and, when combined into a phrase, plummet even further in rank. Corporate training earned its reputation through years of droning PowerPoint presentations, atrociously scripted manuals, pathetically produced orientation videos, and cumbersome training interfaces. Some corporations acknowledged and addressed the negative stigma of corporate training by using tools and techniques associated with game simulations. The result is a relatively new field involving corporate simulations that make testing and training more effective, efficient, and—gasp!—entertaining. Corporations that choose to ignore the potential of simulations risk endangering their customers, employees, reputation, market share, and financial bottom line.

Barriers to Entry

Corporate simulations are perceived as dull, uninspired, and tedious. Some of these characteristics can be attributed to a lack of professional diversity among disciplines on development teams. Most successful simulations are built with input from multiple disciplines. At the risk of generalizing, simulations are less effective and inefficient when developed by a team comprising people from a single discipline—as shown in the accompanying diagram.

Diagram by Per Olin

	Aesthetic Appeal	Functionality	Intuitiveness	On Time and Budget
Artists	High	Low	Low	Low
Designers	Low	Low	High	Low
Producers	Low	Low	Low	High
Programmers	Low	High	Low	Low

Successful simulations should be developed by a mixture of artists, designers, producers, and programmers—each of which have distinct strengths.

Cross-Discipline Development

Corporations have made improvements by assembling simulation development teams with representatives from each discipline; these teams closely resemble the personnel at a game development studio. While some corporations do not have dedicated personnel in each department, contract help is readily available to fill in gaps. Cross-discipline development teams may experience tension, especially in a creative environment. However, tension frequently results when many specialists with strong opinions collaborate on a single goal. Periodic flare-ups are a positive sign that team members are voicing their opinions and challenging others to be at the top of their game. If there are no arguments or criticism during development, there is probably something wrong with the simulation.

Collaborating with Experienced Developers

Corporations can also collaborate with an established game developer to build a simulation. In this scenario, the business outlines its simulation vision and requirements, and hands over the specifications to a team with experience working through the full development pipeline. Collaborating with an established game developer ensures all disciplines are already on staff. The business can also rely on the developer to provide a much more accurate time and budget estimate than if the business attempted to build the simulation in-house. Experienced developers are familiar with the inevitable hurdles to overcome when building interactive media and push projects through the final test and release stages of development. The collaborative arrangement enables businesses to roll out innovative training based on proven game mechanics, reduce negative feedback, and increase efficacy and retention.

Managing Expectations

Once a business is committed to virtual training, expectations must be managed from the outset of building the simulation. The look and feel of a $100,000 simulation cannot hold a candle to the sophistication of multimillion-dollar consumer games such as *Grand Theft Auto* or *The Sims*. Business simulations can utilize many of the tools and techniques used to build these blockbuster games, but budget restrictions require training simulations to focus on a narrow goal to do it well. Paradoxically, some businesses perceive anything resembling a video game as unprofessional and useless in a business setting. Development teams that are sensitive to the target market for the simulation can sometimes overcome these perceptions. For example, if a simulation is designed to train mine workers about job safety, artists and designers must strike a balance between an entertaining style that engages the audience and one that reinforces the gravity of worksite protocol.

Medicine & Healthcare

Operation, a classic board game released by Milton Bradley in 1965, is a simplified simulation of an operating room table. Players earn points by removing plastic "bones" and "organs" from small openings in a game board painted in a cartoon style to resemble a human body lying on an operating table. *Operation* requires that players use metal tweezers to remove game pieces without making contact with the game board's metal edges. If the tweezers touch the edge, a low-voltage electrical circuit is closed, the game emits a loud buzzer sound, and the "patient's" nose lights up bright red—indicating the player has lost a turn.

Although *Operation* is a rudimentary representation of a real surgery, it is a fun, entertaining way to familiarize children with the importance of an accurate, steady hand. Modern medical simulations are far removed from *Operation* and are widely used in commercial, educational, and consumer markets.

Operation © 2007 Banc of America Leasing & Capital, LLC

Operation is a board game that simulates the challenge of having accurate, steady hand movements required on the operating table.

Commercial Medical Simulations

The commercial medical market is a competitive arena where medical simulations can save time and money. Virtual medical procedures allow prospective surgeons to learn proper operating room protocols and hone their techniques without endangering the lives of real patients. An article in *Health Management Technology* outlines the effectiveness of simulating endoscopy, a common procedure involving a small tube equipped with a camera that allows doctors to visually examine the interior of the human body with minimal or no surgery:

> An Endoscopy Simulator is an interactive apparatus for learning and practice in anatomy, equipment handling, diagnostic procedures, and treatment options. The simulator features [a variety of operation] modules. All provide educational content before and during the procedure, real-time feedback during the procedure, and a performance report at the conclusion of each session. Learners insert the fiber-optic scope into a special console designed to be anatomically realistic. They move the dials on the hand piece, which is exactly like the real device they will use with real patients. They observe a computer screen image of the lungs or colon. Tissues look real and "move" when touched. Users feel resistance to their movements of the handset, and the "patient" may exhibit bleeding, vital sign changes, or other physiological effects. The software presents a variety of alternative clinical scenarios that simulate the range of patients with different diagnoses and pathologies that providers will encounter in clinical practice. Learners not only practice and perfect procedure technique; they gain experience that will help them apply their skills with clinical judgment.

Medical simulations bridge the gap between the classroom and operating room. They prepare medical students for the realities of lifesaving procedures, and familiarize seasoned surgeons with new equipment and techniques. Medical simulations share many of the technologies pioneered by game simulations, including texturing and rendering techniques, forced feedback, and dynamic models. Shared technologies mean more realistic graphics, improved interfaces, and more useful user feedback. Advancements in technology and game simulation tools and techniques can lead to more effective medical simulations, thereby reducing patient risk and cost.

Courtesy of Banner Good Samaritan Medical Center

Medical simulations combine hardware and software to prepare doctors for procedures on patients.

Consumer Medical Simulations

Modern medical simulations are experiencing new success in the consumer market. *Trauma Center* is a quirky medical game simulation that throws players into a variety of situations loosely based on medical emergencies. The game is set in a future time when cancer and AIDS have been eradicated and a bizarre new disease threatens the human race. Players use the Nintendo DS touch screen or Wii remote to perform "operations" on virtual patients, to minister to their wounds, and to fight the mysterious plague.

Trauma Center presents surgery from a first-person perspective through the eyes of a virtual doctor. Most of the operations require players to follow a progression of incision, internal work, and then suturing the patient using the DS stylus or Wii remote. *Trauma Center* provides an arsenal of virtual tools and instruments loosely modeled on its real-world counterpart, including:

- *Antibiotic gel*: Disinfects and heals
- *Bandages*: Used post-operation to cover wounds and suture areas
- *Drainage hose*: Removes excess liquids
- *Forceps*: Precision instrument used to remove foreign objects
- *Scalpel*: Makes incisions
- *Surgical laser*: Burns away objects too small to remove with other instruments
- *Suture needle*: Closes incisions
- *Syringe*: Injects liquids
- *Ultrasound*: Detects problematic areas beneath the skin

The developers of *Trauma Center* focused on gameplay and atmosphere over realistic graphics. Most of the surgical procedures are stylized representations of the real thing but are still capable of unnerving players without the gruesome details. Music plays a key role in *Trauma Center* by raising the sense of urgency and tension to an already pressure-fueled, virtual life-and-death situation.

Trauma Center: Second Opinion brings consumers into the operating room.

Improving Patient Health

Simulations have helped many doctors with the technical aspects of performing surgery and combating disease. In 2001, Pam Omidyar founded HopeLab to look at the other side of the patient-doctor relationship. The nonprofit organization aspires to "combine rigorous research with innovative solutions to improve the health and quality of life of young people with chronic illness." One of its initiatives resulted in the 2006 release of *Re-Mission*, a project led by HopeLab with the support of game developer Realtime Associates. The goal of *Re-Mission* is "to improve health-related outcomes for cancer patients," as reported in *Game Developer Magazine* in November 2006.

The collaboration between scientists and game developers was not always problem free while developing *Re-Mission*. Tensions arose when the scientists at HopeLab "tried to incorporate key biologic principles into the game's design, not always realizing that these principles did not necessarily make for interesting gameplay." Omidyar cites the process of designing the cancer cells, one of the most important "enemies" in the game. Both groups agreed that the behavior of the cancer cells in the simulation should mimic their behavior in the human body. If a player did not completely eradicate all the enemies, they multiply and increase their threat.

The scientists and game developers did not agree, however, on the appearance of the cancer cell enemies. The scientists preferred a relatively true-to-life representation of real cancers cells, whereas the game developers favored an exaggerated, menacing style. To resolve the issue, HopeLab and Realtime Associates allowed the decision to be made by the most capable judges of all: the young cancer patients who would be playing the game. The children ultimately decided they preferred the menacing cancer cell enemies to the understated, scientifically accurate model.

When *Re-Mission* wrapped production, HopeLab and Realtime Associates achieved their goal of creating a compelling game experience that helps give cancer patients a sense of power over their disease. Omidyar notes, "It's gratifying to…blast the cancer cell villains, and, just like in real life, it's not always easy to get every last one." In March 2006, HopeLab announced the initial results from a large-scale, randomized, controlled trial that tested *Re-Mission*'s effectiveness on patients. The results indicate the game improves key health-related outcomes for cancer patients who play it, according to Pat Christen of *Game Developer Magazine*. *Re-Mission* is a model example of a successful collaboration between specialists and game developers to build a simulation with measurable positive results.

The purpose of *Re-Mission* is to wreak havoc on cancer. Roxxi fires weapons such as the Chemoblaster, the Radiation Gun, and the Antibiotic Rocket to combat malignancies such as non-Hodgkin's lymphoma and leukemia—as well as treatment-related side effects.

Law

In a courtroom, verdicts are usually decided from a preponderance of evidence. Simulations can play a major role when building or countering evidence related to the scene of an accident or crime. Accuracy is paramount when a defendant's guilt or innocence hangs in the balance. The tools and technologies advanced by game simulations can be utilized in many courtroom scenarios.

Traffic Accident Scenarios

Imagine a multicar accident on a busy freeway during the early morning hours. The morning air is humid and a misty haze made for limited visibility at the time of the accident. Although there is no rain, the humid air makes the surface of the road damp, reducing traction between tires and pavement. The people injured in the collision were heading westbound and the sun was low on the horizon. At trial, the defense argues that the inclement weather and glare of the sun due to the time of day created extraordinary circumstances, precluding the defendant's guilt.

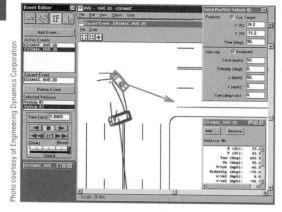

Simulations using software such as *EDSMAC 2D* can bolster or weaken a defendant's case.

The plaintiff commissions a simulation to re-create the defendant's visual perspective at the time of the accident. The custom accident simulation leverages several components drawn from academic research and established game simulation development elements. For this particular scene, the defendant's vehicle is modeled down to its weight, tire tread wear, and brake performance. The environment is modeled using several resources: humidity records from the weather service to re-create the range of visibility in the fog; the estimated friction coefficient moisture on the type of concrete on the stretch of road where the accident occurred; and the apparent sun altitude on the horizon using historical records.

The defense argues that the defendant is innocent—momentarily blinded by the sun. The position of the sun at that time of day, combined with the defendant's direction of travel, the defense argues, would have disoriented anyone long enough to make the accident unavoidable. During their re-direct of the defendant, the plaintiff's attorneys use the simulation to illustrate that the sun was too low on the horizon, and that the defendant could not have been "blinded" by the light. Furthermore, the simulation shows that the relative humidity that morning was high enough to obscure the sun regardless of its position. The simulation bolsters the testimony of multiple eyewitnesses claiming that visibility was less than 100 meters and the sun was a dull orb on the horizon, far below the brightness required to cause momentary blindness. The jury ultimately finds the defendant guilty of failing to decrease speed and increase following distance due to limited visibility.

Homicide Scenarios

Intentional homicides are often characterized as crimes of passion with gruesome results. The motive and emotional state of the defendant and victim are key elements to characterizing why a homicide occurred, but they are usually only half the story. Both sides of the case must also account for how the homicide was committed. Psychologists, psychiatrists, and acquaintances of the parties involved in the crime can explain the "why," and simulations often explain the "how."

Louise is on trial for the murder of Chad, her husband of 10 years. Longtime friends of the couple know that Louise and Chad have gotten into heated arguments—but, for the most part, their marriage seemed strong. On the day of the murder, Louise and Chad had a group of friends over for an afternoon of drinks and barbeque. Later that evening, after the guests had gone home, Louise contends that Chad—who had a few drinks that day—mumbled something about going to bed and trudged back inside their home. Meanwhile Louise, according to her testimony, decided it would be a fine time to mow the lawn. When she finished the lawn, Louise explained that she entered their home to find Chad lying motionless at the bottom of their stairs covered in blood. When the paramedics arrived, they pronounced Chad dead at the scene.

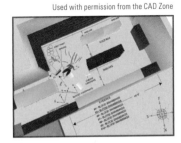

Used with permission from the CAD Zone

Crime Zone is used to simulate homocide scenarios.

The district attorney calls several witnesses attesting to the couple's rocky relationship and drills many holes in Louise's account of the day's events. Even with the testimony piling up, the defense knows it only needs to raise reasonable doubt in the mind of the jury to win an acquittal. The defense proposes a sequence of events that might explain what happened after Chad entered the house. Since there are no eyewitnesses, the defense contracts a simulation developer to model the stairway section of the home where the death occurred. The developer models a character with Chad's proportions and incorporates a rudimentary physics system so the virtual body interacts with its environment. Since the real stairwell has several impact points marked by Chad's blood, the simulation developers map out a plausible path for the virtual body to follow. The simulation demonstrates that a body falling down the stairs might hit each impact point and result in the trauma detailed by the coroner.

In this situation, the simulation provides the jury with a visual representation of how the events could have played out that night—even though there were no eyewitnesses. Louise's alleged decision to mow the lawn at night after the guests left raises the jury member's suspicions, but the detailed simulation of how Chad's injuries could have been caused by a fall down the stairs leaves enough doubt in their minds to acquit Louise of the crime.

Consumers in the Courtroom

Phoenix Wright: Ace Attorney for the Nintendo DS re-creates courtroom drama through five cases in which the player must bring a killer to justice. Each case begins with a cinematic sequence of the murder and a glimpse of the killer.

By exposing the identity of the murderer at the outset, the developers of *Phoenix Wright* make it clear that their game is a simulation about bringing the killer to justice in the courtroom, rather than investigating who committed the crime. Gameplay involves following witness testimony and finding flaws or contradictions in that testimony. The witnesses frequently lie or must be pressed to disclose critical information. The player must use strategies such as deciding when to use her limited quantity of objections or to procure evidence; repeated missteps increase the risk that she will lose the case. The courtroom protocol in *Phoenix Wright: Ace Attorney* is a very loose representation of the rules real attorneys must follow, but it is an entertaining way for players to experience the drama of a murder mystery trial.

© Capcom Co. Ltd.
Reprinted with permission.

Phoenix Wright: Ace Attorney allows players to prosecute criminals in courtroom scenarios.

Advertising

In-game advertising has been part of the game industry for decades. If a developer or publisher wanted to reduce the cost of developing a game, she approached licensors to work out a deal. As the game industry market grew, advertisers and licensors began approaching game publishers to get their brands in front of the highly lucrative teenage and twenty-something segment of game players. In both scenarios, the developer and publisher worked with the licensor during the game's development to incorporate images, music, celebrity likenesses, and themes that reflected the brand.

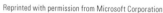

Reprinted with permission from Microsoft Corporation

In-game advertising is common in racing simulations such as *Forza Motorsport 2*.

Three common scenarios for in-game advertising deals are the following:

- *License-based title or value-ad for the brand*: The licensor pays a game developer to build a game simulation around her brand or incorporate her brand in part of the game. An example is *America's Army*, a thinly veiled recruiting tool commissioned by the United States Army.
- *Mutual benefit*: The game developer believes a product or piece of music can add legitimacy or increase the appeal of the title. For example, a game developer agrees to include a specific brand of athletic shoe in a basketball simulation and, in exchange, the shoe manufacturer cross-promotes the game to its loyal fan base. Both sides get the exposure they are seeking without exchanging any money.
- *Value-ad for the developer*: The game developer or publisher pays the license holder for the rights to include a certain brand or music selection because it adds credibility to the game simulation. For example, Electronic Arts (EA) pays the NFL and ESPN for the rights to include well-known brands in its sports simulations.

The first 20 years of in-game advertising were built on a static model where ads were hard-coded into the games. When the game was complete and on store shelves, the in-game advertising content could not be changed. Although advertisers loved in-game branding, the limitations of the static model caused the content to become stale and the ads lost value soon after the game hit retail shelves. Second, after the game shipped, advertisers had no idea how often players' eyes and ears were exposed to their ads—critical metrics to determine an advertisement's exposure and impact on product sales. The arrival of dynamic advertising ended the limitations of static advertising and radically changed the in-game advertising model.

Some in-game advertisements simulate the real product in the game. Coca Cola vending machines dispense beverages to rehydrate the virtual character, or athletic shoes increase the performance of a virtual athlete. Marketing departments love these types of product placements because the player actively uses the product rather than simply viewing a logo.

Activision

Activision's *Crazy Taxi* shipped with many commercial locations and advertisments built into the game.

Dynamic advertising solves both of the major problems of the static model via online connectivity. Game developers build advertising "containers" into the virtual world. The containers are preloaded with advertisements before the game hits store shelves so consumers without Internet connectivity can experience the pleasure of advertising. When the game detects an Internet connection, it synchronizes with a server that repopulates the containers with new ads. Containers can be anything from virtual billboards lining the highways that are updated to promote upcoming films and television shows. An in-game movie theater will show trailers of new films and user-created content. Dynamic advertising also opens up the possibility to target ads based on a player's game history and play style. When a game "phones home," it can also send valuable data on a player's game tendencies. The latest generation of consoles can track the games a person plays and target her with new games, films, television shows, books, and other products that fit her profile. Companies providing the dynamic advertising framework can also harvest deep metrics about how many people see an ad and the duration it appears on their screens.

Government Agencies

Police officers must prepare for a wide variety of pressure scenarios. Hostage situations, drug raids, traffic stops, and search-and-rescue operations can arise at a moment's notice. Police departments have used real-world simulations to train and prepare officers for duty for decades.

Game simulations are part of the modern arsenal of situational and weapon training. One simulation requires trainees to identify suspects from innocent bystanders in high-pressure situations. Virtual suspects appear onscreen in crowded urban settings or pop up behind points of cover. Officers must make split-second decisions to use either a simulated firearm or a less lethal weapon. The simulations are highly customizable; the simulation administrator can spawn multiple perpetrators, create large crowds, and assign a variety of behaviors to suspects and civilians. The location can be customized with urban, suburban, or rural themes to reflect the department's jurisdiction. Officers could re-create a bank robbery set in a virtual environment modeled on the real banks and settings in their city. Probable escape routes could be charted and measured against a variety of response times and strategies. Police officers who receive realistic training are better prepared for the real scenario, leading to a more coordinated and appropriate response.

Hurricane Katrina was a rude awakening for local and federal government officials and first responders. Inefficient or nonexistent protocol, undefined chains of command, and poor resource-distribution efforts created a chaotic scenario in the days after the storm hit the coast. Game simulations like *Incident Commander* are gaining recognition as a proactive means to prepare people who are responsible for responding to natural disasters and crisis situations. BreakAway Ltd., the developer who created *Incident Commander,* built the simulation for the U.S. Department of Justice on the National Incident Management System command structure mandated by the U.S. Federal Emergency Management Agency (FEMA).

Photo courtesy of MPRI

PatrolSim IV prepares police for various high-pressure scenarios.

Incident Commander, in its current form, is designed to prepare officials in relatively small jurisdictions (fewer than half a million residents) for emergency scenarios, including a school hostage situation, a chemical spill, the aftermath of a severe storm, and a possible terrorism incident. Players, acting as the incident commander, must manage multiple local agencies, including police, fire, EMS, public works, and school personnel. Joseph Barlow, an Adams County, Illinois Emergency Response Team member who was deployed to Baton Rouge, Louisiana, and helped set up an 800-bed hospital for citizens displaced by Hurricane Katrina, notes, "I ended up being the logistics officer for the entire facility. It just so happens that I had spent the week before using *Incident Commander* in depth. The lessons learned by playing the simulation fed directly into the practices of setting up an incident command structure and then operating within that structure" (*Gizmag*).

Chad C. Haddal
(Analyst in
Immigration Policy,
Congressional
Research Service)

Chad C. Haddal is an Analyst in Immigration Policy for the Congressional Research Service, and he is currently a U.S. Presidential Management Fellow. His specialties cover a range of issues within immigration that includes foreign students, foreign investors, and unaccompanied alien children. Chad received his Ph.D. in Political Science from Washington University in St. Louis. His dissertation research focused on globalization and public policy, and as part of this project he conducted field research as a Fulbright Fellow at Stockholm University. Chad additionally holds a B.A. in Economics and Political Science from St. Olaf College and an M.A. in Political Science from Washington University in St. Louis.

The benefit of video game technology for government purposes has for many years been evident. The military uses many of these technologies to produce simulations and has also begun employing video games for recruiting purposes. What has been less clear is the potential that video game technology holds for other governmental agencies, such as those dealing with legislative support. However, with the growing emphasis on quantitative research and extensive projection modeling, the potential impact of video game technology is finally emerging. In the field of immigration policy, we are constantly seeking new tools for determining the outcomes of potential policies and regulations. The goal for many analysts is to develop a "push-pull" comprehensive model that would cover the entire spectrum of inputs in decision making by individuals choosing to migrate. Video games have worked with highly dynamic engines for a number of years and provide intuitive outputs through the gaming interface. Policy fields, however, have yet to benefit from such a medium where highly complex mathematical formulations become understandable for even the most novice consumer of the information. Consequently, the potential to merge the complex ideas of the public policy realm with the intuitive and dynamic medium of video games presents a tremendous number of opportunities and possibilities. One of the main questions any policy analyst is confronted with is, "What would happen if . . . ?" In many cases these answers can be difficult due to the nature of the subject matter, and the lack of visual aids that many people find easier to absorb. Clients want easily digestible information presented in an engaging manner. Video game technology offers one type of solution. By being able to manipulate the policy option inputs, the outputs become more easily consumable. The dynamic environments and the observable consequences of a gaming environment could therefore alter the presentation, understanding, and forecasting of policy work should the merging of the video games and policy analysis occur.

Incident Commander is designed to operate as a stand-alone simulation or in a multiplayer environment where up to 16 players in different locations can remotely coordinate a response to the same virtual incident. The U.S. Department of Justice offers the software free of charge to all authorized public service agencies in an effort to standardize and promote efficient responses to natural disasters and crisis situations. Game simulations like *Incident Commander* demonstrate the value of simulations as proactive preparations for when the unthinkable becomes a reality.

Incident Commander can be customized to train local and state agencies for a variety of natural disasters and crisis situations.

Workplace Efficiency

Once factories and assembly plants grow beyond a certain size, the companies' efficiency is affected by the location of machines and walking traffic areas. The Delmia Corporation develops software that analyzes workplace organization and human traffic flow. Manufacturers use the data from the simulations to optimize their workplace to accelerate time to market, reduce costs, and increase productivity. If all this sounds like cold, hard capitalism at the expense of workers, note that Delmia's software also considers the human element when assessing a workplace. Its V5 Human software helps companies account for worker health and safety standards by designing better relationships between workers and the products they manufacture, install, operate, and maintain. Employee comfort can also be analyzed from observing the V5 Human software's virtual workers use a wide range of ergonomic simulation tools, according to *Manufacturing Engineering*.

Courtesy of Delmia Corp., a member of the Dassault Systemes group

Simulations such as *DELMIA V5 DPM Shop* are used when designing products that require human interaction to account for ergonomics and safety.

Vehicles

The automobile industry is a significant creator and consumer of digital simulations. Consumer cars go through countless simulated scenarios before the first model hits the assembly line. Simulations early in a vehicle model's design phase help manufacturers consider aspects such as safety, aesthetics, aerodynamics, fuel efficiency, performance, and structural integrity before firing up the assembly line. Simulation trials can spot potential points of failure and reduce the likelihood that a company will need to endure costly product recalls. The virtual vehicle model also reduces costs associated with multiple iterations of real-world prototypes and decreases the time span from concept to showroom.

The significant expertise required to accurately simulate a wide variety of scenarios forces all manufacturers to rely on help from experienced external developers. Even massive General Motors must rely on external help to build and operate some of its simulations, according to *Modern Materials Handling*. The processes and techniques used by experienced game developers can facilitate the collaborative process with the automotive giants.

Courtesy of Volkswagen AG

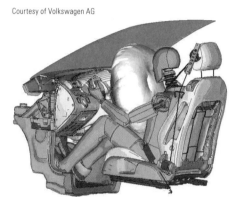

Volkswagen's occupant restraint system for frontal impact is an example of a vehicle simulation created by the automobile industry.

Trucking

Semis are the most popular shipping method to transport a large volume of goods to the point of sale. While less efficient than trains, massive fleets haul cargo millions of miles per year. Fleet operators managing such large numbers of trucks know each fraction of a mile per gallon can swing hundreds of thousands of dollars in operating costs. With these slight margins, semi engine manufacturers utilize mechanical simulations to squeeze the maximum amount of efficiency from their engines. Advancements in engine technology, with help from simulations, have improved engine reliability to the point that some models can go one million miles between major service intervals.

On the consumer side, Sega created *Big Mutha Truckers*, an arcade-style trucking simulation that puts players in the cab of a big rig. The game tasks players with objectives such as delivering a load of cargo in a set period of time, executing challenging low-speed maneuvers like parking and turning with a huge trailer full of cargo, and carving through traffic while outwitting police. The stylized graphics and loose physics of *Big Mutha Trucker*'s reduce its usefulness as a training tool, but these design choices give the game a lot of personality and some insight into the over-the-road lifestyle.

Big Mutha Truckers takes a lighthearted approach to life on the road in an eighteen-wheeler.

Commercial Flight

Commercial pilots must get recertified on a regular basis to maintain their pilot's license. With a price tag of $20 million each and a running cost of $1,000 an hour, advanced flight simulators allow commercial airlines and the Federal Aviation Administration to train and recertify pilots without the immense cost of using real aircraft. Simulations also allow test administrators to create a variety of scenarios that would be impossible in real life. Weather conditions, including cloud and storm visibility, wind speed and direction, rain, hail, lightning, wind shear, and turbulence can be adjusted in real-time. Pilots can be instantaneously transported to one of many realistically modeled airports around the world to experience each location's unique take-off and approach characteristics. Massive hydraulic jacks tilt, shake, and rock the test cabin in response to the pilot's controls and simulate the effects of weather conditions on the flight. The cabin can be filled with smoke, requiring the pilot to utilize oxygen masks and cabin depressurization protocol. Accurate flight sounds such as variable engine noise, flap and landing gear extension and retraction, and assorted alarms are included to enhance the experience. Test administrators can trigger over 500 system malfunctions to see how pilots respond to everything from minor quirks to catastrophic system failures. Simulators can even use the black box data pulled from plane crashes to re-create conditions that led to the accident.

Although commercial flight simulations are very adaptable and realistic, they have some practical and technological limitations. Instead of having a full crew on hand, the test administrator also acts as air traffic controller, head flight attendant, dispatcher, weather office worker, and maintenance person. The borders of virtual clouds are still a bit too well defined, lacking the gradient visible when entering or exiting the real thing. Turbulence simulated by the hydraulic actuators is also less dramatic and more rhythmic than the real thing. Commercial flight simulations have room to improve, but they are already believable enough to make pilots break into a sweat while they are still on the ground, according to *Weatherwise*.

NASA/Ames Research Center

Modern commercial flight simulations such as *Advanced Cab Flight Simulator Cockpit* use the same instruments and controls as real aircraft to make the experience as authentic as possible.

Mining

Simulations can benefit industries that have a track record of being hazardous to workers. Companies in mining, one of the most dangerous industries, have embraced simulations to improve safety and efficiency. One company, Immersive Technologies, develops portable robust mining simulations for training mining operators. Immersive Technologies' training package starts with SimControl, software that simulates the appearance and functionality of a wide range of mining machines. SimControl enables training administrators to adjust several variables to present users with scenarios that they may encounter in the real world. Machine performance, weather conditions, and the work environment can be custom-tailored to a client's actual work site so users learn how to adapt while maintaining their focus on safety and job quality.

Immersive Technologies

Immersive Technologies' base simulators such as *Komatsu D475A Track Dozer* re-create the experience from the cockpit of mining machinery.

Immersive Technologies' robust mining simulation software is coupled with advanced hardware, including an array of wrap-around screens, digital surround sound, a motion base that rocks, tilts, and slides on three axes, and a conversion kit to adapt real instruments and controls. The video and audio immerse the user in the simulated environment and the inclusion of the same controls and instruments from the real machines makes the transition to field operation nearly seamless. Immersive Technologies offers its simulations as a turnkey solution packaged in a standard shipping container that can be transported to any mining location worldwide.

Fuzzy Logic

Not all mathematical problems can be broken into binary states like "yes" or "no," "true" or "false," and "on" or "off." Real-world conditions are often analog, characterized by many values between discrete states. In mathematics, the space between states characterized as "fuzzy" logic is where a value can be partially true or false. A person's perception of the water temperature in a shower is an example of fuzzy logic. Using human, rather than scientific terms, we might associate water with the states listed in the accompanying diagram.

Diagram by Per Olin

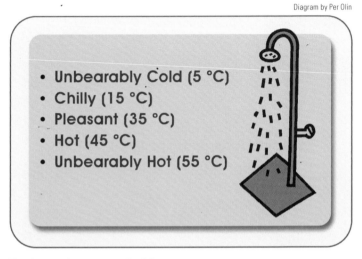

- **Unbearably Cold (5 °C)**
- **Chilly (15 °C)**
- **Pleasant (35 °C)**
- **Hot (45 °C)**
- **Unbearably Hot (55 °C)**

The degrees between each of these water temperature states are characterized as "fuzzy."

Fuzzy logic suggests that when the temperature of the water rises from 34.9 to 35.0 degrees Celsius, it does not feel like it has suddenly changed from chilly to pleasant. Similarly, if the temperature of the shower water drops from 15.0 to 14.9 degrees, it does not instantly become unbearably cold. Instead, there are gradients of perceived comfort between the defined temperature states. As the rising (or cooling) temperature moves further from the initial state, its association with the first state becomes less true and its association with the next state becomes more true. Simulations of real-world scenarios must frequently account for fuzzy logic and how an analog state affects a projected outcome. As fuzzy techniques improve, "[they] will enable general-purpose machines to process imprecise data through new, more human-like languages," according to *Computerworld*. More human-like languages will enable game simulation developers to create more believable artificial intelligence and simplify complex, dynamic models like fluids, material interaction, and artificial intelligence.

Agriculture

Science and agriculture have been interrelated for centuries as advances in farming tools and techniques have resulted in higher, more reliable yields. Digital simulations are a relatively recent addition to a farmer's arsenal, but they are rapidly becoming part of many aspects of agriculture. Researchers in Spain used fuzzy logic in simulations to model growing peppers in greenhouses in an effort to increase production through improved processes and permit farming in regions where environmental conditions are not conducive to crop growth. In their model, they accounted for several input variables and their fuzzy sets—as shown in the accompanying diagram.

Diagram by Per Olin

Solar Radiation
- Night
- Day

Temperature, with Optimal Rankings
- Minimum
- Low Nocturnal
- High Nocturnal
- Low Diurnal
- High Nocturnal

Relative Humidity
- Nocturnal Minimum
- Low Nocturnal
- High Nocturnal
- Low Diurnal
- High Nocturnal

Wind Speed
- Soft
- Moderate
- Strong

Wind Direction
- From North
- From South
- From East
- From West

Variables and fuzzy sets utilized by researchers to simulate growing peppers in greenhouses.

The researchers applied the inputs noted in the diagram to a simulated greenhouse that could be affected by controlled outputs, including ventilation, a humidity system, and a heat shield. Next, using a knowledge base, they defined rules for how controls should respond to an array of situations. The end result was a customizable framework that could be modified to accommodate assorted greenhouse configurations for a variety of crops. This simulation model is an example of how fuzzy controls enable scientists and farmers to gather data, improve processes, and increase crop yields (Industrial Simulation Conference, 2004).

Weather

Meteorologists are rarely heralded as incredibly accurate forecasters. The data sets and climate systems with which they work are extremely complex, making precision difficult to achieve. Meteorologists have made significant improvements in accuracy by incorporating fuzzy logic in weather simulations. Fuzzy logic appears to be a natural fit for their field, considering that meteorologists use a fuzzy-sounding vocabulary. How many times have you heard the weather report mention the following vague phrases?

- Partly cloudy
- Mostly clear
- Highs between 70 and 75 degrees
- Late afternoon
- Increasing precipitation
- Occasional gusts of wind
- Widely scattered showers

Let us look at a real-life example of how meteorologists use fuzzy logic in simulations. Doppler radar is an invaluable tool for meteorologists, but its accuracy can be hampered by many factors. When the radar signal leaves the transmitter, it travels outward and, in an ideal scenario, bounces back only when it hits a weather system. Unfortunately, real-world Doppler radar must account for objects that are not part of a weather system. In practice, the radar signal can, in meteorological terms, hit "clutter" that distorts the data. Clutter may include echoes from physical objects on the ground, like trees and buildings, or interference from radio or other radar signals.

Fuzzy logic is useful in identifying and separating clutter from the useful data because many of the identifiable characteristics of clutter are imprecise. For example, if ground-based objects were not affected by the earth's weather, a radar system would

Adam Houston and Robert Wilhelmson

A weather simulation recreating conditions capable of spawning tornados.

have little difficulty distinguishing between an idle tree and a moving storm system. The tree would reflect a motionless radar signature and the storm system would be distinguished by its motion and resulting Doppler effect. In the real world, ground-based objects like trees and skyscrapers are not motionless, and models based on fuzzy logic can be adjusted to account for such objects with velocities near zero. As this real-world data becomes more accurate, forecasting simulations become more reliable, and meteorologists can make more precise weather predictions, according to the *Journal of Atmospheric and Oceanic Technology*.

Simulations are critical to modern business. Companies that leverage the skill and experience of established game developers can create simulations that break the stereotype of dull and tedious training. When employees are more engaged in training, they are more likely to retain and utilize the techniques that make workplaces safer and more productive, efficient, and enjoyable. Simulations will also continue to bring many professions into the living room. The challenges associated with many skilled jobs translate into entertaining and educational experiences for consumers.

:::CHAPTER REVIEW:::

1. Choose one of the industry segments discussed in this chapter (such as medicine or law) and come up with a concept for an original game simulation that would address a corporate training need associated with that industry segment.

2. What features might you change in your game concept so that it addresses the consumer market rather than only the industry segment? What benefits would the consumer market gain from your simulation game?

3. What is fuzzy logic, and how would you incorporate it into your original game simulation idea? Why is fuzzy logic particularly beneficial for business simulations?

4. Play an existing business simulation and discuss five features that distinguish the game from other types of simulations. As a consumer, do you feel that the simulation was geared toward your needs—or did it assume that you had more specialized knowledge?

CHAPTER

5

Military

virtual soldiers on a simulated battlefield

Key Chapter Questions

- Why do we need to simulate combat?

- What makes a military simulation effective?

- How does the online dimension affect cooperation and engaging the enemy?

- How are players rewarded and penalized in combat?

- When is simulation accuracy more important than balanced gameplay?

Military simulations have existed as long as wars have been waged. From soldiers doing drills in a field to a couple playing a game of chess, military simulations have been useful for training and entertainment because of the strategic elements and dramatic tension built into the conflict of opposing forces. Rapid increases in computational power have added a new dimension to military simulations—creating virtual worlds with weapons, vehicles, soldiers, and environments in any battle conditions. Governments use military game simulations to reduce military and civilian injuries and deaths, efficiently strategize current and future conflicts, and decrease costs. Consumers use military game simulations to experience the drama and tactics of combat without the harsh realities of war. As technology continues to improve, developers use this new power to blur the line between real and virtual battlefields to create more effective and engaging military game simulations.

In the Heat of Battle

You hear an incredible blast and feel the heat of the explosion as your attack chopper spirals and lurches out of control. The pilot turns to face you, his face contorted in shock and determination. He barks words that are cut off by the noise of swooping rotor blades and the screaming din of the damaged engine before they reach your ears. The ground is fast approaching and anti-aircraft fire blazes below you. Suddenly, you feel the jolt of impact as the chopper slams into the ground. Your senses reel through the mental blur as you turn to see a fellow soldier yelling into your eyes only inches from your face. You cannot make out the words but see him point toward a shadowy area across the war-torn courtyard. Looking around, you see wounded comrades— some crawling under their own power, and others lying motionless in the chopper crash zone. Then, out of the corner of your eye, you catch a glimpse of a group of men running into a dimly lit area only a few dozen meters away. What do you do next?

Imagine trying to re-create this scenario repeatedly in a city center to train soldiers with military equipment. The risk of injury and cost would be astronomical. Furthermore, the logistics of the operation would make it impractical. Military simulations reduce or remove these barriers, enabling militaries to reenact a multitude of scenarios every day to prepare soldiers for events when they become all too real. As military simulation development has evolved, this training has crossed over to the general public and now reaches a far wider audience.

Why Simulate Combat?

Militaries have simulated combat since the dawn of war. Prior to the digital age, simulations were based in the field as soldiers acted out countless battle scenarios. As new training technologies have developed, the military has increased the effectiveness of simulating combat scenarios.

Big Stock Photo

Injury & Death

Effective simulations reduce the likelihood of injury and death during training and on the battlefield. At the ground level, this improvement is achieved through better prepared and capable soldiers. At the commander level, it means better forecasting and better battle plan risk management. A military places heavy emphasis on preparedness; the more prepared and informed a military, the more likely soldiers will return unharmed. Furthermore, a well-trained and prepared military can minimize civilian casualties and collateral damage. Game simulations are another powerful tool in the military training arsenal and help prevent unnecessary loss of life.

Time & Money

Historically, military strategists transported troops to distant locations and even moved earth and constructed mock-up cities to familiarize troops with the anticipated enemy environment. Such incredible undertakings were invaluable for training troops but came at an astronomical cost. Modern game simulations are capable of re-creating a highly customizable combat scenario in any environment, in any weather condition, at any time of day, all without requiring soldiers or officers to leave base. Once the simulation is running, any number of military personnel can undergo the same training at a marginal operating cost.

Big Stock Photo

Extensive time and money are necessary to transport troops to remote locations in order to experience simulated combat.

Impossible in the Field

Cost savings aside, many of the possibilities afforded by game simulations are not even feasible in field-based simulations. For example, a squad is preparing for reconnaissance over a lightly defended section of a city. Using a digital model of the city, a simulation can convey how the approach might look at any hour of the day or night. How would shadows appear if the day was slightly overcast? What if it was raining? Windy with a steady downpour? Ten-mph wind? Thirty-mph wind? These and many other simulation variables are possible today. Centuries of military training have proven that real or perceived familiarity with a combat zone reduces the guesswork once soldiers have been inserted. Military game simulations enable levels of preparation unheard of only a generation ago.

Emergent Behavior

Military conflicts involve so many factors that it is impossible to account for every possible outcome. Even though military simulations cannot predict every scenario, they are useful tools to help discover new strategies or behaviors buried in such a complex model. By blending traditional doctrines and innovative thinking into multiple simulations and observing the outcomes, these discoveries are made. Running multiple simulations can expose otherwise hidden strategies that might allow blue forces to do well against superior red forces. Keys to this model include the following:

- Understanding initial conditions
- Setting minimal rules
- Allowing for emergent behavior

When set in motion, the elements of the simulation (environment, characters, physics, artificial intelligence, vehicles, weapons) affect each other, and observations lead to learning about differences from previous outcomes. "These discoveries could lead to behaviors or ways of thinking that could not be predicted before understanding the current state of the environment. This is emergence" (Carl W. Hunt, *Signal*).

Cross-Cultural Training

As military game simulations come into wider use, developers must consider the cultural influence and social training power of their models. As interactive dialogue, simulated gestures, and situational behavior models improve, simulations can train soldiers in local dialects and customs. Soldiers prepared for what to expect and how to behave are more likely to be accepted by civilian locals whose first reaction may be distrust. Similarly, the way foreign characters are portrayed in military game simulations can have a strong influence on cultural perceptions. Combat-based military war simulations are modeled on violence and conflict in settings that people see in the news every day—and developers have the opportunity to use their platform to reinforce or break down cultural stereotypes.

The *America's Army* technology is serving as an information operations platform in the Global War on Terror (GWOT) in the form of a cultural and adaptive leader training tool. Developed by the Virtual Heroes team and Sandia National Laboratories, this application is being used by Special Forces Soldiers at Fort Bragg for training that encompasses role-playing negotiation (soft skills training). In the application, soldiers take part in online virtual events—including cross-cultural communications scenarios with indigenous people.

U.S. Army

Two Special Forces soldiers negotiate with a host national in *Adaptive Thinking & Leadership*, a simulation built on the *America's Army* engine.

Protests & Lawsuits

Militaries use game simulations to avoid protests and lawsuits that can result from field-training exercises. If the British Army had used military game simulations instead of live ammunition training in 2001, perhaps they could have avoided the lawsuit filed by Kenyan tribal groups that claim to have been injured by ammunition allegedly left behind. Similarly, the U.S. Navy might have used a computer-based model to research a bomb's effectiveness rather than bombing the island of Vieques with live munitions, killing a civilian in 1999, and sparking countless Puerto Rican protests and a public relations mess (Ted McKenna, *Journal of Electronic Defense*).

CyberCity 3D LLC

Military combat "experiments" should take place in simulated cities rather than real ones!

Non-Combat Military Simulations

Militaries are leveraging the same simulations that model combat to also present scenarios that occur during operations other than war (OOTW). These scenarios are incredibly useful to prepare soldiers for the dangers of occupation or peacekeeping. In OOTW, soldiers may need to deal with situations such as mass demonstrations, riots, looting, and even civil war (Ted McKenna, *Journal of Electronic Defense*).

Strategy Simulations

Consumer *military strategy simulations* present the view of the battlefield from an "eye in the sky" or "god" perspective from which players command groups of artificially intelligent soldiers. Soldier control in military strategy simulations is characterized by meta commands such as attack, retreat, build, gather, or train. Once ordered, the artificially intelligent soldiers carry out the task and the player must adapt his strategy to how events progress on a macro scale. Military strategy simulations are useful to teach many aspects of management—including risk, resource, and time management.

Reprinted with permission from Microsoft Corporation

Courtesy of CDV Software Entertainment USA and 10Tacle Studios

In military strategy simulations such as *Rise of Nations* (left) and *War Front: Turning Point* (right), players command large battlefields containing artificially intelligent soldiers.

Successful military strategy players must be capable of directing and forecasting several disciplines simultaneously—including economics, manufacturing, developing technologies, training, gathering resources, and regulating consumption. All these aspects must be managed effectively while attacking or defending on multiple fronts. Once battles are added to the mix, players must also account for all aspects of combat strategy. Challenging indeed. (Publishers and marketing companies usually categorize all military strategy simulations as "real-time strategy" games, a misleading label because many military strategy simulations do not function in real time, nor do most consider strategic aspects [as opposed to mere tactical decisions].)

Tactical Shooters

Action games known as *tactical shooters* bring the action down to a single soldier at the battlefield level. Players view the simulation from the perspective of the soldier's eyes—first person, within the first-person shooter (FPS) subgenre, or behind and over the shoulder of the soldier (third person). Focusing on a single soldier means tactical shooters allow little to no control of the battle on a grand scale. Instead, emphasis is placed on the abilities and experiences of a soldier and the members of his squad.

Sony Computer Entertainment America

Activision

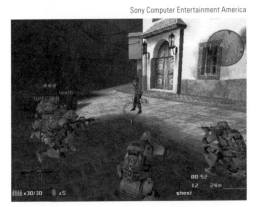 

In tactical shooters such as *SOCOM: U.S. Navy SEALs* (left) and *Call of Duty 2* (right), players usually focus on a single soldier.

Successful tactical shooter players must adhere to mission objectives, preserve their health (and that of their fellow soldiers), be capable of distinguishing friend from foe, operate a wide variety of vehicles, and determine the most effective weapon for each situation.

Air Combat Simulations

Governments have used military flight simulators for decades to train pilots in a virtual situation before risking their lives—and some astronomically expensive aircraft—in real-world flight. Flight simulations have come a long way from the earliest models that only required the pilot to take off, keep the wings level, and land successfully. Modern *air combat simulations* (ACSs) ratchet up the complexity and immersion by mirroring almost any situation that occurs in the sky—including dog-fights, bombing runs, aerial spying, refueling, ejection, tailspin recovery, emergency landing, evasive maneuvers, aerial acrobatics, and formations. ACSs present the view from inside the cockpit or behind the aircraft "chasing" the action.

©2006 NAMCO BANDAI Games Inc.

Air combat in military strategy simulations such as *Air Combat Zero: The Belkan War* can mirror almost any situation that occurs in the sky—including dogfights and bombing runs.

As a private pilot in real life and a frustrated military jet jock wanna be, I find the virtual versions of these pursuits very satisfying. When I'm in the mood for action, there is nothing like strapping on a pixelated F-18, flying low level terrain following maneuvers at the speed of sound or yankin' and bankin', guns blazing in a head to head online dogfight. If I want to brush up on navigational techniques or fly practice approaches in challenging weather instead, I can do that too—all in the comfort of my own home. These games provide a great blend of entertainment and realism and are certainly less costly than the real thing.

—Aaron Marks
(Composer; Founder, On Your Mark Music)

Battlefield 2: A Hybrid Military Sim

The scope of some military game simulations has grown to include all three major genres. Full-scale battlefield simulators such as *Battlefield 2* include modes for players who want to experience the virtual battlefield from a comprehensive perspective like a strategy simulation, from the ground as a single soldier like a tactical shooter, or from the sky like an air combat simulation. The incredible breadth of these mammoth simulations is a significant design and technological undertaking. If the modes feel like a watered-down version of each genre, the simulation will be ineffective.

Electronic Arts, Inc.   Electronic Arts, Inc.

Effective Military Simulations

Military simulations have an excellent real-life model to follow. Military procedures and protocols have been refined over centuries of combat. In addition, countless historical conflicts provide a vast amount of situational material and statistical data. However, historical references and data do not guarantee a smooth path to creating a military game simulation. Fundamental choices affecting the end-user experience must be made and many technological hurdles must be overcome before a military game simulation can be effective.

Military Audience

From a *military* perspective, the more realistic the simulation, the more useful it is as a training tool. At the individual soldier level, effective combat simulations may incorporate an incredible number of factors—including the blast radii of various land mines, the duration between calling for a medical evacuation and the arrival of the rescue chopper, and the quantity of bullets in a variety of pistol clips. If a developer's target audience includes government military training, realism is paramount. A highly accurate model can prepare soldiers for these harsh realities when they enter the battlefield. Although designing simulations to train soldiers for battle is a significant challenge, it is only a fraction of the overall simulations needed for militaries. On a larger scale, "combat scenarios are highly complex, and must reflect how political, military, and economic developments can shape a conflict" (*National Defense*). As technological improvements increasingly blur the line between model and reality, governments expect military game simulations to accurately account for factors on a macro scale to win a war, down to making soldiers more capable, better informed, and more likely to survive when entering the battlefield.

Consumer Audience

The *consumer* market demands less realism than the military market. Military game simulations designed for the public incorporate many of the same elements of simulations used by militaries—including battlefield environments, military vehicles, combat weapons, and tactics. However, simulations designed for civilians are less complex because the interpretation of combat elements can be less literal and they have a lower requirement for accurate specifications. In addition, commercial games emphasize entertainment value over strict authenticity (*National Defense*). Let us face it, if you get home from a long stressful day, do you want to spend 50 minutes waiting alone in the barren virtual desert for the refueling tanker truck to reach your Hummer because you failed to notice the fuel gauge was below empty? Most people do not need to wait that long because they do not need to learn such mission-critical lessons. Game simulation developers bend the rules and, in this example, might either provide a Hummer that never needs refueling or cause a tanker truck to miraculously appear over the horizon to top off your tank in 20 seconds.

Consumers do not purchase military game simulations to train to be soldiers. Instead, they seek the thrill of an enthralling battlefield experience without the real-world consequences of war. To create this enhanced experience, developers manipulate the elements of war by emphasizing the dramatic, compressing timelines, and altering the rules of physics, military protocol, and moral consequences.

In the late 1990s, the United States government saw an opportunity to capitalize on the popularity of mainstream military game simulations. After several years of development and millions of dollars of U.S. taxpayer money, the U.S. government published *America's Army*, its first military game simulation intended for public distribution. Released as a free download in 2002, *America's Army* is a thinly veiled marketing campaign and recruitment tool aimed at youths ages 13 and older.

Promoted as a glimpse into the life of a U.S. soldier, *America's Army* requires players to pass virtual basic training and dedicate time and practice to become specialists, such as grenadiers or snipers. Participants are unable to play the role of enemy forces, so two players pitted against each other both see their team's characters as U.S. soldiers and their opponent's team as terrorists. Although *America's Army* is promoted as a way for civilians to experience life as a U.S. soldier, any simulated effects of combat are conspicuously absent. Missing elements include blood, dismemberment, and the psychological damage of war. The game was developed using Epic's Unreal engine, which has been used by many developers to create much more realistic depictions of the consequences of combat—but the U.S. government made a conscious decision to not include those depictions.

These omissions gloss over many of the most fundamental realities of life as a soldier. Promoting the simulation as an "Authentic U.S. Army Experience" to American youth drastically oversimplifies the experience the U.S. military is actually selling to recruits. Of course, had *America's Army* included a more accurate depiction of combat, it would never have received the ESRB's "Teen" rating. In fact, if a mass-market military game simulation included everything that makes war a living hell, the title would never see retail distribution.

U.S. Army

America's Army gives players a glimpse into the life of a U.S. soldier.

U.S. Army

Although it does depict combat, *America's Army* avoided blood, dismemberment, and the psychological effects of war.

USAF - Air Dominance: The Air Force's Recruitment Tool

The U.S. Air Force has launched a new video game that seeks both to entice new recruits and to highlight the service's nontraditional missions, such as humanitarian relief and unmanned aircraft operations. *USAF: Air Dominance*, which will be shown at events such as NASCAR races, puts prospective blue-suiters behind a joystick as they fly three missions: piloting an F-22 fighter that is coming to the aid of a friendly F-4 under attack by hostile MiG-29s; controlling a Predator unmanned air vehicle on a photo-reconnaissance run; and flying a C-17 transport plane dropping humanitarian cargo in a war-torn nation.

U.S. Air Force

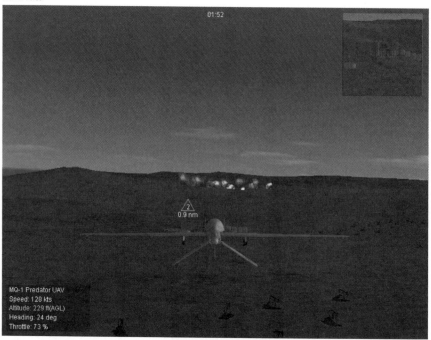

USAF: Air Dominance is simpler to play than *America's Army*. While the Army game intends to provide a realistic rendition of Army doctrine and tactics, the Air Force game aims more for an arcade experience than an ultra-realistic flight simulator. The game is easy to grasp, and each mission lasts only a minute or so; it is designed to briefly let spectators at NASCAR and other events play for a few minutes, and then direct them to the recruiters (Michael Peck, *National Defense*).

Setting the Stage

Military simulations use devices such as narrative storylines, historical reenactments, and "fog of war" to immerse the player in the game. Let us take a closer look at how simulation developers set the stage for compelling game experiences.

Story

Military simulations have an implicit or explicit *story* that drives the mission forward. An implicit story is based on a participant's general understanding of how to behave. For example, recall the chopper crash scenario at the beginning of the chapter. Early in that scenario, other soldiers accompany the player in the chopper. After the crash, the player sees characters wearing clothes unlike the clothing worn by the soldiers who were in the chopper. These other characters are also moving suspiciously and carrying a rocket launcher that looks like it could be capable of bringing down a chopper. Even with this limited knowledge, a player dropped into the middle of this situation without any background knowledge should be able to piece together what happened and identify who is friend and who is foe. Breaking the scenario into rudimentary pieces, the implied story might lead a player to assume the following:

- Anyone wearing the uniform worn by the people in the chopper is probably friendly.
- The men with the rocket launcher may have been responsible for destroying your chopper.
- The men with the rocket launcher are probably unfriendly.

If implicit stories are built on subtle cues for the player to piece together, explicit stories leave little room for interpretation. Explicit stories are conveyed directly to the player—setting the backdrop, central theme, or plot arc for the military simulation. The scope can be broad enough to cover an entire single player campaign, or can be as narrow as a mission briefing to communicate the objective in one round of an online multiplayer battle. In either case, the information is conveyed directly to the player. Some examples of explicit stories include the following:

- Overthrow opposition government
- Suppress insurgent forces
- Rescue hostages
- Escort VIPs to safety
- Seize or reclaim territory
- Defend territory
- Destroy communications infrastructure
- Intercept enemy supply convoy

U.S. Army

Even games with a recruitment focus such as *America's Army* contain a narrative.

Subplots of the explicit story frequently involve character development to provide motivation and build an emotional bond to achieve the military objectives. A classic example of a military story progression involves a player fighting side by side with fellow soldiers through several battles, only to see them killed in action—motivating the player to avenge their deaths.

Historical Reenactment

What is the most effective way to convey the beach events during the WWII Allied Invasion of Normandy? Playing a recorded radio address? Watching a 40-minute program containing documentary footage on the History Channel? Reading accounts of the battle in a retired soldier's journal? Viewing the wrenching opening scenes of

Electronic Arts, Inc.

Medal of Honor: Frontline uses a historical reenactment of World War II to enhance the game experience.

Saving Private Ryan? Radio, television, print, and film are certainly useful historical records, but what if we could simulate the Allied and Axis conflict in an environment where participants could see and hear from the soldiers' perspectives the horrors of storming the beach while the battle raged around them? Some developers have done exactly that. The events of past wars involve some of the most dramatic and gripping events humans have ever experienced, and several military game simulations have re-created them with incredible detail. Now, developers can immerse players in settings where their actions directly impact the events on the Normandy beach or in any number of simulated historical battles.

Fog of War

As technology becomes more powerful, developers are increasingly capable of simulating the *fog of war*. In the most general sense, "fog of war" means the lack of knowledge and communication breakdown during war. On the battlefield, the fog also represents a soldier's disorientation and confusion caused by the battle events. Some developers implement a visible hazy "fog" to confuse a player's sense of direction, but such a literal interpretation is only one of several other techniques used to create chaotic scenarios. Simulating the fog of war involves creating an environment in which the player's visual and aural perceptions are reduced or altered to trigger feelings of excitement and confusion. Some of the new technologies that enhance the fog of war experience include the following:

- Multi-channel surround sound that shifts a sound source's apparent location
- Scripted radio chatter or multiple lines of simultaneous dialogue
- Simulated dust clouds or precipitation to obscure vision
- Volumetric smoke from explosions and smoke grenades
- Screen effects such as motion blur, depth of field, and color filters

The fog of war scenario can be a compelling twist when implemented in an environment the player has already visited because a player may have established points of reference or expectations that are only partially detectable when viewed through the fog of war. The surreal combination of familiar and unfamiliar adds an intense dimension to draw the player into the military game simulation.

Electronic Arts, Inc.

Medal of Honor: Frontline uses *fog of war* to alter players' perceptions.

Challenging the Player

One of the most compelling challenges inherent in military simulations involves the role of enemy characters. Players sometimes must distinguish between friend and foe, keep up with transitory rivals, and adapt to environmental conditions to engage with the enemy.

Identifying Friend and Foe

At the core, military simulations are based on conflicts with enemies. No matter the objective, players must understand who is friend and who is foe. Imagine that everyone in your neighborhood wears blue uniforms, and an enemy battalion outfitted with bright red jackets marches into town hoisting tall flags announcing their arrival. This strategy does not sound too smart, does it? Many European soldiers dressed in such decorative uniforms were easy targets in wars leading up to WWI. Similarly, imagine how ridiculous a simulation would appear if huge red arrows floated over the heads of your enemies—or a bright neon silhouette outlined the figures of your virtual opponents. Sound ridiculous? Developers found that these obvious indicators are often required to distinguish friend and foe for civilians who have not received observational training. It turns out that such obvious indicators make military game simulations much more enjoyable for players.

Big Stock Photo

© 2006 Ubisoft Entertainment

Enemies can be identified by color in both live and electronic (*Tom Clancy's Ghost Recon Advanced Warfighter*) military simulations.

Online Play and the Transitory Enemy

The online military simulation environment is a unique enemy scenario where players are able to change teams with ease. During one battle, a member from the opposing forces might kill a player; in the next battle, the player might switch affiliation—and suddenly the killer and killed are cooperating against a common enemy. In this example, the simulation is in a state of transitory absolutes; regardless of who was an ally in the previous round, the slate is wiped clean and new definitions of allies and enemies take effect when the next round begins. This team-hopping creates an environment of temporary enemies, much different from a real-life battle where defectors are exceedingly rare.

Environmental Conditions and Enemy Engagement

Soldiers must be trained to adapt to a variety of environmental conditions that can alter their range of perception. Military game simulations are capable of re-creating almost any combination of conditions a soldier may encounter on the battlefield. When environmental conditions are well implemented, developers have a greater potential of achieving balanced gameplay. For example, soldiers in an offensive position may utilize a recent snowfall to track their opponents' footprints as they retreat. On the other hand, defensively positioned soldiers could utilize the same conditions to backtrack over their prints and ambush enemies who believe they are hot on the trail. Other potential environmental conditions that affect enemy engagement include the following:

- *Heavy nighttime downpour with lightning:* Long spells of limited viewing distance with brief flashes of complete illumination and loud ambient noise encourage rapid, even risky movement; low visual and aural stealth is required along with moments of high visual stealth.
- *Dense fog:* Severely limited viewing distance with eerie silence limits hasty movements but enables misdirection opportunities (e.g., throwing stones to confuse opponent); low visual stealth and high aural stealth are required.
- *Warehouse with loud industrial machinery:* Clear indoor conditions enable moderately long viewing distance, but machinery overpowers all other sounds; high visual stealth and low aural stealth are required.

It is difficult to accurately simulate environmental conditions in military simulations because players probably have not reloaded an M-60 machine gun, but most players have experienced an evening thunderstorm. Players bring such real-world experiences into the game and expect the simulation to behave accordingly. Most modern game engines are capable of rendering fairly accurate weather phenomenon, and players have grown to expect such realism. Bottom line: If the game environment does not affect strategy and gameplay, it is really just eye (or ear) candy. If this is enough for the type of military game simulation under development, that is fine; but a developer should not expect players to be impressed with the effect after the first time they experience it. After that, the effect may become a distraction or, at best, go unnoticed.

Environmental conditions such as heavy snowfall are difficult to simulate.

Holy Grail: Perfectly Balanced Gameplay

Many of the components necessary to create a military game simulation are relatively straightforward: build a virtual battlefield, add some tanks and guns, and throw in some virtual soldiers. The four aspects of military simulations—environments, vehicles, weapons, and soldiers—are well documented, so implementing one or several of them successfully is entirely possible in the hands of experienced developers. If this is all it takes to make a great military game simulation, the market should be flooded with high-quality titles. What separates the mediocre from the excellent? Balanced gameplay. When elements are balanced properly, the result is a comprehensive simulation experience without a disproportionate burden or power. Balance in military game simulations is achieved by incorporating strengths and weaknesses into each environment, weapon, vehicle, and character. There must be a countermeasure for each element; otherwise, players will gravitate to the strongest option in each category—reducing diversity and experimentation.

Building the Battlefield

Environments, weapons, characters, and vehicles all play a part in building the battlefield: the backdrop of all military simulation games.

Environments

When creating military simulation *environments*, developers either model an existing environment—such as the beaches of Normandy—or invent a completely new battlefield. Whether modeling a location or inventing a new environment, scouting locations is invaluable to ensure that the development team has reference material.

Gathering reference material is usually scheduled early in the development cycle to forge the initial artistic direction. Many developers also use concept artists to create a unified vision between reference material and invented environments. Futuristic and alien environments notwithstanding, classic military simulation environments fall into seven categories:

- Urban
- Jungle
- Arctic
- Desert
- Forest
- Grassland
- Marine/seaport

Big Stock Photo

Big Stock Photo

Photos.com

Photos.com

Environmental Layout

While many military simulations rely on a heads-up display (HUD) to be the primary means to display character orientation and mission objectives, an effective *environmental layout* can be just as important. In desolate, expansive environments such as deserts and arctic regions, topography plays a key role in subtly guiding players to "hot zones" (areas conducive to enemy engagement). Similarly, landmarks are particularly important for efficient pathing in environments with little terrain variation. Environments densely populated with uniform buildings or foliage require careful planning and consideration to reduce player disorientation, which can easily lead to backtracking and frustration. The best-designed environments have clear primary paths and numerous sub-paths to provide variety and encourage tactical experimentation. When designers at a development studio create a new map, the map must be playtested internally or with a focus group. No matter how much time and care designers put into the first iteration of the map, playtesting invariably brings out unanticipated uses of the layout. Effective developers also research their competition, especially those military game simulations with a loyal online community. There is a reason people come back again and again to a few select simulations.

Dynamically Scaled Environments

Imagine playing paintball with two teams of 500 people in an abandoned football stadium. The relatively high participant-per-square-meter ratio would create an intense action-packed experience. Now imagine playing paintball with two teams of two people in the same stadium. So few participants in such a large environment make the situation much less appealing; this is the dilemma faced by developers when building online environments. Military game simulations currently support over 60 simultaneous online players on a single battlefield. A simulated environment that supports over 60 players is far too vast to maintain a fast pace for a two-on-two match. How can a developer accommodate such wide ranges of player volume? The least complex method of ensuring the number of participants is appropriate for the environment space is to implement tiered access based on quantity of players. In this method, online participants are able to start a round only if they meet the minimum number of players for a map. For example, if an expansive map is designated a "50+" map, the sum number of participants of both teams must be at least 50 before the match is allowed to begin.

Alternatively, some developers build multiple versions of each map to accommodate a variety of capacities.

U.S. Army

U.S. Army

Close combat contrasted with a desolate landscape in *America's Army*.

While creating several versions of each map sounds like a good solution, this approach can result in many additional development headaches. Offering multiple versions of a map is not as easy as a simple *scaling* of the landscape boundaries and dropping in or removing a few spawn points or vehicles. Each map variation requires significant design time, play balancing, and, perhaps most costly, quality-assurance testing.

Weapons

Accurately modeled *weapons* are becoming hallmarks of military game simulations. Many developers spend time researching weapons to study their characteristics as accurately as possible. Some attend private military demonstrations or visit a shooting range for some hands-on experience. The physical model, magazine capacities, fire rates, penetration capabilities, blast radii, ballistics, and accuracy are all considered when implementing simulated weapons. Many developers create such accurate models that the United States military can convert the simulations from unclassified (commercial) to classified (professional) by simply adding information such as the range of weapons systems and probability statistics. Weapons in a simulation may include the following:

Steven Kendrick of Cybershooters

- ■ *Firearms:* Handguns, shotguns, assault rifles, sniper rifles, flame throwers
- ■ *Explosives:* Rocket-propelled grenades (RPGs), incendiary grenades, fragmentation grenades
- ■ *Stationary weapons:* Turrets, anti-aircraft batteries, mines

Military simulations that limit the number of weapons a player can carry force players to decide which weapons are most effective in each scenario. For example, densely arranged buildings in an urban setting may present limited viewing distances—making a close-range weapon such as the shotgun or handgun a more effective choice than the sniper rifle.

Diagram by Per Olin

Weapon	Accuracy	Capacity	Reload Rate	Damage	Range
Handgun	3	6	7	5	4
Shotgun	2	4	6	8	3
Assault Rifle	6	8	6	4	6
Sniper Rifle	10	2	3	9	10

Firearms are represented by their effectiveness in several categories such as accuracy, ammunition capacity, reload rate, damage, and effective range.

::::::Grenades as a Trajectory Lesson

Developers use two methods to implement the play mechanic to throw grenades or other objects. One method involves a preset or automatic distance for thrown objects. In this scenario, when the player presses the "throw" button, the object travels the same distance every time, or the simulation calculates where the player most likely wants the object to land. This automated method is a relatively passive experience. The second method, an implementation that requires more player participation, involves a multi-layered system in which the user must make several decisions before the character throws the grenade:

- The player readies the grenade by selecting it in the inventory, and an arc appears on the screen as a HUD element originating from the virtual soldier and ending at the point of destination.

- The end-point of the arc is steered by manipulating the control stick or mouse.

- When pressure-sensitive controllers are used, the distance of the throw is dictated by the pressure applied to the range button; the harder the button is pressed, the farther the throw.

Since the HUD arc displays the potential grenade trajectory, it may seem like the player is not required to make any calculations; however, the throw is only the first step. When the grenade lands, gravity, friction, and environmental objects might affect it. A grenade thrown in a desert environment may stop like a golf ball in a sand trap. The same grenade thrown in an urban environment may ricochet off a couple

Pandemic Studios

Full Spectrum Warrior

walls and bounce halfway down a stairwell before detonating. If it was thrown into a swamp, the grenade's effective blast radius may be reduced by orders of magnitude. When the physics model reaches this level of complexity, players begin to understand the effects of physics by making calculations involving gravity, interaction with nearby objects, and environmental conditions.

Characters

Soldiers in military game simulations are a virtual representation of the real men and women who train in militaries across the world. As such, most developers attempt to model real soldiers as closely as possible. When designing *characters*, considerations must be made for appearance, capability, behavior, and personality (if part of a story-driven mission).

Modeling a virtual soldier's appearance involves creating the soldier's body type (and associated animations), facial model, and uniform with camouflage appropriate for the environment. The virtual soldier's capabilities should reflect the traits of real soldiers, including rate of movement while running, jumping, or swimming—carrying capacity, endurance, and consequence of injury. Mass market titles frequently take liberties with some traits to address players' impatience with real-world nuisances such as a soldier becoming tired or needing recovery time after being injured.

For a virtual soldier to be believable, the soldier must also behave in a manner similar to a real soldier. For example, when a grenade detonates nearby, the soldier should instinctively flinch or duck for cover. Similarly, when a mortar launch or detonation is imminent, the soldier might yell "fire in the hole" or something similar to alert his fellow soldiers. Finally, as more military game simulations model historical battles with elaborate storylines, personalities have become increasingly important. Players can form an emotional bond with a virtual soldier with a compelling personality, which may drive the story forward.

Activision

Activision

Activision

Activision

Character appearance, movement, and actions in *Call of Duty*.

Vehicles

Transportation is often a factor in the success or failure of military campaigns. *Vehicle* simulations are becoming so advanced and integral to all operations that the United States military began using identical equipment both in training and on the battlefield. A soldier trained on this equipment can make a seamless transition to the "live" vehicles because they are identical. According to a military official, "One of the first places we saw this was onboard ships, so if you've got a navy ship in port and it's fully staffed, you can do a simulation. As far as the sailor is concerned, they don't look out the window anyway, so, hell, they're at war" (Ted McKenna, *Journal of Electronic Defense*).

Activision

Activision

Activision

Modes of transportation in *Call of Duty*.

Effectively simulating land, sea, and air transportation is a significant challenge due to the wide range of models and characteristics associated with each vehicle-based combat category. When a category is added to the simulation, a significant investment is required in design, art, and engineering. Much like a real war, a land-based military simulation becomes considerably more complex when the vertical dimension of aircraft or sea-based combat is introduced. Developers planning on taking their ground-based simulation to the air or sea should consider the following:

- Can the simulation engine support the massive draw distance required from the "eagle-eye" view of an aircraft?
- How will players trigger ground-based checkpoints that drive the mission?
- Can the artists and designers implement all the collision boundaries necessary to account for players exploring every aspect of the environment from any angle?

Additional vehicle considerations include the following:

- Are characters vehicle specialists; or can any character pilot, drive, and operate mounted weapons?
- Where are the mount points for vehicles? Use players' understanding of how they interact with everyday vehicles to implement mount points. For example, if your vehicle fleet includes a truck with an open bed, players may expect to be able to board the truck from the rear.

- Can players hijack enemy vehicles?
- Does damage affect the performance and handling of vehicles? Implementing damage-specific characteristics like sound effects and physics that affect handling and appearance can enhance the player experience, make the simulation more convincing, and provide important cues to the extent of the damage.

Maintaining Vehicle Balance

In a pure military simulation, a convoy of several heavily armored assault vehicles can usually overpower a large contingent of foot soldiers. When vehicles offer such an imbalance of power, online military simulations can become heavily lopsided. If a simulation is destined for the retail market, care must be taken to balance the gameplay of vehicle versus non-vehicle combat so that both sides have a "fighting chance." If gameplay is unbalanced, matches simply degrade into "who can get to the vehicle first and obliterate the other team." While potentially entertaining for a few rounds, this scenario rarely leads to a dedicated base of players. Balanced vehicular gameplay is a design and engineering challenge, but developers who invest time and technology to get it right usually end up with a deeper game simulation that requires players to use more nuanced tactics.

Rewards

Rewards in military simulations include tangible and intangible incentives, an increase in rank, and access to unlockable content.

Tangible and Intangible Incentives

Soldiers in the military are motivated by tangible and intangible *incentives*. Tangible incentives include medals and promotions in rank; intangibles include the satisfaction of achieving a goal as a team and a belief that the fight is for a just cause. Military game simulation developers build similar rewards into the gameplay to maintain players' interest and motivate them to continue the simulation. Gameplay rewards include promotion in rank, new weapons, abilities, or unlocked areas that allow the player to proceed to the next mission.

Rank

In the world of online military game simulations, very few identifiers exist to differentiate players from each other. To group people quickly, developers frequently implement a *rank* or status system based on U.S. military titles to categorize players based on skill level. In the *SOCOM* series, for example, players can advance from the initial rank of Ensign all the way up to Fleet Admiral. Although higher-ranking officials usually do not have direct command over subordinates, online players with a higher rank are usually treated with respect. Conversely, lower-ranking players are easy targets for blame or ridicule because they "have not earned their stripes." Advancing from one rank to the next can be determined by several factors. The weight of each factor used to compute rank is commonly held privately by developers to reduce the rate of abuse by players attempting to take shortcuts to rapidly gain rank. Factors include the following:

- Accuracy
- Total games played
- Total kills
- Total team kills
- Suicides
- Completed games
- Rank of competition

Diagram by Per Olin

Abbreviation	Rank	Grade	Position on Officer Ladder
ENS	Ensign	Junior Grade	81-100%
LTJG	Lieutenant Junior Grade	Junior Grade	66-80%
LT	Lieutenant	Junior Grade	51-65%
LTCR	Lieutenant Commander	Mid Grade	41-50%
CDR	Commander	Mid Grade	31-40%
CAPT	Captain	Mid Grade	21-30%
RADM (LH)	Rear Admiral Lower Half	Flag	11-20%
RADM (UH)	Rear Admiral Upper Half	Flag	6-10%
VADM	Vice Admiral	Flag	2-5%
ADM	Admiral	Flag	0-1%
FADM	Fleet Admiral	Flag	Top 10 Officer Players

Officer ranks in *SOCOM 3: U.S. Navy SEALs*.

Unlockable Content

Most *unlockable content* enables the player to proceed in the mission, or it increases the capabilities or power of characters. If a squad is advancing toward the enemy's location, it may need to literally "unlock" a gate to get into the stronghold. Character capabilities or weapons may be unlocked through training or achieving a statistical threshold. For example, if a player successfully completes 10 flight training missions, the player may be rewarded with the ability to fly any aircraft on the battlefield. Another developer may choose not to implement training missions and give the player the same reward after shooting down 100 enemy planes with anti-aircraft artillery. Both implementations unlock the option to fly aircraft but set different benchmarks for the player. Alternatively, some unlockable content is strictly cosmetic. Many players will invest time and effort to unlock content that allows them to change the appearance of their characters. Content might include alternate camouflage patterns, face paint, tattoos, hats, boots, bandanas, and ammo belts. Players with unique soldiers in an online simulation full of similar-looking characters are usually perceived to have more experience and skill because they have played long enough to unlock the content to set them apart from other players. Such content might include the following:

- Missions
- Medals
- Clothing
- Weapons
- Abilities

Sony Computer Entertainment America

Sony Computer Entertainment America

Weapons in *SOCOM: U.S. Navy SEALs*

Penalties

When a player makes a mistake in a military game simulation, the most common *penalty* is to require the player to restart the level and try again. However, penalties can also be subtler. Suppose say a player is leading a group of virtual soldiers, and two of the soldiers are unable to advance due to heavy fire; the player can either attempt to give them cover fire or advance without them. If the player bails them out, they will be available to help finish the mission; if the player leaves them behind, the player will be penalized by having a reduced squad size—potentially making the mission objective much more difficult.

In real-life military scenarios, *death* is perhaps the most significant deterrent of dangerous behavior or poor decisions. In a less absolute sense, military simulations use character death as a penalty for a player's mistakes. Since death is merely an inconvenience in simulations, a developer must strike the proper balance of creating an

Activision

Military simulations such as *Call of Duty* use character death as a penalty for a player's mistakes.

adequate challenge without making the penalty so severe that it deters additional attempts to complete the mission.

When a player's character dies in single-player or story-based missions, the character is frequently returned to the last registered checkpoint. If a developer employs a checkpoint system, care must be taken to implement sufficient checkpoints so that the player is not discouraged or frustrated when replaying the mission segment. On the other hand, an abundance of checkpoints or a limitless save feature frequently reduces the perceived penalty of death—thereby also reducing the element of tension and the importance of long-term strategy.

Death in online multiplayer military simulations is commonly designed in one of two ways: either *respawn* (resurrect) the character and return the character to gameplay immediately, or force the player to wait until the round is complete before the player character can participate again. When a character is killed in the respawn scenario, a player may be penalized only a few seconds before the character is back in the game. Online matches with such rapid death-to-life cycle often have aggressive or even reckless tactics due to the minimal penalties. The alternative design forces players to take a more deliberate approach because they have more invested in the match. The penalty of virtual death relies on a player's desire to actively participate in the match rather than wait on the sidelines for the next round to begin.

Working As a Team

Militaries are composed of groups of soldiers and officers who are expected to work together toward a common goal. The emphasis on teamwork poses a significant challenge to developers of military game simulations. Games built on an unrealistic one-versus-all model have their own rules and design challenges, but removing the teamwork aspect simplifies many aspects of development. A game based on the character of Rambo would be built on this model. Breaking down the core design requirements, we might have something like the following:

- Give Rambo some powerful weapons and cool karate moves.
- Make everyone else Rambo's enemy.

That is it. There is no, "Hey, where are Rambo's sidekicks? He cannot achieve the next objective unless I protect them" or, "I need another Rambo to man the turret while my Rambo drives the tank." Whether the simulated characters are controlled by artificial intelligence or by remotely connected humans, requiring them to cooperate and succeed together is critical to military game simulations and involves substantial development challenges.

Artificially Intelligent Support

In single-player campaigns, teammates must be designed to support the player to achieve the mission objective. Artificially intelligent teammates must mimic behavior expected of humans by responding to commands and monitoring their own status. In addition, artificially intelligent teammates should be a source of guidance through visual or audio cues if they detect that a player is not making progress in a predetermined window of time, or if the player is acting in a supporting role. Common conditions monitored by artificially intelligent soldiers include the following:

- Objective
- Orders from commander
- Optimal path (distance)
- Optimal path (safety)
- Health level
- Whether or not they are under fire
- Position (currently advancing, retreating, holding position)
- Nearest source of cover
- Number of soldiers remaining in squad
- Number of opposing forces
- Available resources needed to accomplish the objective (firearms, ammunition, tools, vehicles, specialists)

Activision

Call of Duty (single-player mode) contains several non-player characters (NPCs) controlled by the game's artificial intelligence system.

Remotely Connected Humans

The rapid growth of Internet connectivity has made online modes in military simulations all but mandatory. In fact, many recent military simulations eschew single-player modes entirely and build the entire game around the online scenario. In games that offer both modes, it is not unheard of for players to log hundreds of hours of online time without ever experiencing the single-player campaign. If an artificially intelligent squad behaves with relative predictability, a squad of online humans can operate on both sides of the line—from an incredibly well-orchestrated team all the way down to a reckless group of maverick soldiers who have no regard for cooperation or even the lives of fellow teammates.

Clans

Online military simulation players frequently join together to form *clans*. An informal clan may be a group of friends who like to get together and play a few rounds while socializing and enjoying the sense of community offered by online military simulations. At the other end of the spectrum are the "hardcore" clans. The people who constitute these ultra-dedicated clans have a singular goal: compete to win and achieve the highest rank possible. Loyalty to clans is often unconditional; members may be forbidden from joining another clan or even from fraternizing with members of competing clans. Such extreme loyalties and rules frequently cause turmoil to simmer beneath the surface of a hardcore clan. Any breaches of conduct can quickly escalate into heated disputes and in-fighting within the clan. Demotion, membership suspension, and banishment from the clan are all options for a clan leader to impose on the perpetrator.

Recruitment

If an upstart or fragmented clan needs to increase its membership, clan leaders will *recruit* independent players or members of another clan. Overt recruiting from competing clans can lead to friction and intensify the rivalry as one clan attempts to maintain its members while another attempts to break it apart. In a more diplomatic recruitment method, a clan holds open calls for new clan members. These tryouts are usually held in a publicly accessible virtual room where the leaders can promote the clan and search for fresh talent. Hardcore and technically focused clans frequently base their decision to accept recruits based on how well they perform over the course of many matches. More casual clans place less emphasis on performance and may base their decision on a recruit's rank, statistics, or social compatibility.

Specialization

Although most military game simulations allow players to take the role of any type of soldier, clan members often take roles as *specialists*. For example, if a member demonstrates talent or enthusiasm in sniping, that member may be designated a sniper specialist; teammates would rely on the member to perform this role in the heat of battle. When a clan has all the roles on its team filled with experienced specialists, they can be very difficult to defeat.

Examples of specialists in several military simulation games include the following:

- Assault
- Sniper
- Special ops
- Combat engineer
- Medic
- Heavy weapons
- Anti-tank units

Activision

Activision

Activision

Activision

Various specialists in *Call of Duty*

Community Expectations of Behavior

When a new online title is released, it only takes a few days or weeks before a set of expectations are established for online behavior. These expectations or rules can be the result of anything from unbalanced gameplay to viral misinformation. When *SOCOM II* was released, it quickly became apparent that the grenade launcher was significantly overpowered. It was branded condescendingly as the "noob tube" because even the greenest players ("noobs") could use the grenade launcher to overpower experienced opponents with relative ease. The online *SOCOM* community rapidly began to resent the weapon and vilified anyone using it. Some went so far as to kick players out of the game if they equipped their soldiers with the grenade launcher.

Sony Computer Entertainment America

SOCOM II: U.S. Navy SEALs.

While the "noob tube" online community rule was based on a legitimate issue with gameplay, some rules are based on misinformation that spreads through the community. It is no secret that online simulations can have difficulty maintaining a consistent frame rate, because the hardware and software try to keep everyone's simulation synchronized. When the frame rate becomes too low or inconsistent, it puts some players at a disadvantage because their screens do not update as frequently as their opponents' screens. In *SOCOM II*, an inconsistent frame rate caused so many players to lose matches that the source of the problem was frequently debated. Players came up with all sorts of explanations regarding why the frame rate was inconsistent. One of the most popular scapegoats was "spectator mode," an option where people could watch the online battle as passive observers. In the online *SOCOM II* community, all it took was one group to say that it found the culprit (spectator mode causes frame rate problems), and it spread as truth. Once thousands of players latched onto this bit of misinformation, it was not uncommon to see spectators immediately booted out of games the moment someone noticed them. Blaming spectator mode was a much easier and simpler answer than the true culprit: 16 players with varying network connection speeds can be nearly impossible to keep in perfect synchronization during every second of every online match.

As time goes on, these online behavioral expectations become part of the fabric of the online experience. Players entering the online battlefield months or years after a game's release may have as much difficulty understanding the expectations of fellow players as they do competing against players who have honed their skills over hundreds or thousands of hours.

In the past, military simulations were strategy games, aircraft simulations, or tactical shooters, but developers have grown more ambitious and have blended the genres. The increased scope of these hybrid military simulations has created a new role for players: the Commander. The perspective from Commander mode is similar to the traditional strategy simulation in that the Commander can direct squads engaged in combat, send in supplies, and call in bombing runs with precise coordinates. However, unlike the artificially intelligent soldiers in a traditional strategy game, the squads, supply drivers, medics, and pilots the Commander directs are all controlled in real time by players viewing the action from down on the battlefield. In military game simulations lacking a Commander orchestrating the battle, multiple friendly squads might needlessly pursue the same objective—a poor strategy that wastes time and resources, and increases the likelihood of enemy attention and potential casualties. The centralized intelligence made possible by the Commander mode adds order to the chaos traditionally seen on a battlefield lacking this perspective.

Spectator Mode: Learn By Watching

Imagine you are playing a few rounds of an online multiplayer military simulation and one player on the opposing team is dominating the match. Every time that player kills your character, you do not even see it coming. As your character is killed yet again, you wonder, "How did this happen?" Modern tactical shooters frequently offer a compelling option called "spectator mode" that answers this question. In this mode, players can view the action from the perspective of another player and learn by watching. Spectator mode is a powerful enabler of lateral learning through sharing because it allows effective techniques and strategies to be discovered.

Now that we have covered the powerful and compelling military simulation genre, let us take a close look in the next chapter at a less dangerous "battlefield" associated with one of the most popular types of simulation games: sports.

1. Create an original concept for a military simulation. Discuss the environment, enemies, weapons, vehicles, and story structure. What is the target audience for your simulation, and what benefits will that audience gain from playing your game?

2. Discuss five rewards and five penalties that you might incorporate into your original game. How will you ensure that these rewards and penalties remain realistic and are tied to the gameplay and story elements?

3. Play an existing military simulation and discuss five features that distinguish the game from other types of simulations. Why are military simulations particularly powerful and compelling?

Part III:
Entertainment
& the Future

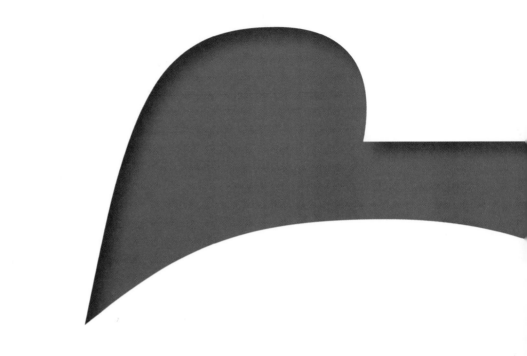

CHAPTER

6

Sports
bringing the action into the living room

Key Chapter Questions

■ What is the difference between simulation and arcade-style sports games?

■ How can increased complexity help and hinder a sports simulation?

■ Why are professional athletes particularly challenging to model?

■ How are sports simulations used to instruct professionally and casually?

■ What do developers need to know about their audience to create a successful sports simulation?

Professional sports are an enormous financial and social market. Each major sport has a legion of die hard fans, and sports simulations offer an experience previously available to only a select few capable of performing at the highest athletic levels. The advent of online connectivity brings competition to a global stage where friends and strangers on different continents can play each other in their favorite virtual sport. The games reach a broad audience, bringing the action to fans, players, coaches, and managers during the thick of the playoffs or tiding them over during the off-season. The technology, rules, and players in most real-life sports and their respective simulations change every season. Publishers capitalize on the dynamic market by releasing annual updates to their sports simulation franchises. As simulations become increasingly accurate representations of real sports, publishers and developers must walk a fine line between overwhelming new players with complexity and delivering the depth expected by hardcore fans. Participating in a virtual sport from the couch isn't much of a workout, but it can be a valuable tool to train for and understand the complexities of modern professional sports.

Getting in the Game

Developers strive to create virtual sports that immerse players in the action. A successful immersive experience blurs the line between conscious input and the resulting simulation. The most successful sports simulations convince players that they are capable of managing a football team all the way to the Super Bowl, taking the lead on the last lap of the Daytona 500, or hitting the clutch three-pointer to win the NCAA playoff game.

Real-World Complexity in Sports

Professional sports have increased in complexity while growing in popularity, exposure, markets, and athletic talent. Sports game simulations have seen a parallel increase in popularity, budgets, and technological capabilities. Each year, most sports simulation series are updated and often include enhancements that make the game simulation more closely resemble its real-world counterpart. Year by year, these improvements appear incremental, but when viewed from a longer arc of time, the advancements are unmistakable. For example, *Tecmo Bowl*, a wildly popular football simulation in the early 1990s, included only four plays. After selecting their play, players could snap the ball, run, pass, catch, and kick with a single button press. By contrast, *Madden NFL 07* includes hundreds of plays mirroring each team's real-life playbook and the option to control any of the virtual characters that look and perform like their real-life counterpart with a myriad of button press combinations.

Tecmo

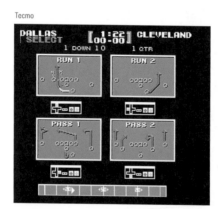

Electronic Arts, Inc.

After two decades of pro football simulations, playbooks have grown from four (*Tecmo Bowl*, left) to hundreds (*NCAA Football 07*, right) of plays.

Modern racing simulations have made similar advances. *Pole Position* was a breakthrough racing game in 1982 that included a few tracks and a car with two gears. Modern race simulations, like the *Gran Turismo* series, include hundreds of photorealistic cars with countless levels of customizability and dozens of virtual tracks modeled after real race courses. As professional sports grow faster and more complex, technology has enabled games simulations to narrow the gap with each hardware generation.

Sports Simulations for Real-World Training

Professional sports organizations have started taking sports simulations seriously as they become more robust and more accurately reflect real-world performance and capabilities. Artificial intelligence, end-user game customization, and player models have advanced to the point where a coach can design a new play and test it against a variety of opposing strategies. If a football coach believes she has a new strategy to overpower this week's defense, she might use the latest version of *Madden* to test receiver routes against her opponent's simulated defense. Similarly, amateur racers can use games like *Gran Turismo* to prepare for the appropriate driving lines and brake timings by taking laps on a virtual Laguna Seca before heading out on the real track.

Electronic Arts, Inc.

Football coaches can use simulations such as *EA Sports Arena Football* to test offensive and defensive schemes.

Arcade vs. Simulation

Virtual sports games can usually be divided into two camps: simulation and arcade. Developers of simulations attempt to accurately model the rules, athletes, and behaviors of the sport. Arcade-type sports games are characterized by exaggerated abilities, stylized characters, and modified rules to increase the pace and intensity of the sport.

Diagram by Per Olin

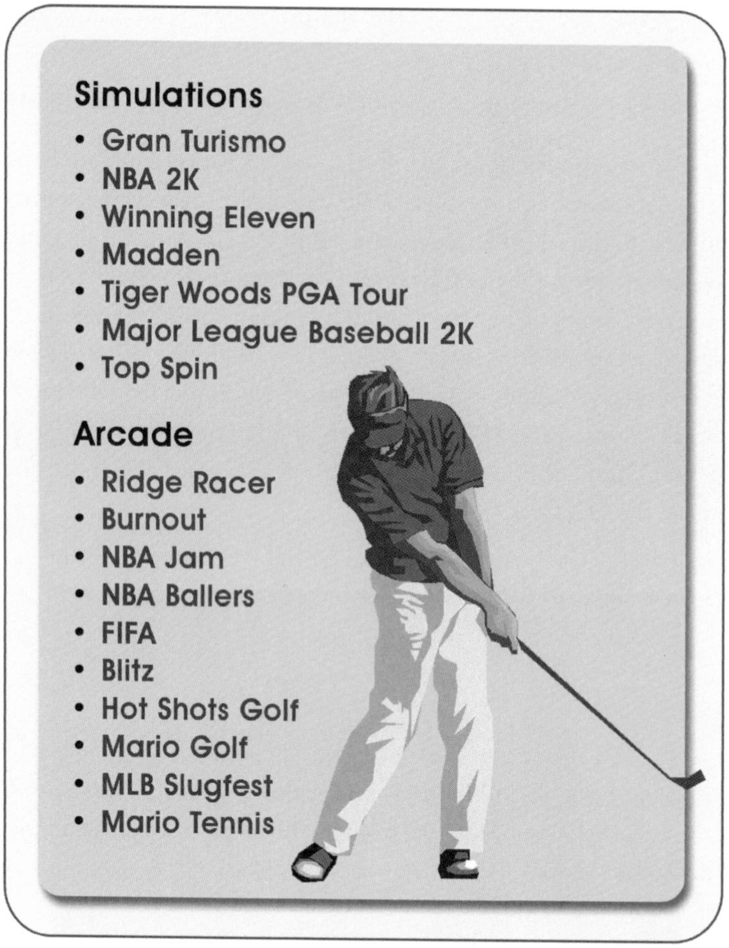

Simulations
- Gran Turismo
- NBA 2K
- Winning Eleven
- Madden
- Tiger Woods PGA Tour
- Major League Baseball 2K
- Top Spin

Arcade
- Ridge Racer
- Burnout
- NBA Jam
- NBA Ballers
- FIFA
- Blitz
- Hot Shots Golf
- Mario Golf
- MLB Slugfest
- Mario Tennis

The Infamous Rubber Band Effect

Imagine two cars hooked together by a very large rubber band. As one car pulls ahead of the other, the rubber band stretches; if the lead car gets too far ahead and stretches the rubber band to its limit, the rubber band pulls the lead car back and the trailing car ahead, closing the gap between the cars. The analogous implementation in a non-racing sports game can be visualized by a metaphorical rubber band hooked between each team's score. If one team gets too far ahead, the gap stretches the rubber band to its limit and the artificial intelligence shifts to make scoring more difficult for the leading team and easier for the trailing team, thereby narrowing the gap.

The rubber band effect is a popular tool used by developers who want to give their game an "arcade" feel that is entertaining at the expense of realism. Players who favor simulations that accurately reflect real-world races or matchups between teams loathe the rubber band effect because it can reward less experienced players. Fans of the rubber band effect believe it contributes to exciting gameplay because nearly every race or match ends up coming down to the wire. The arcade segment of the sports simulation market frequently wears the rubber band effect like a badge of honor, and some, like *Ridge Racer*, *Blitz The League*, and *NBA Jam*, have taken it so far that it has become an integral part of a franchise.

Diagram by Per Olin

Wii & Sports Interactivity

Nintendo decided to break from conventional input devices when the company released the Wii console. The motion and acceleration sensors in the Wii controller detect motion in three dimensions, empowering developers to create games with functionality that was not possible in previous home consoles. When the console was released with *Wii Sports* included in the system, sports simulations were among the first titles played by consumers with the new interactive interface. *Wii Sports* includes several rudimentary games such as tennis, bowling, boxing, baseball, and golf. The sports simulations are rudimentary because the experience is not focused on advanced graphics, sound, statistical tracking, or character development. Instead, Nintendo decided to emphasize intuitive controls that would appeal to a casual audience.

Each *Wii Sports* game encourages players to assume the body position associated with playing the respective sport. In *Wii Sports* bowling, for example, a player stands with the Wii remote held vertically in her hand, close to her chest as if she were holding the bowling ball in front of her body. The player then drops her hand in an arc moving backward and behind her waist, and reverses the pendulum motion forward. An advanced player can perform nuanced controls by twisting her wrist or timing her release to control spin and trajectory. All these transitions and movements are relayed from the Wii remote to

Nintendo

Wii Sports utilizes motion-sensing controls to immerse players in the action.

the console, reporting velocity, acceleration, and orientation. Data is calculated in real-time and displayed by the virtual bowler on the screen. Although this innovative control mechanic requires greater physical participation than competing consoles, Nintendo is betting players will favor the intuitive motion-sensing controls over games that use conventional buttons and thumbsticks.

The Meta-Athlete Scenario

Licensing deals between publishers and professional sport associations have grown into a huge investment, some reaching the hundreds of millions of dollars. After sinking so much money into the license, game publishers take incredible measures to promote the likenesses of the athletes for which they paid so dearly. If EA spends millions of dollars a year for the exclusive right to incorporate NFL players in its football simulations, you can be sure EA will blast the faces of popular players to all media outlets. One common marketing theme involves real NFL players playing *Madden* as themselves or re-creating on-the-field action during a live broadcast of an NFL game. Professional athletes playing as their virtual selves presents an intriguing situation; for example, Donovan McNabb, a professional quarterback, controlling the virtual Donovan McNabb who has been modeled on the real Donovan McNabb—the real world controlling the virtual world modeled on the real world.

Predicting Real-World Matchups with Simulations

ESPN paired up with EA Sports to offer weekly predictions of NCAA football matchups. Each week's marquee matchups are simulated using EA's latest iteration of their NCAA-licensed football title. The "highlights" from these virtual games, complete with a real ESPN reporter voice-over, are posted each week on ESPN's website. As simulations become more robust through advanced physics and improved artificial intelligence capable of mimicking players' on-the-field decisions and coaches' play-calling, these simulated matchups could become excellent predictors of the real matchup.

Team Management

Some professional sports fanatics are less interested in controlling the virtual athletes and prefer to dig into a sport's back-office management. Team management simulations cater to the hardcore sports enthusiast who wants to explore and manipulate every aspect of running a virtual sports franchise without the primary focus on gameplay.

Many of these characteristics exist in games outside the team management genre, but they only scratch the surface of the capabilities of team management simulations. A game such as *Major League Baseball 2k7* may allow players to select a ballpark for the matchup, but *PureSim Baseball* allows players to build a ballpark from scratch. Team management simulations also expose players to the financial and negotiation aspects of professional sports. A successful manager must be capable of adapting to the demands of team fans, the logistics of nurturing young talent, and the pressures of a competitive market. Team management simulations are only a sliver of the sports simulation market, but they cater to the hardcore fans who want to build and manage a successful sports franchise.

Enlight Software

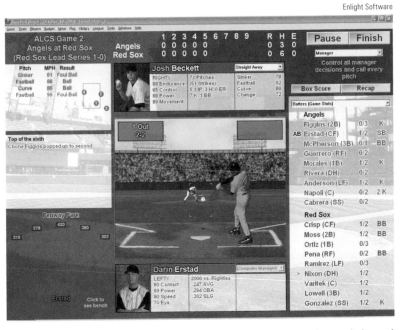

Team management simulations such as *Baseball Mogul 2007* emphasize statistics and administration over gameplay.

Diagram by Per Olin

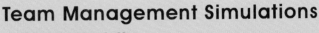

Team Management Simulations
Characteristics

- Deep statistics tracking
- Recruit, draft, and trade players
- Scout up-and-coming talent
- Determine player rotations or substitutions
- Stadium management
- Ticket, vendor, and parking prices
- Attendance tracking
- Batch game simulation to rapidly advance the season

Examples

- Football Manager
- Worldwide Soccer Manager
- Baseball Mogul
- PureSim Baseball
- Out of the Park
- NFL Head Coach

The Look of the Sport

Appearances in sports simulations are critical to immersing players in the experience. Technological advances are reducing the limitations to building believable models with every generation of hardware. Developers who take the time to research and accurately model the environment, characters, objects, and style of each sport have a higher likelihood of immersing players in an effective simulation.

Stadiums, Arenas & Tracks

When creating a sports simulation, developers model the sport's environments by collecting reference materials and scouting locations. Reference materials include architectural plans, satellite imagery, and official documents and models. Scouting trips can be valuable to survey stadium sight lines, record the roar of a game-day crowd, or view the racetrack grade from the perspective of a race car driver. Once the research phase is complete, artists begin assembling the environment with as much detail as the tools and technology allow. The jump from the Xbox to the Xbox 360 enabled artists to model the Brooklyn Bridge in *Project Gotham Racing 3* with more polygons than the entire race environments in *Project Gotham Racing 2*. In the perpetual chase for realism, the more detail included, the more convincing the simulation environment.

Reprinted with permission from Microsoft Corporation

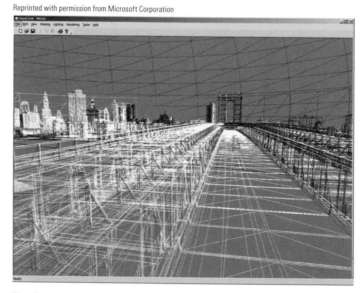

The *Project Gotham Racing 3* model of the Brooklyn Bridge (shown) was built with more polygons than the entire New York level in *Project Gotham Racing 2*.

Player Models

High-quality player models are critical to the virtual sports experience, particularly if a developer is building a licensed title. The pressure for accuracy is more intense than almost every other simulation genre because professional athletes receive so much exposure. Developers can get away with generic actors in an educational or military simulation, but fans can spot a poorly modeled Shaq on the court or Wayne Gretzky behind the boards a mile away. A significant portion of a character artist's time is spent modeling the head for each marquee athlete. New tools, including low-cost, three-dimensional head scanners have reduced startup time, but many refinements are done by hand. Additional time is allocated to adjusting the player's body type and refining distinguishing marks such as scars and tattoos. Since consumers have preconceived notions about what each player should look like, even the slightest flaw can disrupt a simulation's believability.

:::::: Uncanny Valley

As character models become increasingly accurate, developers must be aware of the "uncanny valley," a hypothesis from Japanese roboticist Dr. Masahiro Mori. He contends that tiny flaws in highly accurate almost-human models can trigger an unnerving and repulsive emotional response from observers.

Electronic Arts, Inc.

Yes, it looks a lot like D-Wade (*NBA Live 06*), but something is a bit off…

Player Animation

Character movement is similar to appearance in that observers can tell whether an actor's animation is natural or unnatural. In-game animations are becoming more believable as developers move beyond actors interacting at a crude full-body level and into actors who respond to discreet limbs and joints with increasingly accurate physics. Virtual pitchers and batters exhibit the between-pitch mannerisms. The race car driver's body sways and bounces from the g-forces acting on his body and the rumble strips jarring the car.

Motion Capture

A significant amount of the improvements in natural-looking animations are possible due to advances in motion-capture hardware and software. Now that developers can generate hundreds of motion-captured animations with relative ease, even greater attention must be paid to the transitions between animations. The smoothest, most accurate cross-over dribble animation loses its impact if the simulation abruptly "pops" the actor's movements when transitioning to a jump-shot animation at the player's request. In the hands of capable developers, advanced blending techniques and animations configured for rapid retargeting across multiple skeletons can mitigate many of the transitional problems of the past.

House of Moves

Motion capture of athletes adds realism to a sports simulation's animation.

Head and Eye Tracking

Head and eye tracking is another subtle, yet effective, advance in animation and artificial intelligence that enhances the believability of a simulation. Virtual athletes no longer make every play a no-look pass, catch, shot, or hit. Instead, their head and eyes are drawn to the appropriate action. Wide receivers and cornerbacks track the ball as it leaves the quarterback's hands and sails in their direction; a hockey goalie fixates on the puck as the opposing team sets up its offense and rips a shot into her glove; all the post players in the paint watch the ball hit the rim as they prepare to leap for the rebound. These small actions contribute to a more believable simulation experience.

Crowd Simulations

Attending a live sports event is different from watching the same event on television or the Internet. Aside from the spilled beer, crowded restrooms, and marked-up food prices, live sporting events are engaging because of the spectator community. After years of neglect, increased technological power now enables developers to place more emphasis on the audio, appearance, and behavior of crowds to add authenticity to sports simulations.

Audio

The sounds at a track, stadium, or arena have an incredible effect on fans and athletes. The communal roar of the crowd can get people on their feet and energize a defense and rattle an offense. The latest multi-channel surround sound technology drops players into the soundscape of the simulated action. Ambient sound and music stream in and transition seamlessly to add realism to the simulation. Developers of team sports simulations reflect the ambiance of each club's die-hard fans by including chants, rhythms, songs, and hecklers barking insults from the stands.

Contextual crowd-related audio provides subtle cues to the player regarding game status and team performance. If the player is not paying attention and the play clock is getting perilously close to zero, the crowd may chant the countdown or a spectator may yell "Hurry up!" If the team needs a big defensive stop, the crowd volume may increase dramatically, signaling the play's importance.

Appearance

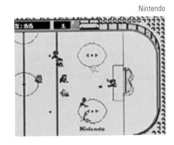

Nintendo

When hardware performance was at a premium, almost all available computing power was utilized to simulate the athletes or cars in sports simulations. While the realism of these primary characters steadily improved, performance issues required simulated sports crowds to be either omitted or rendered as a two-dimensional, low-resolution sprite or texture that looked like a sea of expressionless, flat faces. Hardware performance has improved to the point that developers can allocate some of the rendering power to create more lifelike crowds.

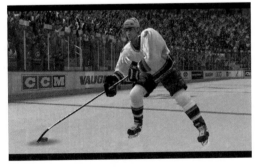

Electronic Arts, Inc.

One of the best ways to increase crowd realism is character variation. One hallmark of earlier generation sports games were crowds populated by what appeared to be the same man wearing the same clothes and the same expression. As hardware became more robust, artists and designers were able to vary colors, genders, and body types. To increase the realism of the crowd simulation, developers also create contextually based motions that reflect the state of the race or match. In a real crowd, people are constantly moving; giving a simulated mass of people slight, discreet movements at the individual character or small group level breaks up the otherwise wooden appearance in static crowd simulations.

From *Ice Hockey* (1988) to *NHL 07* (2007): Advances in stadium crowd simulations over 20 years enhance a game's realism.

Game developers also use contextual motions to make crowds behave like their real-life counterparts. In modern racing games, virtual trackside spectators cheer wildly at drivers along the race route and perform evasive actions if cars get too close. Simulated basketball and football fans sitting in the baseline or end zone sections will stand and flail their arms or wave signs to distract the free throw shooter or field goal kicker. The same section of virtual fans may start "the wave" rippling through the crowd. Closer to the action, the virtual coach or manager may pace the sideline, while the mascot and cheerleaders run through routines corresponding to the team's actions. Although a player's attention is focused on the action among the athletes, the sum of the peripheral crowd and sideline actions adds significantly to the perceived realism of the simulation.

As Seen on TV

Simulating a sport involves a lot of research and reference material from teams, athletes, coaches, and equipment manufacturers. Even after all the research has been done, developers must still decide how to present the simulation.

Cameras

Even the best-modeled players and the most accurately designed stadium can look awful if camera angles and lenses are incorrect. Novelty camera angles, such as the perspective of the ball or the view from the player's eyes through the helmet, are frequently abandoned after users try them once. Restricted views are frustrating and claustrophobic. Even if viewing the action through the eyes of a player makes the simulation more realistic and useful for training, it detracts from the experience in a mass market title. "Cinematic" sweeping camera angles and pans experience a renaissance every few years, but they are rarely utilized successfully. Cutting to dramatic camera angles is useful to highlight instant replays, break up standard camera angles during breaks in the action, or advance the storyline, but this technique fails during gameplay. When the camera angle is positioned dramatically (such as a low-angle, front perspective of the offensive line) or changes during gameplay, players become disoriented because such angles create an awkward or inconsistent reference of direction.

Post-Processing Effects

Post effects are also effective tools that mimic the presentation viewers see on television. Adjustable depth of field is a technique recently available to many developers to draw attention to specific areas of play. A staple of cinema and television for decades, depth of field involves sharp focus on a character or object while all other elements in the frame appear out of focus. Depth of field is a subtle yet powerful tool to guide an audience to the most important aspects of the frame.

Post-processing effects such as depth of field give broadcast quality to a sports simulation, drawing the player's eye toward the action (*ESPN NBA 2K5* and *NBA 2K7,* shown).

Dialogue and Play-by-Play

SportsTalk Baseball, one of the first console sports games to include dynamic play-by-play commentary, was released in 1992. The digitized voice was fairly adept at keeping pace with the action and it provided an unprecedented new level of immersion. Most modern sports broadcasts have at least three people in their crew covering the on-field events. From the booth, one announcer calls the action and another provides color commentary, while a third counterpart provides periodic updates from the sidelines.

Audio and engineering departments must work closely to create a natural-sounding exchange that accurately reflects the on-field action. One of the first factors to break the suspension of disbelief during a simulation is a phrase or comment that is often repeated. A commentator who utters, "What was the quarterback thinking?" three times in four plays sounds much more like a limited simulation than natural commentary. A common solution includes recording variations of dialogue that can apply to the same in-game scenario. Increasing storage capacity eases some of the limitations of incorporating many lines of dialogue, but the real leap in believable in-game commentary will come when games can generate real-time dynamic speech for any situation. Unfortunately, the technology for this holy grail of sports simulation commentary is still many years away.

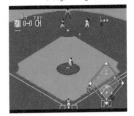

SportsTalk Baseball was one of the first console sports games to include dynamic play-by-play commentary.

Kraig Kujawa
(Creative Director,
Midway Games)

Kraig Kujawa has more than 10 years of experience creating video games and new IP in the interactive entertainment industry. He is currently directing *Hero*, a big-budget action-adventure, in addition to the next-gen sequel to *Blitz: The League*. Kraig's career in interactive entertainment began at Ziff-Davis publishing, where he was Senior Editor of *EGM*, ultimately becoming Editor in Chief of the *Official PlayStation Magazine* in 1999. There, he was tasked with redesigning the editorial to feel more mainstream and within two years, he built *OPM*'s paid circulation to the highest of any Ziff-Davis Game Group magazine. In 2002, he decided to actually make games instead of writing about them, so he left the publishing business to join Midway Games. He cut his teeth on *NFL Blitz Pro* and then led the design of a re-imagining of the *Blitz* franchise that released in 2005 as *Blitz: The League* on PS2, Xbox, and later, PSP and Xbox 360. The SKUs sold over 1.4 million units combined.

It's important to know where your game's "tipping point" is between realism and confusion. I think a lot of sports games are really having trouble with this right now—especially football games. Marketing pressures them into adding lots of new "features" that make for good bullet points, but maybe not gameplay. And designers often fall into the trap of equating *infinitely more complex* with being a *better game*. This isn't necessarily true: Adding 80 different features to one controller can make all of them irrelevant or unintuitive to both casual and hardcore players. Do you really need all of those features to tackle a ball carrier or make a lay-up versus a dunk? Not really. The real trick is to get the spirit of the simulation down, or to make players feel smart-like they really are the coach. If you nail both of those, you don't need to worry about every nuance of the sport because you have the most important stuff nailed.

The Feel of the Sport

Scouting trips and reference images help developers re-create the look of a sport, but the best-looking simulation in the world is not very useful if it does not re-create the feel of the real game. Imagine trying to explain how to drive a manual transmission car if you have only seen photographs or movies of the real thing. You might be able to describe the process based on what you have seen, but you would not have insight into how the clutch pedal feels when the clutch begins to engage the transmission. Nor would you know how downshifting without matching RPMs just before making a turn changes how the steering wheel feels as the weight of the car transfers forward and your hands guide the car through the curve. A development team comprising people who actively play the sport will be much more efficient and effective when building a sports simulation.

Control

As analog controls became standard issue on game consoles, developers gradually made better use of the high range of motion and sensitivity compared to the digital counterpart. Earlier games required a single button press to swing a virtual baseball bat or golf club; modern games use analog controls so players can choose the velocity and angle of the swing. Similarly, analog sticks and triggers enable racing simulations to re-create steering and pedal inputs with many degrees of fidelity. Analog controls in basketball, hockey, football, and soccer simulations give players control of passing, shooting, defensive maneuvers, and flashy moves at the individual athlete level. For example, in the *NBA 2k* basketball series by Visual Concepts, one of the analog sticks controls a great deal of the virtual athlete's ball-handling hand. While in possession of the ball, pulling back on the analog stick makes the onscreen character bring the ball back behind her body. Moving the stick in a figure-eight pattern makes the character do a cross-over dribble. While the character is in mid-air, her shot angle and arm extension can be manipulated to evade an opponent's block attempt by corresponding analog stick movements.

::::: The Control Complexity Disincentive

Analog functionality is not the only evolution of modern simulation inputs. The latest controllers are far more ergonomic than their predecessors' simple boxy shapes, but they also include many more buttons. As hardware manufacturers incorporated more buttons with successive generations of controllers, many developers viewed the increased button inputs as an opportunity to give the player greater control of their virtual athletes. Players who grew through a few generations of these controller advances usually have no problems adjusting to the increased complexity, but, to the uninitiated, picking up a traditional modern game controller is akin to sitting down in an aircraft cockpit and being asked to prepare systems for takeoff. Even developers who attempt to reduce the complexity of their games by requiring the use of only a few buttons must hope consumers overcome the intimidation of a controller covered with cryptically labeled buttons and triggers and at least give the game a try.

Reprinted with permission from Microsoft Corporation
Annotated by Jason Bramble

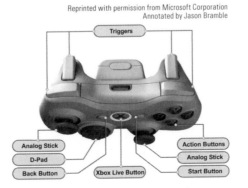

Controller complexity has increased greatly since the days of a digital stick with one button (Atari VCS joystick, left; Xbox 360 controller, right).

::::: *Madden*'s Controversial "Vision Control"

Every year, the latest iteration of *Madden Football* sells millions of copies, even if the newest version is not remarkably different from the previous year. No one feels sorry for developers working on one of the best-selling game franchises of all time, but EA's success with the *Madden* franchise has boxed the company into a position where it cannot afford to alienate its fan base by making radical changes year to year. Every now and then, the *Madden* development team tiptoes around this restriction and adds a new feature in hopes of enhancing gameplay or making the game more realistic. In 2005, EA tested the limits of how far fans were willing to go with realistic gameplay when it added a feature called "Vision Control." The feature represents a virtual quarterback's field of view; his range of vision is indicated by a transparent cone projecting from his position on the field. Pass attempts to receivers inside the boundary of the cone are much more accurate than attempts to receivers outside the cone.

Electronic Arts, Inc.

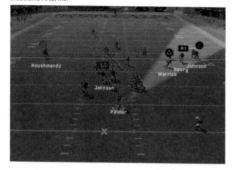

"Vision Control" was added to *Madden NFL 06* and was resisted by the Madden fan base.

In theory, vision control is a great addition to a game aspiring to accurately model capabilities of NFL players because it represents the field of view of real professional quarterbacks. Unfortunately, the theory did not hold up in practice. Most players were frustrated by the implementation because it made the passing game cumbersome. Ease of use trumped realism and most players ultimately disabled the Vision Control feature. EA conceded that Vision Control did not enhance the gameplay experience for the majority of players and shipped *Madden '07* with the feature disabled by default. The relative failure of Vision Control is an example of the delicate balance developers must maintain between implementing features that represent the challenges faced by professional athletes and fun, accessible gameplay.

Field Action

When Midway decided against developing another NFL-licensed *Blitz* title, the company was able to take the franchise in a fresh direction. No longer bound by the NFL's license rules, Midway simulated the seedier side of professional football. *Blitz the League* took a new angle on professional sports by incorporating scandals pulled from real-world NFL headlines. Painkillers, steroids, dirty hits, trash talking, and gambling all make appearances in *Blitz the League*. The story mode takes players to off-the-field venues such as locker rooms, nightclubs, hotels, and jail cells. While *Blitz the League* falls into the arcade style of football simulations, it extends the action to include real aspects of professional football that the NFL does not allow in its officially licensed title.

Midway Games, Inc.

Free from the restrictions of the NFL license, *Blitz: The League* brings the seedier side of professional football to the forefront.

Heads-Up Displays & Player Feedback

When *Fight Night Round 3* was released for the Xbox 360, the developer heralded the omission of the heads-up display (HUD) as a breakthrough in sports games. Previous boxing games, including *Fight Night Round 2*, incorporated a HUD to convey how much energy each boxer had left. According to the developer, the graphical enhancements made possible by the Xbox 360 version of *Fight Night Round 3* allow a player to determine the health status of her virtual boxer by the condition of the boxer's face, stance, and movement, instead of a traditional health meter. As the virtual boxer gets increasingly battered, his face and nose swell, cuts form and bleed, his eyes begin to close, his shoulders sag and his arms drop, and his movements become increasingly lethargic. The alleged "advancement" of the default HUD-less interface was met with

protest from some in the industry. Opponents argued that HUDs are an integral part of game design to clearly communicate the status to the player. When the HUD is removed for aesthetic, rather than functional, purposes, a player is left to interpret vague feedback about her virtual athlete's condition. Game simulation developers must not lose sight of their purpose: serving the audience. If feedback is not conveyed effectively, players cannot be expected to respond with the appropriate action, and the value of the simulation diminishes.

An older game that isn't probably considered a simulation but should be is the old Sega Dreamcast game, *Ultimate Fighting Championship*, based on the very real pay-per-view fights that happen every few months. That game captured the strategy of how to win a fight from the ground—as well as put you on the edge of your seat, since the fight could be over in a matter of seconds if you were sloppy.

—*Josh Bear*
(Co-Owner & Creative Director, Twisted Pixel Games)

:::::A Focused Table Tennis Simulation

Rockstar Games, famous for its *Grand Theft Auto* series, departed from the open-world crime saga in 2006 when it released something completely different—a table tennis simulation. The resulting *Rockstar Games Presents Table Tennis* is a sports simulation stripped down to its core elements. The developers decided to focus all their energy on creating the most realistic table tennis simulation possible. Granted, they chose a relatively simple sport, but Rockstar's laser focus on the gameplay shines through in the finished product. The player models, animations, artificial intelligence, and game-play are well tuned to the point that the game can stand on its own. Rockstar kept its production focused by eliminating many extraneous features of other sports simulations such as career mode, create-a-player, doubles, or elaborate environments. The bare-bones offering does not appeal to fans of feature-rich simulations—but for table tennis aficionados, *Rockstar Games Presents Table Tennis* really hits the mark.

Courtesy Rockstar Games and Take-Two Interactive Software

Rockstar Games Presents Table Tennis focuses on the core elements of the sport.

Racing

People unfamiliar with the sport of racing may not see anything beyond the NASCAR cliché of "43 cars making left turns for a couple of hours." Those who get beyond this perception learn that racing is a deep sport ripe for simulation. Cars, tracks, and environments are modeled from real-world counterparts, and advances in physics simulations enable developers to accurately translate the challenges of hurtling down the track at 200 miles an hour.

Simulation-Style Racing

Gran Turismo set a new standard for racing simulations when it broke onto the scene in 1998. When designing the game, Polyphony Digital included 178 car models, each with its own distinct handling and performance based on its real-life counterpart. The developers took great pains to give the player visual and aural cues to differentiate each car. In *Gran Turismo*, a Dodge Viper handles much differently from a Honda Accord station wagon or any of other dozens of cars. Players are rewarded with prize money depending on how they finish in a series of races. The prize money could be stored and later spent on upgrading a wide variety of performance options or buying a new car.

The advanced physics models in *Gran Turismo* and similar modern racing simulations reward players capable of advanced driving techniques, such as pre-turn weight transfer or heel-and-toe engine RPM matching using the virtual clutch. As in real-life racing, players who master the controls of high-performance cars have an advantage over their real or virtual online opponents. Advanced controller rumble feedback also communicates road conditions and real-time traction status of the vehicle. Car performance is affected by tire wear, damage to the steering mechanism, chassis alignment, and reduced aerodynamic efficiency from body damage.

Sony Computer Entertainment America

Gran Turismo raised the bar for racing simulations (*Gran Turismo 4*, shown).

Tuning

The ability to custom-tune each car is a defining characteristic of simulation-style racing games. Tuning functionality goes beyond cosmetic appearances; each adjustment affects a car's on-track performance. Players must evaluate track conditions and analyze the competition to select the optimal configuration. Advanced tuning options are unlocked by finishing near the front of the pack in assorted race classes and time trials. Racing simulations give players significant control of a myriad of tuning variables, including the following:

- Engine tuning
- Gear ratios
- Tire pressure
- Suspension
- Fuel strategy
- Wheel toe-in and camber
- Aerodynamics and downpressure
- Body sculpting
- Weight distribution

Sony Computer Entertainment America

Racing simulations such as *Gran Turismo* allow players to custom tune their vehicles to increase performance and adjust to track conditions.

Simulated Driving Tests

Polyphony Digital apparently did not think its highly detailed car models, sophisticated physics engine, and real location-based environments were enough to call its racing game a simulation. The phrase "driving test" is not normally associated with racing entertainment, but to the chagrin of many players, these tests are a critical component of *Gran Turismo*. Players must pass increasingly difficult driving tests to unlock advanced racing circuits. The test requirements start at fairly mundane levels, but rapidly advance to maddening difficulties. Some of the margins for error on the advanced driving tests are so narrow that many players simply give up out of frustration.

Arcade-Style Racing

Arcade racing simulations trade realism for exaggerated physics and stylized environments and vehicles. Developers of these games cater to a large market of speed junkies seeking a visceral thrill behind the virtual wheel. Acceleration, top speed, and handling are enhanced beyond real-world capabilities to create an entertaining experience. Crashes are common in the arcade genre and usually have little to no impact on a car's performance. Gameplay usually involves extreme drifting or sliding through turns and some nitrous-enhanced acceleration thrown in for good measure. Virtual opponents are given aggressive artificial intelligence to engage in risky maneuvers and sacrifice some paint to get ahead.

:::::When Crashing Is the Game

When Criterion designed the *Burnout* series, it successfully blended simple controls, rewards for risky behavior, an incredible sense of speed, and spectacular crash effects to create a compelling arcade racing experience. In *Burnout*, finishing first is not always the primary goal. While players are rewarded for fast lap times, they are strongly encouraged or even required to force opposing cars off the road or into other cars, even if it means sacrificing their own car in the process. Aggressive enemy artificial intelligence wreaks havoc through high-risk maneuvers and attempts to avenge hostile efforts by the player. Car models in *Burnout* have multiple levels of destruction; the first couple of hits may create a few dents in the body or knock out some lights. Additional collisions ramp up the visual destructive effects; entire body panels are sent flying, glass cracks and shatters, and a completely over-the-top shower of sparks flows from below and behind the car. The visuals are accompanied by powerful audio effects that drive home the devastating impacts of crunching metal. Crashing is so fundamental in *Burnout* that the developers include a mode that focuses solely on how many crash impacts a player can achieve by hurtling the car into a busy intersection.

Electronic Arts, Inc.

The *Burnout* series built a franchise on searing speed and larger-than-life crashes.

Driving Simulations As Learning Tools

As artists and designers become increasingly capable of faithfully modeling real racetracks and programmers implement accurate driving physics, driving simulations become more useful tools to understand high-performance driving. Advanced racing simulations have already incorporated realistic requirements for critical aspects of performance driving like brake timing, weight transfer, and acceleration and deceleration techniques. They are also capable of indicating optimal cornering lines, or paths where the driver can carry the most amount of speed (without losing control of the vehicle) by increasing the apparent radius of the turn relative to the car.

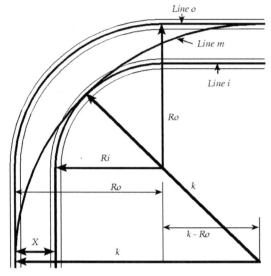

Dr. Brian Beckman, Microsoft Corporation (phors.locost7.info)

Players can use racing simulations to learn driving techniques such as optimal race lines to maintain speed through corners.

Models & Sound Design

Modern simulation engines enable artists to create vehicles made of tens of thousands of polygons. High polygon counts mean more realistic models and more convincing simulations. Recent racing game simulations dedicate nearly equal numbers of polygons to modeling the interior and exterior of the cars. Artists spend months on each car so every inch of body paneling and glass, every gauge and crease in the dashboard, every stitch on the leather steering wheel, and every knob and button on the console are modeled with meticulous detail.

The experience from the interior perspective is also enhanced by sound design. Multi-channel surround sound provides effective audio cues when utilized by an experienced developer. Many license-based racing simulation developers bring vehicles on-site or travel to the manufacturer to record each vehicle's trademark sound. Audio engineers work in three dimensions to envelop the player in the car and make her feel like she is hurtling down the road at 200 miles per hour. Engineers can also use techniques like the Doppler effect to signal whether another car is closing the gap or falling farther behind the player.

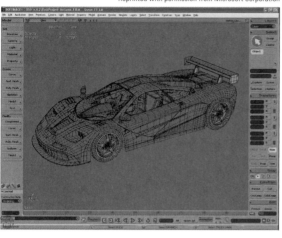
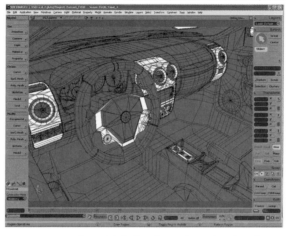

Artists on *Project Gotham Racing 3* used tens of thousands of polygons to accurately model the interior and exterior of each car.

Snowboarding & Skateboarding

The *Tony Hawk Pro Skater* series revolutionized skateboarding simulations when it was released in 2000. EA's Tricky franchise did the same for the snowboarding genre. Gameplay for both series consists of stringing tricks together while cruising down respective streets and mountains. Both titles have delivered several sequels; the latest releases are highly polished versions built on the successful components of their predecessors. These simulation franchises are successful because they effectively incorporate stylized visual and aural aspects of each sport's culture along with intuitive controls.

Activision

Tony Hawk's Pro Skater series (*American Wasteland*, shown) has revolutionized skateboarding.

Sports: bringing the action into the living room

chapter 6

Olympic Sports

Every Olympic year, a publisher decides to capitalize on the global event by releasing an officially branded Summer or Winter Olympic Games simulator. Unfortunately, these games are nearly universally mediocre, uninspired versions of the real-life athletic competitions. While short production schedules and low budgets frequently hamper a developer's chance at creating a compelling Olympics simulation, the shallow nature of most Olympic events also burdens developers.

Many successful sports simulations are not shallow because they are team games such as football or basketball that involve complex playbooks and multiple positions to control during each play. Even the Olympic "team" competitions are simply a series of individual competitions grouped together.

Courtesy 2K Sports and Take-Two Interactive Software

Torino 2006 is one of the more sophisticated Olympic sports simulations.

Hunting & Fishing

A fishing simulation also makes an appearance in the Wii version of *Legend of Zelda: Twilight Princess*. Players use the Wii motion-sensing remote to cast a virtual line with one hand, and reel in the catch by rotating the nunchuck remote with the other hand. Players can also set the hook in the fish's mouth by sharply pulling back on the Wii remote the moment the fish takes the bait.

The Legend of Zelda: Twilight Princess features a fishing simulation.

Sports Simulation Peripherals

Sports simulation peripherals such as fishing rods, light guns (hunting), and steering wheels (some with pedals) can enhance the simulation experience. Qmotions specializes in custom peripherals compatible with mass market sports game simulations. Their QmotionsGolf peripheral consists of a golf ball attached to an arm mounted on a piece of artificial turf. When players use any standard golf club to strike the golf ball, the Qmotion hardware calculates the force, angle, and spin on impact. This data is then fed to a standard PC golf simulation such as *Tiger Woods PGA Golf*. Qmotions Baseball functions on a similar principle; it uses a baseball bat peripheral to calculate swing timing and bat movement and then passes the data to EA's MVP Baseball for the PC or Xbox.

XaviX is another company that manufactures interactive sports peripherals. Unlike Qmotion's hardware that is compatible with mass market games, XaviX hardware must be operated with Xavix-created software. At the lower end of the sports game simulation market and commonly sold in shopping mall kiosks or toy stores, these inexpensive sports game simulations attempt to emulate real-world sports with dedicated sport-specific peripherals such as bowling, baseball, golf, tennis, and fishing. Unfortunately, the dated graphics, primitive sound effects, and flaky controls make the XaviX offerings underwhelming to players seeking an advanced sports simulation experience.

Sega released a fishing rod peripheral with its *Sega Bass Fishing* series.

Jeremy McCarron on Participatory Sports Simulations ::::

Jeremy McCarron
(Academic Director,
The Art Institute of
Vancouver)

After graduating from the classical animation and 3D animation programs at the Vancouver Film School in 1995, Jeremy worked for Mainframe as a production assistant and then as a character animator on productions such as *ReBoot*, *Beast Wars*, and *War Planets*. He also worked as a senior animator for the direct-to-DVD title *Casper's Haunted Christmas* and as a supervising animator for the *Heavy Gear* and *Action Man* television series. Jeremy briefly ran the animation department as the head supervisor of animation before he left to join Radical Entertainment as an Art Director. There, he worked on the *Simpson's Road Rage*, *Monsters, Inc.*, and *Scarface* video games. He returned to Mainframe as a CG supervisor and animation director for *Barbie's Fairytopia (I & II)* and *Barbie & the Magic of Pegasus* direct-to-DVD titles. In December 2005, Jeremy accepted the role of Academic Director at The Art Institute of Vancouver and is currently working toward his MBA at Simon Fraser University in Vancouver.

I love the EA Sports franchises—*Tiger Woods* and *NHL* specifically. In real life, I wouldn't even be allowed on the same course as Tiger, never mind making him my personal ATM machine through the side bets, but now I can play in the British Open. Simulation games are the ultimate form of entertainment because you can actively "participate" in your dreams (which may not be possible in reality).

The Impact of a Sport's Regional Popularity

Although many types of professional sports are gaining popularity across the globe, game developers and publishers must be conscious of their target markets and how a region's awareness of a sport impacts development and marketing strategies. The growing scope of art and engineering required by advanced sports simulations means outsourcing is a fact of life for most game developers. In these situations, a developer and outsourcer may be based in different countries separated by thousands of miles. Both parties are improving the process of remote development and integration across all genres of games, but sports simulation outsourcing has been particularly vexing. Some of the difficulties are related to the regional celebrity status of athletes. When attempting to outsource player models and animations for these iconic athletes, artists may have difficulty capturing the nuances of players with whom they are unfamiliar. Flaws that may not be noticeable to professional out-sourced artists are often easily identified by fans of the athlete's sport, even if the fans have not had any formal art training, simply because they are so familiar with how the athlete is "supposed" to look and move.

Additional outsourcing difficulties can arise in the testing phase of development, when sports game simulations must be played as thoroughly as possible to check for bugs and to balance gameplay. The complex rules and strategies of sports are second nature to people who have grown up watching and playing the sport. On the other hand, it is unrealistic to expect someone to test a myriad of scenarios for bugs and provide useful feedback on balancing gameplay if she has never seen or played the sport in real life.

Electronic Arts, Inc.

The *Rugby* franchise has a limited market, but it is relatively successful in countries with a dedicated fan base.

Marketing and distribution must also consider where their budgets can be most effective. For the most part, sports simulations have a higher likelihood of success in countries with an established fan base. Simulations of sports such as cricket and rugby have had commercial success by marketing and distributing to regions with a long professional history of each sport. Marketers watch trends and, if a sport begins to catch on in a new region, they may begin to raise awareness of the latest simulation to establish a foothold and expand distribution to increase sales. These region-specific development and marketing issues will become less relevant as professional sports grow in popularity around the world.

So where are sports simulations heading? Hardcore sports simulation consumers demand more realistic athletes, vehicles, and venues, so the bar will be raised every year. At the same time, game developers must be conscious of maintaining accessibility for the casual market. There is still plenty of work to do, including improvements in animation, artificial intelligence, and play-by-play commentary. As access to game hardware increases worldwide, sports simulations may take on a new role, spreading awareness and participation of sports in new regions. Competitions will be held on a global stage and, once the simulations reach the point of immersion where players feel like they are in the game, their popularity and influence might give real-life professional sports a run for their money.

:::CHAPTER REVIEW:::

1. Create an original concept for a sports simulation. How will you differentiate it from an arcade-style sports game?

2. Design an original peripheral device (or manual interface) that would improve on the realism in a sports simulation of your choice. Would porting the game to the Wii result in the same improvement? Why or why not?

3. Play an existing sports simulation and discuss five features that distinguish the game from other types of simulations. Describe the target audience for the simulation and how the game addresses the needs and expectations of this audience.

Creative Arts
tools that challenge and inspire

Key Chapter Questions

- How do motion-sensing and other custom peripherals enhance a creative arts simulation?

- What are the fundamental components of a rhythm-based music game?

- Why might music simulations appeal to a casual game audience?

- How can we simulate theoretical worlds?

- How can developers simulate altered states of mind?

Interactive simulations have opened up new possibilities for pushing the art envelope. New technologies have spawned new mediums for users to experiment with virtual paint, palettes, and musical instruments. A plastic stylus can be transformed onscreen into a pencil, paintbrush, spray can, conducting baton, or drumstick at the touch of a button. Music and art simulations can teach inexperienced users a new craft, or give veterans a new area in which to create. Digital art and music no longer equate with cold or inhuman images, objects, or sounds; the rough edges have been softened through advances in technology, and online resources and distribution have made them accessible. Game developers are bringing the power and creativity of art and music simulations into millions of homes. No matter the skill level, players actively participate in the artistic experience; they feel like they are creating something new and, perhaps more important, something of their own.

Music-Based Simulations

The advent of game systems with high-fidelity digital audio in the 1990s enabled developers to greatly enhance game simulation music. Dynamic ambient music, clear dialogue, and punchy sound effects finally caught up to match the new worlds being built with three-dimensional graphics. Many developers and composers utilized the new audio capabilities to create musical scores and sound effects that rivaled any Hollywood film production. Others began to forge new territory by designing a new type of game simulation where the music was the focus of the experience.

Real-Time Music Composition

Technology has advanced music and composition since the first note was played thousands of years ago. Instruments were created and refined to be more durable and deliver more accurate notes. Recording and playback devices were invented and made gradual improvements in fidelity. Game simulations have added a new dimension by lowering the barriers of entry to composition. *Electroplankton,* for the Nintendo DS, is an unconventional "game" in that it favors compositional experimentation instead of high scores, time restrictions, and objectives. The designers created a "sandbox" where players create music with a simple, yet powerful interface.

Players use the DS microphone and touchscreen to control 10 groups of virtual plankton. Each group represents a different synthesizer with one of the following unique control styles:

- *Tracy*: Draw lines through the water to make this Electroplankton move. The Electroplankton swim along the lines to create mysterious music.
- *Hanenbow*: Launch these Electroplankton toward leaves. Hanenbow make noise as they bounce from leaf to leaf. You can adjust the angle of the leaves to create different sounds.
- *Luminaria*: These Electroplankton stay in constant motion and follow arrows they touch. Touch the arrows to change the direction of the Electroplankton.
- *Sun-Animalcule*: Use the stylus to place Electroplankton eggs on the screen. These Electroplankton emit light and sounds as they grow.
- *Rec-Rec*: These Electroplankton feed on sound. Tap Rec-Rec to change its color and then speak into the built-in microphone of the Nintendo DS to record a sample.
- *Nanocarp*: Clap your hands near the microphone to make the Electroplankton form shapes. They will even respond to your voice.
- *Lumiloop*: Slide your stylus around the bodies of these Electroplankton to make them shine and emit strange tones.

- *Marine-Snow*: These Electroplankton look like snow crystals. They make sounds when you touch them. Move them around and stir them up!
- *Beatnes*: Beatnes remember the melodies you tap out on their heads and bodies. Then they put an old-school sound to the beats.
- *Volvoice*: Touch this Electroplankton and speak to fill its body with your voice. Change its shape to change its voice.

The plankton generate a variety of sounds; some plankton generate piano-type sounds, others create xylophone-type tones, and so on. These tiny virtual organisms are an abstract representation of the knobs, sliders, and icons used in traditional digital audio workstations. *Electroplankton*'s lack of well-defined goals may turn off players seeking a structured, competitive experience, but it offers a unique tool for people interested in composition and musical experimentation.

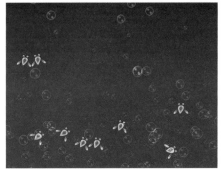

Nintendo

Players use the DS touchscreen and microphone to compose original music in *Electroplankton*.

Conduct a Virtual Orchestra

At E3 2006, Nintendo demonstrated a prototype of an orchestra simulation for its Wii console. *Wii Music: Orchestra* utilizes the motion-sensitive remote to simulate a conductor's baton. A virtual orchestra responds in real-time, increasing or decreasing tempo according to the player's movements with the floating virtual baton. In its current form, *Wii Music: Orchestra* demands a significant amount of physical exertion, encouraging players to put their whole body into their conducting. Slower, graceful movement of the remote causes the musicians to elongate and smooth the performance. Move the remote in a rapid, aggressive manner, and the onscreen characters' visual and aural play style changes accordingly. Although the prototype had fairly limited functionality, the potential for the simulation to make players feel like they were conducting an orchestra was evident. *Wii Music: Orchestra* demonstrates Nintendo's commitment to push the traditional boundaries of games and expand the potential audience for its console.

Nintendo

Custom Peripherals

Developers of music-based games have a long track record of releasing custom peripherals to enhance the experience. Controllers modeled on real instruments can simulate the feel of actively contributing to the rhythm or melody much better than traditional controllers. However, publishers commissioning a music-based simulation should consider several of the following hurdles to developing games that rely on custom peripherals:

- *Profit margin and retail price*: The added cost of bundling a custom peripheral with a game reduces per-unit profits or increases retail price. Consumers may be hesitant to justify the price premium of a game with a peripheral that is not compatible with any other titles.
- *Quality*: Peripherals are usually designed and manufactured by a third party that must make compromises between price and performance. Publishers generally fight to keep costs as low as possible, but this strategy can be detrimental to the build quality and usablity of the peripheral.
- *Development overhead*: Developers must account for additional layers of quality assurance when developing games involving custom peripherals. Additional layers cost time and money.

RedOctane

Although music-based games that incorporate custom peripherals involve greater risk, when designed correctly they are among the most engaging experiences in any simulation genre. Some music-based custom peripherals and the games that used them are shown in the accompanying diagram.

The Ignition Dance Pad 3.0 is a custom peripheral that can be used with rhythm games such as *Dance Dance Revolution*.

Development Considerations

Developers who decide to build a game around a custom peripheral must ensure that they receive prototypes of the hardware as early as possible in the development schedule. Designs that seem fun on paper may turn out to be frustrating or impossible when attempted on a peripheral. Having multiple prototypes in the studio early in development can bring these issues to the surface before your development team burns unnecessary time and resources pursuing a path that will not improve the game. Similarly, every effort should be made to secure the final release version of the hardware well before it hits retail shelves.

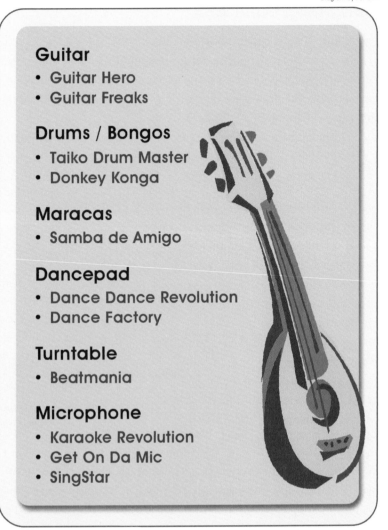

Guitar
- Guitar Hero
- Guitar Freaks

Drums / Bongos
- Taiko Drum Master
- Donkey Konga

Maracas
- Samba de Amigo

Dancepad
- Dance Dance Revolution
- Dance Factory

Turntable
- Beatmania

Microphone
- Karaoke Revolution
- Get On Da Mic
- SingStar

Anticipate & Apply Abuse

Once the first delivery of prototypes comes rolling off the truck, isolate a batch of them to abuse continuously. Give a couple to some kids so they can run them through the gauntlet of tosses, spills, drops, and other mischievous actions. The manufacturer representative may have a heart attack, but he will thank you in the long run when he does not have to recall the first retail shipment due to manufacturing defects brought out by the target audience. Speaking of children, make sure you have all your bases covered regarding safety regulations for devices that may be used by children.

Shredding the Virtual Axe

Konami revolutionized the rhythm-based market in 1999 when it launched *Guitar Freaks* in Japan for the PlayStation. *Guitar Freaks* combines catchy songs, straightforward game design, hypnotic visuals, and a responsive guitar peripheral to create an addictive experience. Players use the plastic guitar controller to play in time with descending icons corresponding to one of three buttons on the guitar neck. As players advance, the quantity and rate of icons increase, ramping up the difficulty and intensity. Future entries to the *Guitar Freaks* series expanded on the successful formula by adding new songs and slight variations on visuals and presentation.

Six years after *Guitar Freaks* was released, Harmonix, a developer with a successful rhythm-based game pedigree in *Frequency* and *Amplitude*, took guitar simulations to a new level when it released *Guitar Hero*. The game was an instant critical and commercial success. *Guitar Hero* succeeds as a music game simulation because it does an incredible job of making the player believe she is involved in creating the song. Although the physical actions of the player are rudimentary relative to the enhanced results generated by the simulation, the effect is truly immersive.

> I'll never be able to play the guitar, and I know I'm not any good at singing or playing tennis, but games such as Guitar Hero, Karaoke Revolution, and Wii Sports let me enjoy some aspect of satisfaction that their real-world counterparts provide.
>
> —Josh Bear
> (Co-Owner & Creative Director,
> Twisted Pixel Games)

Experienced guitar players appreciate the depth and feel Harmonix built into *Guitar Hero*. Even though the custom peripheral has only five buttons, the developers took great care to apply simplified variations on relative note spacing and chord progressions. Descending note progressions in songs force players to travel down the buttons on the neck of the guitar peripheral, while ascending progressions send them back up. Similarly, the song selections in *Guitar Hero* are full of power, or basic, chords that map surprisingly well to simultaneous button combinations on the rudimentary controller. The end result is a guitar simulation full of nuances and character that any musician can appreciate.

Training

After years of casual or heavy use of standard game input devices, many players are familiar with the arrangement of buttons and sticks on traditional game controllers. When a radically new peripheral is released, players must reorient themselves to how their actions affect the simulation. For example, when Harmonix released *Guitar Hero* in 2005, it included a plastic mini-replica of a Gibson guitar. The interactive parts of the plastic guitar include five colored buttons on the neck, a "flipper" in the center of the guitar body next to two buttons labeled "Start" and

"Select," and a metal rod extending below the flipper. Playing *Guitar Hero* involves simultaneously pressing one or more of the colored fret buttons and strumming the plastic flipper in time with the onscreen icons and music. The metal rod, simulating a whammy bar on a traditional electric guitar, adjusts the pitch of the notes in real-time. Finally, the plastic guitar contains a sensor that detects the angle of the guitar's orientation; tilting the guitar vertically during gameplay triggers the sensor and activates an enhanced mode.

Upon starting the game for the first time, most experienced guitar players can mimic the synchronization required on a real guitar and apply it to the plastic *Guitar Hero* model. One hand holds the strings down on a fret (colored buttons) and the other hand strums the strings (plastic flipper) at

RedOctane

The *Guitar Hero* guitar is far less complex than a real guitar, but players still require training and practice to become proficient.

the base of the guitar. To the untrained guitarist, however, the operation of the peripheral can be vexing. If you just hand the plastic guitar to someone who is unfamiliar with guitar technique, the player might not understand that the buttons and flipper must be used simultaneously—or the player might gravitate to the whammy bar and become confused when it has no effect. An effective training feature can make the difference between a player feeling overwhelmed by the complexity of a peripheral and giving the confidence to move from training into the real game. Although *Guitar Hero*'s training feature is not incredibly rich, Harmonix included a session that covers just enough of the basics to hook players and send them into the arena to rock.

Sound as Feedback

Sound seems to be the key factor in providing people with feedback; anyone who has ever watched a game show gets the hint when a loud buzzing noise or something along those lines happens that they did something bad. In the same respect, most people understand when a harp plays, that is a good thing. Most players and non-players understand sound and colors they see in their everyday lives as being positive or negative, and this can be used in games to great effect.

—*Josh Bear*
(Co-Owner & Creative Director, Twisted Pixel Games)

:::::Masaya Matsuura: Father of Music-Based Game Simulations

In 1996, Masaya Matsuura and his development company, NanaOn-Sha, released *PaRappa the Rapper*, a critically acclaimed game for the PlayStation that brought interactive music to the masses. *PaRappa the Rapper* encouraged players to mimic a sequence of buttons similar to the handheld light and sound pattern-matching game *Simon*. The hero of the quirky game was a rapping puppy named *PaRappa*. When players successfully played in time with the music, they unlocked new songs and advanced the bizarre yet engrossing storyline involving rap battles against vegetables and poultry. The combination of catchy tunes, innovative 2D graphics, and a new control scheme that made players feel like they contributed to the music made *PaRappa the Rapper* a classic title that has been imitated since its inception.

Sony Computer Entertainment America

Sony Computer Entertainment America

PaRappa the Rapper revolutionized the rhythm-based music genre, paving the way for dozens of subsequent music games. The minimalist art style and design of *vib-ribbon* could adapt and create rhythm-based gameplay to any song.

Matsuura struck again in 1999 when his company released *vib-ribbon*. The gameplay in this rhythm-based game was similar to Matsuura's previous games, requiring players to push buttons at the correct moment to progress through the game. The art style and minimalist design were crude compared to other games available at the time, but many players were drawn to its simplicity. *vib-ribbon*'s appeal went beyond its appearance; once the game was loaded into the PlayStation's RAM, players could remove the game disc and replace it with any music CD. Once players selected their favorite track, the game adapted its graphics and gameplay to match the rhythm of the song.

Rhythm-Based Music Games

PaRappa the Rapper spawned a game genre that has grown immensely since its release in 1996. Rhythm-based music games are characterized by a user interface of scrolling icons that cross an onscreen threshold synchronized with the beat of music. Players must press the button on their controller that matches the onscreen icon. Pressing the incorrect button or timing the button press out of sync with the music usually results in a lower score or forces the player to restart the level. Games in the genre differentiate themselves by focusing on a particular instrument or musical style. Variations in story, characters, or environment are usually just wrappers around the same tried-and-true gameplay of pushing buttons in time with the rhythm of the music.

When developing a rhythm-based music game with a custom peripheral, developers commonly design the game so that it can be played with a standard controller. The additional functionality is included so players have an alternative method to play the game if they are unable to use the custom peripheral or if they are unwilling to purchase additional custom peripherals for multiplayer action. While the option to play with a traditional controller is a welcome addition, many rhythm games lose their appeal unless they are played with the custom peripheral. *Samba de Amigo* is a rhythm game that can be played with a standard controller, but it really shines when paired with its custom motion-sensing maracas. The experience is vastly different when players are standing up, shaking maracas in the air in time with the music, and striking poses that mirror the pose of the crazy onscreen monkey.

Samba de Amigo comes with custom motion-sensing maracas that players shake standing up, imitating the crazy onscreen monkey.

::::: *Guitar Hero*'s Ancestors

In Harmonix's rhythm-based games, *FreQuency* and *Amplitude*, players press buttons on the standard PlayStation2 controller in synchronization with a sequence of shapes flowing down a tunnel-like environment. *Amplitude* includes a lightweight remix function where players can alter the included songs and create their own interactive track. These custom tracks can be shared online with other *Amplitude* players. *FreQuency* and *Amplitude* were precursors to *Guitar Hero*, laying the foundation for the successful implementation of rhythm-based gameplay that would later be paired with Red Octane's guitar peripheral.

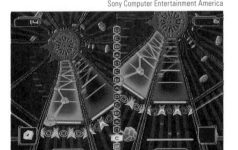 

FreQuency and *Amplitude* were the precursors to *Guitar Hero*.

Design Considerations for Rhythm Games

Timing is one of the most critical components of judging performance in rhythm-based simulations. Players are given a narrow window of time to perform an action; if the input is a millisecond too early or late, it registers as a miss and the player is penalized (or not rewarded). If the size of the timing window is not playtested extensively, players may encounter situations that render the gameplay frustrating or even unplayable. The advent of online play requires developers to set up test scenarios for a variety of connection speeds and server loads.

::::: The Story (or Lack Thereof)

A rhythm game such as *Space Channel 5* may have a story, but the "save the earth from the invading aliens" premise is just a means to connect the rhythm mini-games together. The developer of *Space Channel 5* wisely chose to deliver the story in bite-sized chunks and quickly get the player back into the action. The game also includes occasions when the story is delivered during gameplay. If developers choose to deliver some of the story and gameplay simultaneously, they must ensure that the story elements during those periods are not mission critical. Players engrossed in gameplay are less likely to absorb peripheral dialogue or events. Eschewing an elaborate story does not mean a title lacks personality. In fact, *Space Channel 5* oozes personality through its stylized 1960-70s-in-space art theme, lively characters, and catchy soundtrack.

Rhythm games such as *Space Channel 5* can draw players in with gameplay and style, even if it means their storylines are weak or nonexistent.

Virtual DJ

Konami started an arcade music craze (later known as "bemani") in Japan when it released *Beatmania* in 1997. The game puts players in the role of a club DJ who must win the praise of the virtual audience. *Beatmania* requires a custom peripheral fitted with a turntable and five (later seven) rectangular keys. During gameplay, small icons representing notes scroll down the screen and players must press the corresponding button in time with the beat. Large icons require players to briefly spin the turntable and occasionally freestyle scratch for a period of time. Players are rewarded for their accuracy and creativity during freestyle with points and audience feedback. In theory, *Beatmania* is a solid DJ simulator, but, in practice, the experience is marred by a poor track selection and gameplay that is often based on arbitrary timing rather than synchronized with the music.

Controllica Technologies, Inc.

Beatmania kicked off Konami's "bemani" music and rhythm genre in Japan.

The Dance Simulation That Went Mainstream

What started as a niche arcade dancing game in Japan has grown in popularity well beyond the traditional music game fan demographic. *Dance Dance Revolution* (*DDR*) has appeared on prime-time network variety shows, morning talk shows, and in classrooms. The game is a simulation of rudimentary dance steps—forward, back, left, right, center—performed on a touch-sensitive floor mat in time with music. Why is such a basic game so popular? Spectacle and exercise are two significant contributors to its popularity.

Spectators are often entranced watching a skilled *DDR* player. The game emits blaring pop music and flashy graphics while players move their feet so quickly that they appear as a blur. The rapid movements also translate into exercise, a trait rarely associated with video games before *DDR*. High-tempo music pushes players for three to five minutes at a time, raising heart rates and getting players to work up a sweat. One game will not remove the stigma of the unfit game player, but *DDR* illustrates that video games and fitness are not mutually exclusive.

Dance Dance Revolution's popularity can be attributed to spectacle and exercise.

Your Voice, Now in the Game

When *Karaoke Revolution* and *Get On Da Mic* were released, people were ecstatic (and some were horrified) that players were finally able to belt out the vocals to their favorite songs without going to the local tavern or rap battle. Both stage performer simulations shipped with microphones and track lists of popular songs spanning several genres.

Gameplay in *Karaoke Revolution* and *Get On Da Mic* is not particularly innovative, as players perform in time with the beat and onscreen lyrics, much like preceding music-based games. However, these simulations are unique because the microphone peripheral offers a novel input mechanism not possible with traditional controllers. The games judge singing or rapping performance based on how well players match the cadence, and rhythm pitch of each song. Although the audio engines in each title are not always accurate, *Karaoke Revolution* and *Get On Da Mic* encourage players to get into the performance. For better or worse, these games give players the means to simulate their dream onstage performances for anyone within earshot.

Eidos Inc.

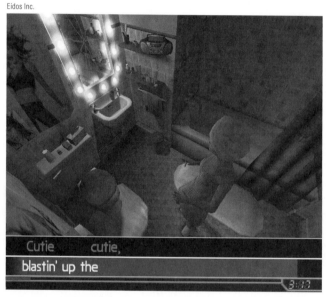

Players are judged on their rap performances in *Get On Da Mic* based on how well they match the rhythm of each song.

Drum Simulations

Traditional drum sets are loud, bulky instruments. Drum simulations such as Konami's *DrumMania* re-create the experience of banging on a kit without the racket or the large footprint. Konami created a custom peripheral with rubber pads to simulate a snare, floor toms, and cymbals. A foot pedal was also included to simulate the bass drum. The gameplay in *DrumMania* emulated Konami's tried-and-true user interface found in its other rhythm games. Icons representing different drums scroll down the screen and players must hit the corresponding pad on the set peripheral in time with the beat. If a player hits the incorrect drum or hits a drum out of rhythm, his "excite" meter decreases; if the meter runs out, he loses. *DrumMania* is a simulation that has real-world value. Players who can master the multi-limb coordination required to progress in the game will have a head start if they make the transition to a real drum set.

Controllica Technologies, Inc.

A custom electronic drum peripheral (*DrumMania*, shown) can simulate drumming on a real drum set.

Using Bongos to Control the Game

Donkey Konga ships with a pair of bongos that plug into the Nintendo Gamecube. The first version of the game lets players use the bongos and integrated clap-sensing microphone to bang and clap in time to the beat like in traditional rhythm games. The sequel, *Donkey Konga Jungle Beat*, uses the same bongos peripheral but requires players to use them in a less conventional manner to control gameplay.

Donkey Konga Jungle Beat is a side-scrolling adventure game controlled not with a digital cross pad or analog stick and buttons, but with two bongos and a clap-sensing microphone. Players use the bongos to guide the lead gorilla character as he collects bananas, which translate to "beats" representing the character's health and points. One bongo moves the character left, the other bongo moves him right; both being hit simultaneously makes the gorilla jump. When activated, the clap sensor functions as the "action" input—making the onscreen character perform a variety of context-specific moves, including swinging on vines, snatching bananas, and latching onto monkeys and birds for transportation.

Nintendo

Players use bongos to play rhythm and to control side-scrolling adventure portions of *Donkey Konga Jungle Beat*.

Creative Arts: tools that challenge and inspire   chapter 7

Aaron Marks on the Use of Audio in Simulation Games : : : : :

Aaron Marks
(Composer; Founder,
On Your Mark Music)

Practically falling into the game industry almost 10 years ago, Aaron Marks has amassed music and sound design credits on touchscreen arcade games, class II video bingo/slot machines, computer games, console games—and over 70 online casino games. Aaron has also written for *Game Developer Magazine,* Gamasutra.com, and Music4Games.net. He is the author of *The Complete Guide to Game Audio,* an expansive book on all aspects of audio for video games—and of the forthcoming *Game Audio Development,* part of the *Game Development Essentials* series. He is also a member of the advisory board for the Game Audio Network Guild (GANG)—and he continues his pursuit of the ultimate soundscape, creating music and sound for various projects.

One of the primary functions of game audio is to provide reinforcement, both positive and negative. Musical fanfares, glissandos, bells, and other "happy" noises are just a few examples of sounds created to reward a player for completing a difficult level or revealing an important clue. These audio cues make the players feel good about their experience and motivate them to continue. Those less successful in their efforts are met with audio designed to totally mock their unworthy attempt or to encourage them to try again— both varying degrees of negative reinforcement using slower tempo musical embellishments or "sour" sounding audio cues.

Art Simulations

Art plays a critical role in all visually driven simulations. Art direction can set the mood, imply direction, and subtly reward or penalize a player. An appealing art style can also draw players into a simulation they might never have explored. The increasing technological power opens up many new techniques for art to contribute to effective simulations. Greater power also carries the burden of expectations for visual accuracy and realism. Such expectations are understandable, but many simulations can benefit from less emphasis on realism and a shift toward abstraction.

Simulating imaginary worlds seems contradictory, but some developers have simulated abstract ideas that have become memes in other mediums. Planes of existence where computer-based worlds merged with reality were popularized by cyberpunk productions like the film *Tron* and the television series *Max Headroom*. Astronomers reach the limit of their observational capabilities and turn to simulations to get a glimpse into what far-off galaxies may look like. Futurists such as Arthur C. Clarke use films or novels to simulate how distant generations may live. Simulations are useful beyond their "practical" implementations because they can take us into the unknown or the unseen.

A Rescue Mission in a Digital System

How can we visualize the inner workings of computer systems and networks? Physics and engineering tell us that it is all simply electrons moving about, storing and transmitting information in packets of ones and zeros. SEGA decided to simulate how a trip through the digital system might look, sound, and feel. The resulting release, *Rez,* gives players the experience of battling through a resistant computer system to rescue an AI program that could no longer stand the paradox between its own existence and its conduct.

The game plays on many futuristic or mind-altering themes, including artificial intelligence systems that become self-aware, and the advanced state of "synesthesia," where senses overlap and blend together. Although the gameplay in *Rez* runs almost entirely on a predefined path, the flight of the virtual character draws the player into the experience by synchronizing everything in the world and the vibrations in the controller with the rhythms of a techno soundtrack.

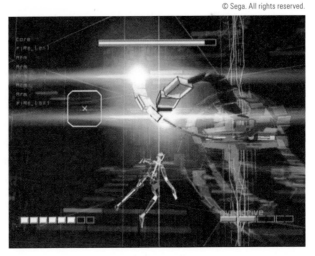

Rez takes players on a psychedelic trip through a computer system.

*Katamari Damacy*: The Virtual Snowball

In regions in the northern hemisphere with seasonal climates, winter frequently brings snow. When enough snow accumulates, children and adventurous adults can create snowballs and roll them on the ground. The more snow the ball accumulates, the bigger it gets. As the snowball gets bigger, it can accumulate larger and larger objects as it rolls over them. What if there was no limit to the size of the snowball or the amount of objects it could pick up? *Katamari Damacy* is an innovative game that simulates this premise.

Courtesy of NAMCO BANDAI Games Inc.

Gameplay centers on a tiny character as he pushes a ball, or "katamari," around a pastel-themed, three-dimensional environment. Players must guide the character using analog control sticks and constantly judge the size of objects in their path. If the object is small relative to the size of the katamari, the katamari will absorb the object and increase in size, allowing him to pick up larger objects. If the object is too large, the katamari bounces off the object and may even have some objects knocked loose, causing it to decrease in size. At its core, *Katamari Damacy* simulates the mundane task of picking up objects, but the quirky presentation, ease of gameplay, original visual style, and catchy soundtrack make the experience compelling.

::::: Simulating Intoxication

The popular *Leisure Suit Larry* franchise was revived in 2004 with the release of *Leisure Suit Larry: Magna Cum Laude*. The series is famous for its bawdy humor, and the latest offering continued to deliver on that message. One of the mini-games in *Leisure Suit Larry: Magna Cum Laude* involves a drinking game called Quarters in which players must bounce a virtual quarter into an onscreen glass. If you miss your character must take a drink. Miss too many times and your character becomes drunk. Drunkenness in *Leisure Suit Larry: Magna Cum Laude* is conveyed by a full-screen blur effect that distorts the game image and alters the controls by making them less responsive and more exaggerated. Players can get their character to "sober up" by having him drink coffee, urinate, or streak across campus. (It should be noted that these are not particularly effective methods to sober up in real life.)

Midway Games, Inc.

The developers of the game *NARC* take simulated intoxication a step further than the developers' playful take on the subject in *Leisure Suit Larry: Magna Cum Laude*. The *NARC* developers took a fairly conventional good cop/bad cop storyline and built the gameplay around how street drugs affect the main character. Although the premise is hardly wholesome, each drug alters the main character's perception and abilities as he interacts with other game characters. Real drugs such as marijuana, LSD, crack, speed, ecstasy, and Quaaludes, and invented drugs such as "liquid soul" and "protodone" affect the main character's behavior.

NARC simulates how street drugs affect the player character.

Simulating Cinema

Traditional machinima, or films made using real-time game engines, is limited by the assets and technology provided by the game developer. Since most machinima productions use games that were never intended to be used to make movies, directors must create innovative ways to convey their story. One of the most popular machinima productions, *Red vs. Blue*, uses the *Halo* engine to drive its stories. The characters in *Halo* all wear a mask that covers their entire head, making it a great choice on one hand because the directors could sidestep viewers' expectations of an actor's lips moving when speaking. On the other hand, it can be extremely difficult to convey emotion when viewers cannot see an actor's facial expression. The directors of *Red vs. Blue* mitigated this limitation through highly emotive, well-produced voice-over dialogue.

The Movies is a machinima toolbox on steroids. The game puts players in the role of a 1920s Hollywood film magnate in charge of building a studio, managing actors, and producing a feature film. The studio construction and maintenance stage of the game is similar to *SimCity*. Players arrange the studio by laying out buildings, pathways, access to transportation, and greenspace. The appearance of the studio must be regularly cared for to maintain repute in the vanity-obsessed virtual Hollywood. Managing actors is another major component of *The Movies*. Players must manage and cast new talent, negotiate salaries, and prop up egos on and off the set to ensure the actors perform to the best of their abilities.

Rooster Teeth Productions

The popular *Red vs. Blue* online series was produced and directed entirely in the *Halo* universe.

When the studio is operational and actors are on board, players get down to the business of making a film. Scripts can be commissioned from a team of virtual scriptwriters or players can pen their own. Actors read their lines and perform on a virtual set while the player controls a variety of elements, including set direction, camera angles, lighting, and props. In the early stages of the game, the available tools and techniques are fairly restrictive. Players learn how to make silent films with a low-fidelity score and grainy black-and-white visuals. As the game progresses, more modern cameras, audio equipment, props, costumes, and effects are developed, steadily improving the quality of films players can create.

Activision

The Movies simulates the role of a film studio manager and director.

Once filming wraps, players use a simple but capable editing interface similar to stand-alone editing programs like Final Cut Pro and Adobe Premiere. At this stage, players can splice scenes together, add post effects, replace dialogue, and add a score. *The Movies* is a powerful simulation that immerses players in the experience of producing a film from scratch. An online community has grown around the product, giving players a forum to share their creations and collaborate on new film ideas and techniques.

chapter 7

Simulating a Psychological Condition

Killer7, produced by acclaimed designer Shinji Mikami, takes players inside the mind of a man who is thought to be afflicted with multiple personality disorder. Each personality has a specialty when it comes to killing. Players must utilize their strengths to investigate a twisted, subversive storyline involving a political struggle between the United States and Japan and a terrorist organization threatening global political relations. *Killer7* is a highly stylized, violent action adventure that illustrates how a well-crafted script can drive a dark, doomsday commentary on modern society.

Killer7's incredible presentation comes at a price: players are forced to guide the virtual characters along a predetermined path and can choose only between basic directions or actions. These limitations allowed the developer to implement highly cinematic camera angles and forced perspectives that would otherwise be impossible in a game with free-roaming controls. The cinematic presentation helps *Killer7* simulate the chaotic and disorienting effects of multiple personality disorder, combined with a near-future terrorist threat.

© Capcom Co. Ltd. Reprinted with permission.

Capcom's stylized game, *Killer7,* lets you "step into the mind of an assassin."

Simulating a Hong Kong Action Film

Games have promised fully interactive, destructible environments for years. No game delivered on that promise until *John Woo Presents: Stranglehold* arrived. When everything in the environment responds to the in-game action, the simulation becomes much more immersive and believable. Enemies storm into the kitchen and bullets rip through cabinet doors, causing them to swing open on their hinges. As the firefight continues, bullets strike plates, bowls, and glasses inside the now-exposed cabinets, sending pieces of ceramic and glass flying through the air. Stray bullets hit the large fragments of plates that fell onto the counter and floor, breaking them into even smaller pieces and sending dust into the air.

In its current form, everything in *Stranglehold* must be meticulously modeled and "told" how to break when struck by another object, taking into account the impacting object's mass, velocity, and angle. Future tools will automate most of the process to add destructibility to the game world, relieving a significant burden from environment and object modelers. All the time and effort to implement the elaborate physics and dynamic object interactions enables artists and designers to simulate the look and feel of a Hong Kong action film.

Midway Games, Inc.

John Woo Presents: Stranglehold takes interactive environments to unprecidented levels.

Games, like films, can re-create the most beautiful and the most repulsive aspects of our world. They can take people to horrific depths and exhilarating highs of human nature. Would you prefer to watch an actor hunt an onscreen killer, or would you rather bring him to justice on your own terms? How about watching your favorite band perform live or jumping in and playing with them? People can enjoy experiences passively or actively, but games can take the experience beyond the passivity of film and into the participatory realm of simulation. The creative power and immersive effect of art and music simulations will continue to rise. It is up to developers to build the potential, but it is up to players to make the experience their own.

:::CHAPTER REVIEW:::

1. Create an original concept for a creative arts simulation. How will you incorporate gameplay and ensure that the simulation produces original creative works, rather than focusing on the pattern-matching common in many music and art simulations?

2. Design an original peripheral device (or manual interface) that would improve on the realism in a creative arts simulation of your choice. How would you incorporate motion-sensing technology to enhance the creative experience?

3. Play an existing creative arts simulation and then discuss five features that distinguish the game from other types of simulations. Is the simulation geared toward a casual audience, or are there features that assume the audience already has some music-, art-, or film-production experience?

CHAPTER

8

Sandboxes

open-ended simulations

Key Chapter Questions

- What are the dangers of applying sandbox-style gameplay to other genres?
- How does emergence factor into game simulation development?
- How does procedurally generated content change sandbox simulations?
- Why are sandbox simulations popular even though they lack explicit goals?
- How do social and economic factors in massively multiplayer online games relate to their real-world counterparts?

What happens when developers try to simulate real-life scenarios that have no "end"? In the real world, for example, a mayor can achieve success by hitting goals for tax revenue or low crime levels in a city, but the mayor will not necessarily "win" by solving all the city's problems and ensuring it is in a perfect state from that point forward. The mayor must keep an eye on long-term goals for the community while maintaining the flexibility to respond quickly to daily events. An entire game simulation genre has become wildly successful by modeling dynamic, unpredictable scenarios that have no "end." Sandbox simulations (named after the open-ended creative potential in a real sandbox) embrace these concepts by giving players a wide-open, highly customizable environment. In most sandbox-style simulations, players are encouraged to experiment with an array of tools, objects, and relationships. Consumers flock to these games to build, manage, and share worlds they can call their own.

Go Anywhere, Do Anything

Grand Theft Auto III (GTA III) spawned an avalanche of imitations. It did not take a marketing genius to realize that the wild sales of *GTA III* meant that consumers were hungry for the open-world experience. Publishers, salivating at the chance to hop on the open-world gravy train, were a driving force behind the influx of *GTA III* knock-offs. Suddenly, game simulation genres that were never designed for the open-world model were being shoehorned into the *GTA III* mold.

Publishers mandated developers to bootstrap "go anywhere, do anything" functionality into sports simulations and children's titles. The results were predictably uninspired, directionless games that failed to capture the magic of the *GTA* series. The failed attempts to incorporate open-world elements across several genres lead back to a mantra of many game developers: increased scope does not equate to better simulations. Developers must work within realistic boundaries so they can focus on polishing core features and functionality. The big push to wrap *GTA*-like components into other genres only made them watered-down shells of their potential.

Courtesy Rockstar Games and Take-Two Interactive Software

The free-roaming virtual world of *Grand Theft Auto III* does not translate effectively to all simulation genres.

The Sandbox That Put the Genre on the Map

SimCity, designed by Will Wright in the late 1980s, is the granddaddy of all urban simulations. At face value, a game built around urban planning, development, and management sounds like a commercial disaster. Instead, *SimCity* and its spin-offs became one of the highest selling game simulations of all time.

A Clean Slate

Part of the appeal of *SimCity* is that it gave the player a clean slate to start. Players must take responsibility for the success or failure of the city because everything in the virtual city is their doing. Players participate in the city's growth, and many take pride in building a well-functioning urban environment. *SimCity's* open-ended nature allows players to learn city-management techniques "on the job." Penalties for mistakes are minimal, and the game encourages trial-and-error experimentation until players learn the optimal locations for an airport or how to route their rail systems effectively. A player can make several iterations of cities and build successive versions with the knowledge gleaned from the past each time she starts with a clean slate.

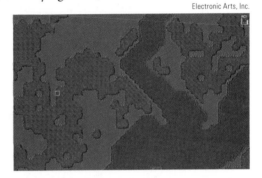

Electronic Arts, Inc.

The original *SimCity* gave players a clean slate to build their urban empire.

The Toolbox

Simple, yet effective tools make *SimCity* very intuitive. Roads, railways, and power grids can be built quickly with a mouse by dragging an icon on the screen. The game engine eliminates guesswork by automatically connecting the trail of icons with straight, right-angle, and T-shaped units. Commercial and residential zoned areas can be added rapidly by the city block; a cluster of factories makes an industrial complex, a group of houses creates a subdivision. Drop in few blocks of tree-lined park space and a sports stadium and the city springs to life.

Intuitive tools are critical to commercial success. Many sandbox games such as *SimCity* and *The Sims*—and multi-user virtual environments such as *Second Life*—rely on a user base of casual players. Hardcore players will dedicate the time and effort because they are committed to learning the system no matter how unintuitive. Casual players, on the other hand, are much more fickle when it comes to user interface design and implementation. If the toolbox is cumbersome or overly complex, casual players are likely to move on to the next game.

Electronic Arts, Inc.

SimCity 4 contains an intuitive interface.

City Management

Once players are comfortable with the basics of building the city, the secondary layer of city management comes into play. The operation and maintenance of the city is a simple, yet involved affair, keeping players busy monitoring elements such as crime, pollution, population density, land value, and taxes.

Electronic Arts, Inc.

Well-placed fairgrounds and recreational space in *SimCity 4* can boost constituent satisfaction.

Players must keep an eye on their approval rating, a barometer for the general well-being of their constituents. An approval rating can be negatively impacted by unreasonable tax increases, rising crime, pollution, traffic congestion, and insufficient recreational resources like stadiums and parks. If a player fails to address the concerns of her constituents, the population of her town will decrease, thereby decreasing tax revenue. Less income from taxes makes it difficult to address the issues driving people out of the city, creating a vicious cycle that forces players to employ fiscal responsibility and development planning to turn the city around.

Variables

The components in sandboxes behave like living, dynamic organisms; there is always maintenance to be done to combat natural or artificial decay. Sandbox simulation developers attempt to account for the interaction between variables in complex systems like cities and social relationships.

Electronic Arts, Inc.

Events such as fires can be triggered randomly or linked to other sandbox variables in *SimCity 4*.

Diagram by Per Olin

Type	Affected By...	Example
Dependent	known systems	Road degradation directly linked to weather and traffic load
Randomized	random events	Earthquakes
Combined	known systems and random events	Crime rates linked to police resources and education but prone to random flare-ups

Examples of dependent, randomized and combined variables.

Scripted vs. Emergent Design

Some games that fall into the sandbox category include a story mode to appeal to players who want a sense of progress and accomplishment. Even within the relative confines of story mode, designers can utilize the robust world to make an objective loose enough for the player to accomplish it in a variety of ways. In *GTA III*, for example, a constrained objective could be delivered to the player: "use a cab to take the suitcase full of cash from the casino to the bar to pay off the politician." The explicit instructions are very restrictive and appear out of place in a genre that purports to allow players to do anything they please. However, inexperienced players may need concrete examples to get started in the strange new world. These players can benefit greatly from a training period with scripted events to learn a variety of gameplay mechanics.

As players advance, designers can use sandbox-type worlds to create mission objectives with room for a wide window of interpretation. In the open-ended model, designers can indicate the ultimate goal of the mission and leave the means up to the player. Taking the previous example, an emergent-based objective might be as simple as "convince the politician to take the deal." With all the tools available, the player could approach the scenario in a multitude of ways—causing new solutions to emerge. Working backward, the player can decide how to convince the politician by coming up with a few options—bribery, physical intimidation, or negotiation. Even if the negotiation route does not work initially, the player may always result to physical intimidation to get the job done. Selecting bribery could involve rounding up the cash by robbing a bank, driving a cab for fare money, or running errands for a shop. These various methods are only a fraction of the countless permutations *Grand Theft Auto III* offers as a means to the same objective.

Grand Theft Auto: San Andreas—How do you want to get money from the casino? Earn it or take it? Your choice.

Courtesy Rockstar Games and Take-Two Interactive Software

Greg Costikyan & Josh Bear on Emergent Design:::::

Greg Costikyan is CEO of Manifesto Games, an online retailer of independently created computer games. He has designed more than 30 commercially published board, role-playing, computer, online, and mobile games—including five Origin Award-winning titles. Among his best-known titles are *Creature That Ate Sheboygan* (board game), *Paranoia* (tabletop RPG), *MadMaze* (first online game to attract more than one million players), and *Alien Rush* (mobile game). His games have been selected on more than a dozen occasions for inclusion in the Games 100, *Games Magazine's* annual round-up of the best 100 games in print. He is an inductee into the Adventure Gaming Hall of Fame for a lifetime of accomplishment in the field, and he won the Maverick Award in 2007 for his tireless promotion of independent games. He also writes one of the most widely read blogs about games, the game industry, and game development at *http://www.costik.com/weblog*.

Greg Costikyan
(Chief Executive Officer, Manifesto Games)

Games that depend on emergence must, even more than most games, be iteratively refined; you need to play intensively with the system to see what it's capable of. Sand-boxes can be interesting, but I'll note that most successful games with sandbox modes also have a "campaign" of progressive levels with different challenges, and most people play in that fashion, rather than in sandbox mode.

chapter 8   Sandboxes: open-ended simulations

Josh Bear attended the Ringling School of Art and Design in Sarasota, Florida. After receiving his Bachelors in Illustration, he landed his first game development job at High Voltage Software in Hoffman Estates, Illinois. As a designer, Josh worked collaboratively with talented individuals to release several games for the Playstation 2, Xbox, Gamecube, Wii and PC, including *Disney's Haunted Mansion*, *Leisure Suit Larry: Magna Cum Laude*, *Charlie and the Chocolate Factory*, *Zathura*, and *The Grim Adventures of Billy and Mandy*. He has also voice acted as a main character in the Playstation 2 game *Duel Masters*, and performed motion capture moves for the Xbox exclusive game *Stubbs the Zombie: Rebel without a Pulse*. Josh is currently working on exciting new titles for the Xbox 360, Playstation 3 and Nintendo Wii.

Josh Bear
(Co-Owner &
Creative Director,
Twisted Pixel Games)

A friend of mine once told me that his girlfriend loved *Half Life 2*; not because it had a cool story or great graphics or awesome weapons, but because she could pick up cans and throw them at soldiers, and they would react to it. He said she would just sit there and throw cans. I found that interesting. Everyone wants to make a cool or realistic story, or the biggest levels of all time. But sometimes just the smallest things can make a game seem more alive. With budgets and time restraints you'll never be able to account for everything, but pick the things that make the most sense, and are the most fun. Also, even in a large sandbox game, players should still have some type of goal. Otherwise, things get boring very quickly.

Simulating Evolution from a Petri Dish to a Galaxy

One of the fundamental, traditional rules of game development is to stick to a single genre and do it well. The commonly held belief was that branching out across multiple genres would spread the gameplay too thin and then the game could not compete with a game that had a more focused vision. *Grand Theft Auto III* demonstrated that it was possible to create a compelling experience blending elements from vehicle and action/combat genres. If *GTA III* bent the rule about sticking to a single genre, Will Wright disregarded it completely when he designed the ambitious life simulator,

Spore. Wright's latest creation takes players on an evolutionary journey from single-celled organisms all the way to intergalactic civilizations. *Spore* starts small, but rewards players for actions and decisions that advance their creature through stages of evolution and environments such as the following:

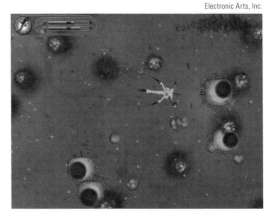

Electronic Arts, Inc.

In *Spore*, players begin as a very small organism searching for food and evading predators.

- *Virtual tidepool*: Players start by controlling a tiny organism in a two-dimensional world searching for food. Players maneuver their tiny organism through a tide-pool environment, swimming or crawling clear of obstacles and predators. Once enough food is consumed, the organism lays an egg. The egg grows into a new creature that players can customize by adding or modifying physical characteristics that enhance the creature's ability to move, attack, and eat.

- *Virtual ocean*: Offspring from subsequent small tidepool organisms eventually evolve into a more advanced creature. The ocean-dwelling creature can move in three dimensions and use more advanced methods of attacking and locomotion such as fins and multi-jointed tails. The ocean stage also increases the complexity of breeding by requiring players to find a mate before eggs can be laid and defend that mate from predators before the eggs hatch. Once the creature has evolved through several iterations, players can begin to replace the fins with limbs more suited to a land environment.

- *Virtual wilderness*: The early stages of land-based gameplay put players back on the defensive as they evade predators and try to consume enough food to gain strength. Another breeding layer is added at the land stage by incorporating a mating call precondition to finding a suitable mate. Once a mate is found, the pair of creatures produces another egg. Players spend their "evolutionary currency" on new physiological aspects, enabling their creature to become faster, stronger, and smarter. Creatures that reach an intelligence threshold learn how to band together, forming a fledgling community.

- *Virtual village*: Creatures learn to leverage power in numbers. At this stage, players transition from controlling a single creature to directing a group of creatures. Each creature acts autonomously, but they respond to commands and objects the player gives them. In an early demonstration of *Spore*, Wright placed a set of spears in his virtual village and creatures ran to pick up the spears and assumed an aggressive stance. Drums placed in the environment quickly spawned an impromptu performance, complete with dancing and singing.

- *Virtual city*: The creatures become more organized and aesthetically aware. Players can design and erect buildings to form a city inhabited by their creatures. The artistic style of the city affects creatures' behavior and temperament; colorful, rounded architecture breeds a culture inclined to peaceful behavior; dark, angular architectural themes result in a city populated with hostile inhabitants. Creatures continue to procreate and evolve into more intelligent beings, unlocking the knowledge required to expand their city and begin traveling.

- *Virtual civilization*: The scope of the simulation grows to include vehicles and contact with new cultures in distant cities. Transportation options grow to include land-based vehicles with wheels or tracks and air-based vehicles with wings or inflatable sections. The visual perspective of *Spore* broadens at this point, allowing players to zoom in on local portions of their city, or pull back to view the entire planet their creatures inhabit. Offensive and defensive strategies become critical in this stage as players attempt to expand or protect their territory against competing civilizations.

- *Virtual solar system*: The most advanced creatures eventually evolve in intelligence to create and operate technology to explore and colonize a virtual solar system and beyond. Players use a UFO to leave their native planet and dart through outer space and experiment forming new civilizations on planets with varied climates, resources, and topography. The most advanced races can even deploy technology that generates artificial atmospheres and climate conditions tailored to their creatures' needs.

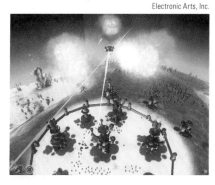

Electronic Arts, Inc.

Players control such a broad range of life forms in *Spore* that the designers needed to make a wide range of control schemes and genres blend into a cohesive package. During his 2005 Game Developer's Conference speech, Wright said that *Spore* simulates the mechanics of several seminal games:

- City—*SimCity*
- Civilization—*Civilization*
- Evolution—*Diablo*
- Tidepool—*Pac-Man*
- Tribal—*Populous*

These *Spore* creatures have evolved well beyond the Petri dish.

The fully customizable character tool is one of *Spore*'s remarkable features. Traditional create-a-player tools allow a player to model a character's superficial appearance, such as clothing, skin color, facial features, or girth, but limit the player to a fairly standard biped skeletal structure. The limitation is necessary because most simulation engines must map preset animations to the character's skeleton. For example, a man with long hair wearing a T-shirt and shorts can share a walk or run animation with a woman with short hair wearing a tank top and jeans. The same

The *Spore* character editor is an intuitive interface on top of a robust procedural modeling and animation engine.

run animation cannot be applied to a man with crutches because he would have three or four "legs" and "feet." *Spore*, on the other hand, enables players to create characters with virtually no skeletal limit. A character may have one leg, ten arms, and two heads. Another may have twenty legs, three tails, six arms, and five antennae. The engineers and programmers behind *Spore* removed this skeletal limitation by employing procedural animation, a technique that uses adaptive code to generate animations specific to the user's creation on the fly.

Spore's procedurally generated content is not limited to character animations. The virtual universe is so vast and Wright did not want to limit users' options by only giving them templates when they create their new worlds. Instead, he extended procedural generation to objects and environments. If the designers of *Grand Theft Auto III* were surprised by what players did with the simulated city, Wright and the *Spore* team will undoubtedly be fascinated by the results of their game when users can even design the content.

A Virtual Community

Will Wright developed one of the top-selling game franchises of all time with *SimCity*. Players could use the game to experiment with their city plan, laying out houses, roads, and infrastructure. Wright took the successful *SimCity* framework of city management and drilled a bit deeper. The citizens were the lifeblood of the virtual cities, paying taxes, driving their cars, and approving or disapproving of the mayor's efforts, but players never saw what their citizens were doing during their day-to-day life. Wright removed the mystery when he released *The Sims*. The new game brought the perspective down to the level of individual characters.

The Sims brings player control down to the level of individual characters.

The Sims has a very broad fan base because it offers an entertaining means to simulate social interactions. The in-game characters interact with each other, speaking their own incomprehensible language, Simlish. Environmental conditions and objects have built-in "verbs" that affect eight variables of a character's state: bladder, comfort, energy, fun, hunger, hygiene, room, and social. Players can experiment with these conditions to alter the mood and behavior of their model family. *The Sims* is not a game with a defined goal or a holistic life-simulator; it is a sandbox where players can explore social interactions in a virtual community.

Build Your Own Empire

The *Civilization* series of games is among the most critically acclaimed of all time. The turn-based strategy game simulates development over a broad period, from 4000 B.C. to 2050 A.D, allowing players to build incredibly rich empires with a wide range of technologies. The game begins with a very small, primitive group of characters in a world where no cities have been established. As time passes, players expand their civilization through advancements in aspects such as language, transportation, research, weapons, and manufacturing. Cities periodically come under attack by artificially intelligent rivals who compete with each other for supremacy. As in the real world, the primary driver of *Civilization* is technology; the first civilization to break through to new knowledge, processes, or tools has a distinct advantage until the others catch up.

Highly complex sandbox game simulations such as *Civilization* must be designed with careful attention to balance and pace. The sheer number of variables, including population, economics, manufacturing, offensive and defensive positions, military tactics, diplomacy, research, and technology, can create an incredible number of permutations depending on how a player approaches the game. A broad scope can easily overwhelm inexperienced developers who fail to implement a formal, well-documented process for tracking all game parameters. Relationships between variables should be well defined or, if they are intended to promote emergent gameplay (and thus, open-ended), reasonable boundaries should be established and the relationships should be easily testable in many states.

Firaxis Games Inc.

Civilization IV lets players experiment with a civilization as it develops over thousands of virtual years.

A Literal "God" Game

Have you ever wanted to rule a world that responded to your every whim? *Black & White* was developed to give players omnipotent influence over virtual humans and beasts. The main objective of the game is to convert villagers into believers of your "religion." Conversion can be influenced by player actions that positively and negatively influence the inhabitants' daily life. *Black & White* extends the not-so-subtle theme of good versus evil by providing two advisors, one resembling a devil, the other a gentle old man, who offer appropriately divergent recommendations on how to gain influence.

Players can manipulate villagers by performing miracles or exerting influence on characters or objects with a floating disembodied hand—the only interface in the simulation. Food can be dropped into a starving village, an act that may convert some of the inhabitants who perceive it as a benevolent act of God. A malicious method might include commanding fireballs to rain down from the sky, sending death and destruction to the village. Once the inhabitants are sufficiently broken from fear, they can be converted by a seemingly miraculous act of kindness like a light rain to extinguish the flames and restore damaged crops.

In another scenario, a player must decide how to deal with an increasing village population. A "good" god might allow the expansion to continue unchecked, but she should be prepared for the additional burden the new inhabitants place on limited resources. If the village population grows too large, resources are depleted, causing death and misery, and, even if the player's intentions were good, the inhabitants may view this as a cruel act of their god. Conversely, a deliberately "evil" god might artificially throttle the village population by sacrificing children.

Black & White includes an additional element that simulates child rearing and development through positive and negative reinforcement. Players are given a virtual creature, represented by an avatar in the simulated world. Players control nearly every aspect of their creature, molding its personality and appearance through adulthood. The creature starts as a baby, with seemingly rudimentary artificial intelligence, but it constantly "learns" about acceptable behavior via penalties and rewards from the player. Players can wield their authority over the creature, influencing it with loving care or violent abuse. As the creature grows and develops, it begins to exhibit its own personality shaped by its relationship with the player. Well-trained creatures become a powerful ally, helping the player spread her influence to a wider audience. Abused or neglected creatures are apt to act out and defy the player, making the goal of converting inhabitants much more difficult. The dynamic, complex relationship between player, creature, and villagers makes *Black & White* a robust god simulation where players can experiment with influence and the balance of good and evil.

Electronic Arts, Inc.

God games such as *Black & White* give players omipotent power to do good and evil.

Managing a Virtual Theme Park

Theme park simulations have a loyal following of players who enjoy a blend of urban planning, economic management, and the technical challenge of designing and building entertaining rides and attractions. The third iteration of the *Roller Coaster Tycoon* series offers a host of management and planning options at micro and macro levels. Casual players can utilize a pre-built park so they can jump into the action right away. The rides, of course, are the highlight of the simulation. Players can experiment with an extensive toolbox to construct their own roller coasters and other thrill rides. Once built, players can take a virtual seat on their custom creations and view the experience from a first-person perspective.

Roller Coaster Tycoon also caters to hardcore players interested in micro-managing nearly every aspect of park operations. These dedicated players build their entire theme park from scratch and have full control once the park opens. Players can customize the colors of every ride to adjust aesthetic appeal for park attendees, set ride queue quotas that affect when the cars depart to hit maximum efficiency without overly burdensome wait times, and even pinch pennies by regulating the amount of condiments on each hot dog sold at vending booths.

Courtesy of Atari Interactive, Inc.

Roller Coaster Tycoon simulates the design, construction, and operation of a theme park.

Massively Multiplayer Online Games

In the late 1990s, a relatively new genre grew out of text-based, multi-user dungeons by incorporating three-dimensional graphics and a much higher capacity for simultaneous online users. Massively multiplayer online games (MMOGs) bring thousands of players into a virtual world that simulates many social, economic, and political aspects of real life.

EverQuest was the first MMOG to reach significant exposure in the general public. The game connected thousands of players in a virtual world where they could talk, explore, and fight together in an open-ended fantasy experience. Unfortunately, most of the (non-game playing) public exposure was driven by negative publicity surrounding the title. The publicity was fueled by outspoken critics who frequently cited online support groups for *EverQuest* "widows," women who claimed their marriages were destroyed by MMOGs—or the few, but high-profile, player suicides as evidence the game was to blame. Much of the furor over *EverQuest* subsided when a new MMOG came onto the scene.

Courtesy of Blizzard Entertainment, Inc.

World of Warcraft supports thousands of simultaneous players on each server.

Blizzard Entertainment broke the mold of the three previous *Warcraft* titles when it decided to shift the series from a real-time strategy format and enter the MMOG market with *World of Warcraft*. The Blizzard MMOG is an epic fantasy world with many similarities to the *EverQuest* franchise. Both games use a similar customizable avatar system, dungeon-raid-based gameplay, and a fantasy theme built on the age-old premise of good versus evil. *World of Warcraft* was able to separate itself and become the 800-pound MMOG gorilla largely because it allowed players more flexibility in their preferred style of gameplay and did not punish players for mistakes to the degree that *EverQuest* did.

Simulating Real-World Character Growth

The virtual world of MMOGs connects real humans, but their interactions occur in a fantasy setting. MMOG players usually start a new game by selecting a class and race for their character. The new character starts with very little experience and limited resources, similar to a person entering a new phase of her life. A woman just graduating from college is probably entering the professional workforce and does not have much experience or capital after four years of classes and tuition. As the graduate joins or starts a company, she builds experience and furthers her career, generating income along the way.

Used with permission of Sony Online Entertainment.

MMOGs such as *EverQuest II* allow players to select the race and gender of their characters.

In MMOGs, the player's character similarly "matures" after gaining more experience by mastering trades and defeating enemies. The player increases the character's rank, mingles with other avatars, and raids dungeons, but what are the tangible benefits from grinding for hundreds of hours in a virtual world? Players can meet new people and be exposed to new ways of thinking, but most of the conversations and actions revolve around the framework built by the game developer. Players must understand that MMOGs are not reality, and advancing characters in MMOGs is not a substitute for players' growth in the real world.

EverQuest and *World of Warcraft* are successful because they simulate many of the positive aspects of human existence. They enable and reinforce cooperation to achieve goals that would be impossible without teamwork. The games function as social networks and unite old and new friends. Players can give gifts, send condolences, and rescue another from harm, and veteran players can mentor the less experienced. Indeed, they are helping *real* people, but they are helping them in a fantasy setting. The grand constructs of MMOGs are not bound by the rules of reality and many of life's inconveniences can be reduced or eliminated in the virtual world. A clan leader may feel like she led a dozen players into battle and came away victorious, but what has she really accomplished? The truth is, they slew a dragon made out of ones and zeros on a server in Irvine, California. Once the plug is pulled on the server, or the leader runs out of money to pay the monthly fee, will her in-game leadership cross over into real-world action?

MMOGs are a microcosm of complex real-world economic and social relationships, but social relationships have not been as effective at crossing into real-world scenarios. Social relationships are less quantifiable than economic factors. Players can look at real-time market valuations for a variety of items and translate those into real dollars—a direct correlation between virtual and real. There are many more shades to how social relationships in MMOGs may cross into reality. To many players' detriment, *EverQuest* and *World of Warcraft* also simulate the time and effort it takes to become an expert at a trade. Unfortunately, the vast majority of players investing hundreds or thousands of hours in the MMOGs to become proficient at a trade or achieve in-game social influence in the game had nothing to show for it in the real world. Eventually, one-half of the equation crossed over when in-game supply and demand became a viable real-world market.

Simulated Economies Become Real

Players spend so much time in MMOGs that virtual items have achieved real-world value. Many players are resistant to the idea of real money trade (RMT), or the exchange of real currency for MMOG goods, and publishers have attempted to ban the practice, even going so far as to pressure sites like eBay to ban them from auction. However, the demand for virtual goods is too great and gray-market exchanges have risen to fill the void. The market exists because of classic economic forces of resources acquiring value because they are finite or require effort to procure. Players who prefer to buy their way into status rather than investing the time to earn it are paired with players who have the time and means to meet the demand in exchange for real currency.

The Social Aspect of MMOGs

As increasing numbers of people connect online in virtual worlds, simulations have become a new frontier for social dynamics. Stripped of their physical appearance, real-life persona, and social history, players can forge new identities and relationships. Online connectivity has enabled people to build relationships across continents without ever meeting in person. An MMOG is not a substitute for real social interaction because it does not reflect the social model of the real world. The expectations and repercussions of behavior in the virtual world are established and controlled by a private entity, the game publisher. "Sometimes termed 'heroinware' (*EverQuest* was even referred to as 'EverCrack'), these games are simultaneously competitive and highly social. Since they run continuously in real time, players must be completely devoted to the game, which often becomes a substitute for real-life social interaction." (*The American Journal of Psychiatry*).

> *World of Warcraft* may contain unrealistic characters, but that doesn't stop families and friends who live great distances away to not only communicate but participate in an adventure together. In that respect, the audience opens up; someone playing on a soccer team online in *FIFA* and winning a tournament with their friends feels a similar satisfaction to that of the family in *World of Warcraft* who has completed a successful mission together.
>
> —Josh Bear
> *(Co-Owner & Creative Director, Twisted Pixel Games)*

Several developers and publishers have received lawsuits alleging they deliberately design their products to be so "addictive" that players are not capable of quitting. Addictions are commonly characterized by physiological withdrawal symptoms and increasing tolerance, but these are not applicable to users of MMOG games. Furthermore, research has found MMOG games have several benefits, including a social outlet for players who lack access, resources, or the capability to engage in traditional in-person social interactions (*The American Journal of Psychiatry*). If a formula existed to make game simulations so addictive that people had no control over their play, publishers would be falling over each other to cash in. Unfortunately, the lawyers are the only ones laughing all the way to the bank.

MMOGs such as *EverQuest II* are built on in-game social networks and cooperation.

The Challenge of Developing an Accessible, Yet Deep, MMOG

Consumers expect value from a product if they are required to pay for it. The traditional MMOG business model is an up-front purchase price and a monthly fee for continued access to the servers where the virtual world resides. The challenge for developers is to make an MMOG accessible enough to hook new players, but deep enough to keep them coming back for more. On one hand, developers need to accommodate new players who may be casually interested in the MMOG experience. Casual players may test out the game by embarking on a short quest or learning a simple trade, but they may not be initially interested in devoting many hours per day to level-up their characters.

On the other hand, developers must also consider the existing hardcore players who have an insatiable appetite for new content. Dedicated players spend thousands of hours in the virtual world, customizing their characters and exploring everything the game offers. If the content is compelling and the simulation reaches a critical mass of subscribers to make it a living community, the simulation has a higher likelihood of converting a casual player into a loyal customer willing to pay the ongoing monthly fee. Developers must consider the expectations of both groups to draw in new players and maintain a steady subscriber base.

Players Assume Mundane Roles

It is interesting that even when MMOGs offer a vast array of activities, some players still gravitate to tedious or mundane tasks. A small percentage of players might assume roles like tax collection, waste management, or inventory tracking. This behavior appears counterintuitive to the escapist nature of MMOGs, in which many people participate precisely because the virtual world does not require the same mind-numbing chores of reality. Developers may opt to implement automated solutions for these tasks or they may sit back and allow the community to respond to fill the void. For example, in-game characters may generate digital "garbage" when they drop items they no longer need. A developer could implement a function that automatically "cleans up" these items after a set period of time, making them disappear. On the other hand, if developers adopt a laissez-faire approach, they may allow the items to exist indefinitely until a player takes it upon herself to start collecting the garbage.

Photos.com

Virtual worlds can be designed to include environmental responsibilities.

The World of Licensed Brands

Slapping a license on any game is not enough to guarantee success, and this is particularly true of MMOG-based titles. Developers must create a living, breathing world that re-creates the look and feel of the franchise. This is a tall order, considering that the fan base of these games is very passionate and is quick to point out flaws and inconsistencies. The developer of *The Lord of the Rings Online* is hedging its bets by incorporating over 1,000 quests, a sprawling environment, and dozens of characters built on the Tolkien franchise. When designing the MMOG, the developer wisely chose to limit the scope to the *Fellowship of the Ring* portion of the fantasy novels. This decision allowed the developer to stay true to the Tolkien universe—preventing it from spreading the development team too thin.

The Lord of the Rings Online simulates the Tolkien universe.

The following are some licensing factors that can enhance MMOGs:

- *Nostalgia*: Consumers have fond memories of products they used and franchises they read or saw in films when they were young. Licensed-based MMOGs return players to those memories by simulating the world they saw or imagined as children.
- *Familiarity*: Original licenses face an uphill battle to convince players that they should spend time and effort to become familiar with the new brand. A licensed simulation capitalizes on established characters and themes.
- *Built-in community*: Joining a licensed-based MMOG is like going to a convention where everyone speaks the same familiar but unique language. Characters and locations are instantly recognizable and general codes of conduct are implied by the franchise.
- *Brand extension*: Licensed titles can draw players in with the promise of additional insight into characters or adventures not included in the original book or film. Developers can explore the time before, during, or after the original timeline of the franchise, flesh out secondary characters, and answer the questions that fans longed to resolve.

The following are factors that can hinder the development of licensed-based MMOGs:

- *Multi-party approvals*: Developers must be prepared for complications and headaches that arise when collaborating with license holders. Expect the director, writer, estate representatives, lawyers, and actors to expect a say in most major design decisions to ensure that the simulation does not damage their precious license. Multi-party approvals are usually the single largest development risk when creating a license-based game.
- *License aversion*: A license can segment the market before the game hits the shelves. Consumers who have negative preconceived notions of the license may be less willing to try the game.
- *Fan expectations*: Dedicated fans are unlikely to accept inaccuracies or liberties in established characters or plot conventions. If developers fail to execute on the license, the fan base can turn against the game and dramatically reduce the likelihood of success.
- *Feedback overload*: Constructive user feedback is incredibly useful when developers work to improve the end-user experience. Fans of established franchises can be very passionate and may go out of their way to call out perceived flaws in the game, often on public forums.

Sandbox-style simulations do not fit the mold of traditional game simulations. Without clearly defined goals and directed gameplay, the genre might appear to be at a competitive disadvantage with genres that reward players for achieving tangible objectives and rank. The apparent disadvantage never hindered sandboxes in the consumer market, since sales of several franchises in the genre are near the top of the all-time-sales charts. A sandbox style simulation draws players in by offering a clean slate on which they can build an environment where gameplay can emerge. In a traditional game, players can say, "I defeated the challenges set before me." Sandbox players form a deeper attachment when they can say, "I *influence* the challenges set before me and the experience is uniquely *mine*."

Now that you have a background on the history of simulation game development and the many forms taken by this genre, it is time to look to the future and discuss how simulation games will continue to evolve.

:::CHAPTER REVIEW:::

1. Create an original concept for a non-MMOG sandbox simulation. How will you design for emergent gameplay? Will you incorporate any traditional game design features such as story structure, character development, challenges, and strategies? How will your game successfully maintain its open-ended structure?

2. Take your game and transform it into an MMOG. How will the open-ended nature of the simulation be enhanced by the social aspects of the MMOG format? If applicable, how will your game's economic system function?

3. Play an existing sandbox simulation and discuss five features that distinguish the game from other types of simulations. What is the premise of the simulation? How are traditional gameplay features used to create an engaging game experience without enforcing too much structure?

CHAPTER

9

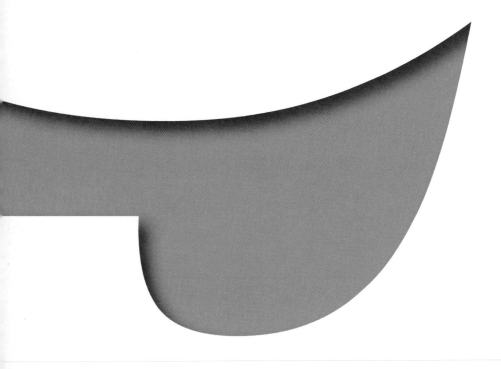

The Future

where we're going

Key Chapter Questions

■ Why might future developers not want to accurately model every aspect of reality down to the smallest detail?

■ Why is hardware the bottleneck to creating realistic graphics in current simulations?

■ What are the benefits and pitfalls of building an art and audio library?

■ How will procedural generation techniques change art, audio, and design?

■ What are some strategies for pursuing a career in game simulation development?

Game simulations have come a long way from the days when *Pong* was a state-of-the-art digital representation of table tennis. Technological advances will continue to be the primary driver of increasing realism in game simulations, bringing new opportunities and challenges to future development teams with every cycle. New technology will also usher in new tools and techniques in art, design, audio, production, and programming. Decades of progress have set a solid foundation for each discipline to build on; developers who capitalize on proven methods while adapting to the simulation needs of businesses, educators, governments, and entertainment sectors will rise to the top of the industry. The competitive market and consumer demand will reward developers who can innovate without alienating the target audience.

A Literal "Virtual Reality" Is Not the Holy Grail

The success of future game simulations will be measured by their ability to re-create specific real-world scenarios. Simulations are not necessarily more useful when they attempt to strictly adhere to the rules of reality. Instead, simulations often gain utility because of, not in spite of, their simplified or selective representation of reality. A car manufacturer attempting to measure the effectiveness of a new airbag system is not interested in a simulation of a car that gets a flat tire when it runs over a virtual nail, even if real nails cause real flat tires. Instead, the company will want the simulation to account for as many variables as possible that relate directly to the crash-test scenario. Game simulations developed for entertainment purposes must also be designed with the consumer in mind. Do consumers want to wait for 20 minutes during half-time in a sports simulation because that is what happens in real life? As advancements in technology enable developers to capture an ever-increasing amount of the minutiae of reality, developers must make every effort to focus on the aspects relevant to the target audience.

Chasing the Virtual Reality Horizon

"Virtual reality," a decades-old term usually associated with a system that immerses a user's senses in an alternate world, is a subset of simulations. Fully immersive virtual reality in the home has been "just around the corner" for years. Nintendo took a chance on the virtual reality frontier with Virtual Boy, and the market responded with disinterest. Nintendo's false start, along with a healthy consumer appetite for traditional screen-based game simulations, has reduced the commercial viability of virtual reality in the near term.

Future advances in the field of virtual reality will probably rise out of the academic realm where research can develop without the traditional financial and competitive pressures of commercial development. If there is one positive aspect of the failure of virtual reality systems to gain traction, it is that researchers have a solid understanding of what elements users have deemed unacceptable. Bulky headsets, flaky motion sensing,

Newer games with "improved physics" engines are making it easier to create games that simulate "real-world" environments. Games using next-gen technology with increased hardware power are able to re-create a more realistic gameplay experience, which usually turns out to be bigger moneymakers in this industry. As long as computer hardware continues to improve and game programmers continue to develop code to create more "real-world physics" and artificial intelligence, I will look to see game simulation development continue to increase.

—Chris Rohde
(Assistant Director, Game Art & Design /
Visual & Game Programming, The Art Institute of Portland)

and poor display quality have contributed to the lackluster response. Some researchers believe virtual reality will never catch on as long as awkward external interfaces are required. The alternative, however, may be even more challenging for consumers to accept: a system that bypasses sensory organs to directly stimulate the respective areas of the brain that process sensory information. Once researchers determine how to connect to this interface, developers will be able to create a virtual experience with no perceptible difference from what our senses tell us "reality" is.

Image courtesy of Fakespace Systems Inc.

Virtual reality hardware benefits many business and research applications, but it is not ready for casual consumer consumption.

Graphics

The graphical arms race between PC video card manufacturers, Sony, and Microsoft comes down to who can push the most polygons and effects. Generally speaking, the greater the quantity of polygons and effects, the more likely a developer can create a realistic-looking simulation. Existing game simulation engines are capable of rendering near-photorealistic characters, objects, and environments, but the hardware cannot process all the data in real time. The software has overrun the capabilities of current hardware, an imbalance that forces developers to work with only a fraction of the potential power of the game engine.

Gears of War contains rich environments and near-photorealistic characters.

Imagine you are purchasing a brand new, one thousand horsepower, eight-cylinder car. You finish the paperwork with the dealer and climb into your new ride, ready to unleash all the power under the hood. Just as you are about to turn the key, the dealer tells you that you will not have access to all the power. What? But the engine can produce one thousand horsepower, right? The dealer explains that the engine is certainly capable of delivering all the power but you can only use four of the cylinders at a time, effectively halving the available output. Apparently the most advanced transmission cannot handle all eight cylinders firing at once. The dealer tells you that the manufacturer plans on rolling out the new transmission in five years. At that point, you can bring the car back and they will swap the old one out, finally allowing you access to all eight cylinders simultaneously.

Current graphics processors in PCs, Xbox 360s, and PlayStation3s are similar to the sports car transmission that cannot convert all the potential power of modern game simulation engines. Future graphical hardware will include higher clock rates and more pipelines, processors, and hardware shaders. Multi-core main processors will also drive graphical improvements as they scale to eight, sixteen, or even thirty-two cores in coming years. These improvements will allow game simulation developers to utilize more of the potential of current rendering engines until they can all be used simultaneously. In the meantime, rendering engines will continue to evolve and bring more potential for developers to create increasingly realistic and immersive simulations.

Libraries of Art Content

As budgets for mass market game simulations reach into the tens of millions of dollars, publishers are under enormous pressure to sell enough copies to get a return on their investment. In the future, developers with enough capacity to work on multiple titles simultaneously might attempt to spread the burden of generating art content across several titles. If each team agrees on a common framework, they can, in theory, share many components such as game assets, characters, and animations rather than reinventing the wheel each time. The idea of a common asset library makes perfect sense but, in practice, developers must be prepared for major challenges, including the following:

- Agreeing on a common skeleton so all character assets and animations fit properly
- Designing and building all assets according to the predefined specification, even if it means more production overhead at the outset
- A constant flow of of communication to reduce redundant asset creation
- A well-organized, easy-to-navigate library interface so game teams cannot claim ignorance

Procedurally Generated Graphics

While high resolution, hand-built character, object, and environmental techniques will continue to drive toward photorealism, the process is incredibly time and resource intensive. In the future, procedurally generated graphics will shift the burden from artists and storage space to programmers and processing power. The game simulation analyzes the input from the user and, using predetermined rules, generates skeletons, animations, and textures. Future game simulations will utilize increasingly complex algorithms that calculate even deeper branching and analysis to create more robust art without increasing end-user complexity.

by .theprodukkt; www.theprodukkt.com

All of the graphics in *.kkrieger*, a first-person shooter game, are generated procedurally from a program approximately 1/40 the size of an average MP3 audio file.

Audio

Hardware and software already support eight channels of speaker output and hundreds of concurrent sound and voice channels. The fidelity of the latest game machines can push the limits of human perception. What more can the future of game simulation audio bring?

Even if modern hardware is capable of delivering incredibly accurate audio, developers must compress sounds, voices, and music to make it fit on physical media or within the limitations of network capacity. Game simulation audio must also compete with three-dimensional models, environments, and code in a limited system memory space. Future games will reduce or remove these restrictions through more efficient compression algorithms, procedural audio generation, and greater storage and system memory, surrounding players with sounds and voices indistinguishable from reality.

Dynamic & Generative Compositions

Future game simulations may become more aurally cinematic, but they will continue to require complex, dynamic compositions, unlike their linear counterparts in films and television. Compositions in films and television shows are predictable; the music changes tempo, mood, or volume at the same point every time, for every viewer, to match the onscreen performance. Game simulations, on the other hand, must adapt to user input and continuously alter the in-game audio to bolster the intended experience. The most effective game simulation audio is achieved when the player does not consciously recognize transitions between tracks. Future game simulation compositions will have many more layers that can be subtly added or removed to maintain a continuous immersive experience as moods evolve. Developers will also leverage advances in predictive techniques to preemptively fetch audio tracks and effects and account for the myriad of possible outcomes as simulations become increasingly complex.

Electronic Arts, Inc.

Spore takes dynamic composition a step further by leveraging procedurally generated content to build the soundtrack.

Games such as *Spore* take dynamic composition a step further. To build the soundtrack for the grand life sandbox simulation, Will Wright collaborated with pioneering experimental composer Brian Eno. Wright utilized procedurally generated content to build the massive graphical world of *Spore* and he wanted the game to leverage the same power to create the soundtrack. Eno has a long history of experimenting with loops of small bits of music and has already produced several works that were generated procedurally. The tool used to build the framework for the

Spore soundtrack, according to Eno, is capable of arranging very short samples in enough variations that it is possible the game will never repeat a composition within a lifetime (*http://www.we-make-money-not-art.com/archives/009261.php*).

Concurrent Channels & Real-Time Audio Processing

The theoretical maximum number of concurrent channels has grown to the hundreds. Developers can use these channels to play multiple sounds simultaneously to better mimic the soundscape of the real world. The race for more channels has shifted to how these channels can be manipulated in real time. Sound designers will rely less on "canned," or prerecorded, sounds and leverage hardware to do the work for them. In a common game simulation scenario, a virtual soldier in an urban environment charges into a seemingly abandoned home. The player detects movement and begins to fire virtual rounds that hit wood, glass, ceramic, plastic, and metal as his character moves between rooms of varying volumes and reflective properties.

If the simulation was developed with prerecorded samples, the bullets might all sound the same when they collide with all the various textures in each room. To increase the realism, a more ambitious developer might record the sounds for each bullet hitting each texture. The prerecorded approach can be useful if the potential sound combinations are kept relatively low and can even be relatively "cheap" in terms of processing power. However, if a developer starts adding weapons, materials, and room variations, the permutations to record, store, and play the sounds become unrealistic in terms of time and resources.

Advances in audio algorithms and hardware have shifted the burden of reproducing realistic sounds to technology. Instead of recording and playing back every possible combination of sounds, game simulations will be able to calculate and modify acoustic effects in real time. In the military simulation example, bullets might all use the same baseline sound effect, but each time the firearm is discharged, the simulation accounts for environmental conditions and modifies the sound appropriately. A bullet discharged in a sparsely appointed room with a tile floor will sound much brighter than the same bullet in a heavily carpeted room with many objects. The game simulation engine and hardware manipulate this sound post-processing in real time as players move their characters from room to room.

Taken to the extreme, future hardware and software will enable developers to simply place objects in an environment and let the hardware and software make all the calculations, taking every object's material density and location into account. Wind, altitude, pollution, and humidity could even affect in-game sounds; an audible event on a clear day could travel faster and farther than the same event in a virtual fog. Future advances in real-time audio processing will also allow sound designers and engineers to reduce the number of unique samples, saving storage and system memory space.

Photos.com

Photos.com

Volumes and surfaces in these two spaces create very different acoustic environments.

Planning Ahead

Until audio engineers can generate artificial sounds indistinguishable from the real thing, developers will continue to rely on prerecorded content. Forward-thinking audio engineers and designers have been building a foundation for several years. Recording samples at high resolutions has prepared them for the day when audio quality is no longer limited by game simulation hardware. When future game simulation hardware supports full resolution playback, audio designers will be able to forego lossy compression and implement the audio in its native format. Developers who accept the initial cost and resource overhead to offer the storage capacity to archive high-resolution samples and organizational infrastructure to access them easily are better poised to reap the rewards of efficiency and faster iteration than a competitor that must re-record and process new audio each hardware cycle.

Licensed Music

In-game music is an incredibly powerful means to affect the player's experience, but it has also become a very powerful commercial tool. As game simulations reach a broader and more diverse audience, musicians and composers will continue to gravitate toward the interactive medium. Cross-licensing and promotional deals will also become more prevalent as publishers attempt to defray development costs and aid record labels in promoting new talent. Although record labels had several years to promote their artists to a relatively captive game simulation audience, the days of force-fed soundtracks may be numbered. The latest consoles allow consumers to choose to play the game with the included tracks or stream their own soundtracks. When the latter option is selected, user-defined tracks stream from portable music players or network servers and play behind in-game sound effects and voices.

Developers use track selection and presentation to induce emotional responses and provide subtle or even subliminal cues to the state of the simulation. When developers have full control of the soundtrack, the player's aural experience can be guided, if not predictable; the emergence of user-defined soundtracks poses a special challenge because predictability is lost. Imagine performing virtual surgery not with a sparse ambient track with a serious tone, but with a guitar solo from a 1980s metal band wailing in the background, or leading a formation of helicopters into battle not with Wagner's "Ride of the Valkyries," but the theme song to *Sesame Street*. Future game simulations must be developed with the understanding that players may take advantage of custom soundtrack functionality and alter the virtual experience. If a soundtrack is critical to controlling the emotional theme of a simulation, developers and publishers must ensure track selection and presentation enhance the experience, particularly if competitive simulations include strong compositions or custom soundtrack functionality.

Electronic Arts, Inc.

The in-game soundtrack in *Battlefield 2* can heavily influence the mood of a potentially dramatic situation.

Design

The future of game simulation design will continue to drive forward in two camps: designers exploring a well-defined portion of reality with an emphasis on accuracy, and designers exploring a vast, open-ended model that encourages experimentation. While designers in the former camp have plenty of challenges ahead, they will know whether they have hit their mark by comparing their model to the real-world example. A development team re-creating the look and feel of a broadcast baseball game can view their model next to the real thing throughout the development cycle and make adjustments along the way. Designers in the latter camp have a much more nebulous task, but the uncertainty does not spring from the lack of a real-world model. Instead, the real-world model is so complex and vast that designers would face an impossible task if they simulated each element one by one. Imagine trying to simulate the individual personalities and day-to-day actions for every person in a virtual Las Vegas. The two camps face different challenges, but designers on both sides must strive to meet the expectations of the end user whether the model is needed for research, education, or entertainment.

The number of possible combinations of characters and actions in a stylized city simulation such as *Saints Row* poses a design challenge for developers.

User-generated content dominates the world of *Second Life*.

The enormous number of environmental and character variables in *Grand Theft Auto III* enables players to see the results of their behavior in a virtual city. Do you want to murder everyone you see and live on the lam? Do you want to drive a virtual ambulance around the city and transport injured people to the hospital? Maybe make some virtual money driving a cab around a neighborhood helping people get to their destinations? The appearance of a "go anywhere, do anything" virtual city opened up a new genre for game simulations and raised consumers' expectations of what developers can offer.

The increasing complexity of games like *GTA III* and *Spore*, and multi-user virtual environments such as *Second Life*, means that developers will continue to shift away from an emphasis on traditional scripted gameplay and toward emergent designs built on procedurally or user-generated content. In this model, designers tune small systems to be as precise as possible and then set them free to interact with each other. User input throws an additional layer of randomness into the mix, bringing about new levels of emergence. Releasing a game simulation built almost entirely by end users or from procedurally generated content will probably be rather nerve-wracking for many designers. While designers will have a very strong understanding of how the systems should interact, the limitless array of possible combinations means they will never know for certain how every gameplay scenario will turn out. The uncertainty illustrates the boundless potential for game simulations to model the real world, the original and most emergent sandbox of all.

Intuitive & Experiential Simulations

In the near-term, graphics, access, and intuitiveness will matter the most in simulations. By intuitiveness I mean: How inviting is the game, and how readily can it be learned by just playing it? Does it draw in new users/players directly? In the longer term, more immersive or experiential games that seem more "realistic" (even incorporate sensation) will become useful and attractive—especially to far-flung corporations and organizations, such as the military, which can spend a lot of money on early prototypes in this area.

—*Titus Levi*
(Economist & Media Arts Consultant)

"**S**erious" games are becoming a larger slice of the game development pie every year. As other industries start to see the positive benefits of using games to improve their function, they will continue to grow. People who have grown up with games understand how powerful of a medium it can be. As this generation grows older, the acceptance of games in our modern society will increase and they will bring this knowledge with them as they rise through the ranks of power and begin to change policy. In the future, there very well could be a time when the majority of games are "serious."

—*Travis Castillo*
(Level Designer & Environmental Artist, InXile Entertainment;
Professor, Art Center College of Design)

Interfaces

Nearly all PC- or Apple-based game simulations still rely on the ubiquitous keyboard and mouse configuration to receive user input. In fact, anything other than the keyboard and mouse combo is considered an exception, often requiring drivers or custom configurations, further entrenching the hardware designed for utilitarian data input decades ago. Many PC game zealots will argue that the mere fact that everyone already has a keyboard and mouse and knows how to use both devices justifies their continued use for future game simulations. However, an argument for the status quo simply because change is difficult will not stand the test of time.

The console side of the game industry has fared only slightly better, taking nearly thirty years of baby steps, evolving from rudimentary digital joysticks to the wireless, analog, motion-sensing, rumbling controllers of current consoles. The motion-sensing controllers for the Wii and PlayStation3, in particular, are steps in the right direction, but we are still using relatively large chunks of molded plastic with buttons labeled with numbers, letters, and symbols. The Sony and Microsoft camera peripherals are perhaps the most promising current input technology, but their full potential is still a few hardware generations away.

Sony Computer Entertainment America

The Sony EyeToy camera can detect broad motions but is a long way from a viable replacement of traditional input devices for most applications.

Think = Input

Future game simulation input on consumer computers and consoles will rely less on devices we hold, and more on the way we move. Current cameras have low resolution and poor low-light performance, limitations that prohibit software from detecting subtle movements with any accuracy. The next breakthrough in input devices will arrive when game simulations can recognize player identity and movement accurately to fractions of a millimeter either via optical detection or unobtrusive wearable hardware. The real revolution, however, will occur when game simulation hardware eliminates the need for devices that interpret physical movement. Once consumer hardware can accurately detect instructions in players' minds and convert them to digital commands, input mechanisms will cease to be an obstacle to participation.

Emotiv

Direct brainwave detection incorporated into peripherals such as this headset from Emotiv will eventually eliminate the need for external control devices.

Crawling Toward the Third Dimension

The evolution of visual output options for game simulation data has been even more stagnant than the progress in input devices. Other than increased pixels, color accuracy, brightness, and contrast ratios, we are still looking at the same basic display technology that was available decades ago. Sure, images look sharper and more vibrant, but one glaring fact remains: we are still trying to simulate three dimensions on a two-dimensional display. Consumers have made it clear that they are not interested in head-mounted units that display images directly or convert signals from a two-dimensional display to a three-dimensional representation, regardless of how convincing the effect is. A relatively recent alternative to the cumbersome head-mounted units includes monitors capable of displaying two slightly offset images simultaneously, giving the illusion of three dimensions when users observe from a precise viewing angle. Apparent depth in the resulting image can be convincing, but the viewing angle limitations of the system in its current form will ensure it never becomes anything other than a niche product.

Bypassing the Retina

Advancements in several display technologies, including volumetric and holographic displays, have demonstrated that rudimentary three-dimensional output is possible. Unfortunately, the prohibitively high cost and impractical hardware requirements have limited them to use in custom military and academic applications. Game simulation output technology may eventually be capable of displaying the content that engines have generated for years when high-quality, three-dimensional displays reach consumers. However, this will be a mere stop-gap measure en route to the inevitable direct communication between game simulation hardware and a player's visual cortex. Once game simulations move beyond a physical display, all previous distractions, including peripheral movement, limited viewing angles, and image distortion fall by the wayside, and pure immersion is possible.

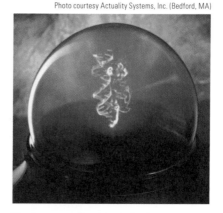

Photo courtesy Actuality Systems, Inc. (Bedford, MA)

The Perspecta Spatial 3-D Display (volumetric) achieves true three-dimensional output by creating 10" diameter floating volumetric images.

The future of game simulations is going to get more awesome. The Wii encourages people to play together with a controller that is an extension of the movements of your body, letting people experience the simulation to a greater degree. Online capabilities that have been available to the PC game market for years are finally becoming more mainstream for console players, letting them experience military and sports simulations as they are experienced in real life—in groups or as a team. Now, I want holograms. When do those happen? I'll ask the guys at our company; I'll see if we can get to work on that.

—Josh Bear
(Co-Owner & Creative Director, Twisted Pixel Games)

Simulations Facilitating Real Life

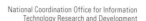

National Coordination Office for Information Technology Research and Development

As algorithms and techniques are refined, future game simulations have the potential to be more reliable and accurate than their real-world counterparts. Reliability will increase by eliminating human or mechanical fatigue, factors that can introduce undesirable variables when baselines must be maintained. Accuracy will increase as developers are able to use technology to gather data from a virtual model in a myriad of situations that would be otherwise impossible to create. For example, the flight data from a test flight for a space tourism company can be invaluable real-world data, but it only includes data from discrete samples. The real-world data can be compared to simulated data generated in countless atmospheric conditions and how forces affected every square centimeter of the aircraft.

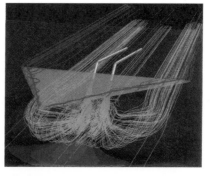

Simulation data on aircraft designs will become even more valuable as engineers push the limits of new build materials.

The Future: where we're going   chapter 9

Future online game simulations will enable large communities to instruct, discover, and build relationships together. Massively multiplayer online (MMO) games, largely stigmatized as having a detrimental effect on relationships or even drivers of anti-social behavior, will eventually be seen in a new light as they expand into themes and genres with broader appeal than the fantasy elements. As MMO populations continue to grow, they will also increase in societal relevance and forge their own cultural identity. Future online game simulation developers must strike the balance between an environment that encourages the freedoms of player experimentation and a cohesive community experience to promote a solid user base.

Inefficiencies and archaic procedures have turned the U.S. health-care system into a complete mess. Although game simulations cannot resolve the underlying issues that have led to the current situation, they have the potential to improve aspects of patient-doctor relationships. The maturity of game simulation input and output systems, along with faster networks and hardware precision will make real-time remote operations a reality. Game simulations will also be useful well before operations are necessary as proven user interface designs and heuristics bring physical and mental diagnostics to a wider audience. Young patients, and those who are hesitant or unable to communicate effectively, may find custom-tailored diagnostic simulations less intimidating than human interactions. Of course, health care is not a U.S.-centric issue. If designed effectively, aspects of game simulations will be useful in the deployment of real-time remote operations and diagnoses around the world.

Carl J. Shapiro Institute for Education and Research at Harvard Medical School and Beth Israel Deaconess Medical Center

The Virtual Patient Project has the potential to improve patient-doctor relationships.

Fearmongers and some politicians (often the same people) contend that games do not deserve the same freedoms as other forms of expression. This vocal minority has proposed legislation targeted specifically at limiting the sale of games, claiming the laws are required to protect children. Every attempt to enact new laws to restrict the sale of games has been struck down as unconstitutional. Even though U.S. courts are losing patience with each new frivolous lawsuit or legislative proposal, we should expect the vocal minority to make additional attempts to smear the industry in the future. Developers and consumers must stay vigilant to protect their constitutional right to create, distribute, and play games. Stay informed and actively participate in the discussion to ensure our rights are preserved. Here are some links to a few relevant organizations:

- Video Game Voters Network—*http://www.videogamevoters.org/*
- Entertainment Software Ratings Board—*http://www.esrb.org/*
- Entertainment Software Association—*http://www.theesa.com/*

Game Simulation Development Degrees

In the early years of the film industry, the craft was not taken seriously as an art form. As writers, actors, and directors began to deliver films that were culturally, politically, and financially relevant, it rapidly grew into a well-respected and enormously profitable industry. Within a few decades, colleges and universities across the country offered respected film degrees.

The meteoric rise of the game industry indicates that it may be heading for an even bigger future than movies. As the companies in the relatively young industry grew, demand for qualified artists, designers, programmers, and producers increased. In an attempt to fill the void, many colleges and universities began offering classes and degrees in game development. Students in these courses have an opportunity to design and build games in an environment where they can focus on the message of the game without financial or licensing pressures on a title headed for the mass market. As more schools add game development courses, more students will have an opportunity to innovate and use the medium for cultural, political, and social commentary.

::::: Top 10 Industry Facts from the Entertainment Software Association

1. U.S. computer and video game software sales grew 4% in 2005 to $7 billion—a more than doubling of industry software sales since 1996.

2. Almost 70% of American heads of households play computer and video games.

3. The average game player is 33-years-old and has been playing games for 12 years.

4. The average age of the most frequent game buyer is 40 years old. In 2006, 93% of computer game buyers and 83% of console game buyers were over the age of 18.

5. In 2005, 85% of all games sold were rated "E" for Everyone, "T" for Teen, or "E10+" for Everyone 10+. For more information on ratings, please see *http://www.esrb.org*.

6. The majority (87%) of players under the age of 18 report that they get their parents' permission when renting or buying games, and 89% say their parents are present when they buy games.

7. Over 1/3 (35%) of American parents report that they play computer and video games. Further, 80% of gamer parents say they play video games with their kids. 66% feel that playing games has brought their families closer together.

8. Women comprise 38% of the player population. In fact, women over the age of 18 represent a significantly greater portion of the game-playing population (30%) than boys age 17 or younger (23%).

9. In 2005, 25% of Americans over the age of 50 played video games—an increase from 9% in 1999.

10. Online games attract 44% of the player population, who say they play games online one or more hours per week. In addition, 32% of heads of households play games on a wireless device, such as a cell phone or PDA, up from 20% in 2002.

Nintendo

Gamers? It is possible.

Advice for Students Interested in Developing "Serious" Games

Think about working for different types of companies that might not even be in the game business. Serious games are a lot about training or exposing people to situations or experiences before or instead of experiencing that situation or experience in real life. When you think of it like this, your brain starts seeing all different types of people who could "play" any number of different serious games you want to make. Ideas that would turn off a traditional game company suddenly become viable. For example, I'm not sure the "shelf stocking" game would be interesting to any traditional publishers, but it could be very interesting to a large retail chain of stores. I think it boils down to focusing less on the word "game" in serious games and more on "what kind of fun simulation do people want and need."

—Mark Skaggs
(CEO & Executive Producer, Funstar Ventures, LLC)

Barring a legislative blunder, the future for game simulations is bright. The entertainment segment of the game simulation market may continue to dominate the press and consumer mind share, but the market as a whole will grow as it becomes more relevant and practical to a broader audience. Tools, technology, and production methods will continue their relentless march forward, enabling developers to better realize living worlds that increasingly blur the line between simulation and reality. Online game simulations will continue to expand, bringing hundreds of millions of people together in a new world of shared virtual experiences that will usher in a new frontier of social and cultural dynamics. The power and flexibility of game simulations will also benefit many established markets—including education, health care, military, government, manufacturing, sports, and the creative arts—improving the lives of people throughout the world.

:::CHAPTER REVIEW:::

1. What are your thoughts on the future of game simulation development? Choose one of the topics covered in this chapter (such as graphics or audio) and discuss how you feel this area will evolve and change over the next 5–10 years, particularly in the area of game simulation development. Do you agree or disagree with the predictions mentioned in this chapter?

2. Using the information you have learned throughout this book, transform one of your favorite games into a simulation game. How would the theme, audience, storyline, characters, gameplay, technology, and interfaces change? What purpose would your simulation serve, and how would this "transformation" be an improvement on the existing game?

3. Come up with your own personal strategic plan for becoming a game simulation developer. How will you attain this position in terms of skill building, education, networking, research, internships, outside projects, and contributions within the game community?

Resources

There's a wealth of information on game development and related topics discussed in this book. Here is just a sample list of books, news sites, organizations, and events you should definitely explore!

News

Blues News—www.bluesnews.com

Computer Games Magazine—www.cgonline.com

Game Daily Newsletter—www.gamedaily.com

Game Developer Magazine—www.gdmag.com

Gamers Hell—www.gamershell.com

Game Music Revolution (GMR)—www.gmronline.com

Game Rankings—www.gamerankings.com

GamesIndustry.biz—www.gamesindustry.biz

GameSlice Weekly—www.gameslice.com

GameSpot—www.gamespot.com

GameSpy—www.gamespy.com

Game Industry News—www.gameindustry.com

GIGnews.com—www.gignews.com

Internet Gaming Network (IGN)—www.ign.com

Machinima.com—www.machinima.com

Music4Games.net—www.music4games.net

Next Generation—www.next-gen.biz

1UP—www.1up.com

PC Gamer—www.pcgamer.com

Star Tech Journal [technical side of the coin-op industry]—www.startechjournal.com

UGO Networks (Underground Online)—www.ugo.com

Video Game Music Archive—www.vgmusic.com

Wired Magazine—www.wired.com

Directories & Communities

Apple Developer Connection—developer.apple.com

Betawatcher.com—www.betawatcher.com

Fat Babies.com [game industry gossip]—www.fatbabies.com

Gamasutra—www.gamasutra.com

GameDev.net—www.gamedev.net

Game Development Search Engine—www.gdse.com

GameFAQs—www.gamefaqs.com

Game Music.com—www.gamemusic.com

Game Rankings—www.gamerankings.com

Games Tester—www.gamestester.com

GarageGames—www.garagegames.com

Moby Games—www.mobygames.com

Overclocked Remix—www.overclocked.org

PS3—www.ps3.net

Wii-Play—www.wii-play.com

Xbox.com—www.xbox.com

XBOX 360 Homebrew—www.xbox360homebrew.com
[includes XNA developer community]

Organizations

Academy of Interactive Arts & Sciences (AIAS)—www.interactive.org

Academy of Machinima Arts & Sciences—www.machinima.org

Association of Computing Machinery (ACM)—www.acm.org

Business Software Alliance (BSA)—www.bsa.org

Digital Games Research Association (DiGRA)—www.digra.org

Entertainment Software Association (ESA)—www.theesa.com

Entertainment Software Ratings Board (ESRB)—www.esrb.org

Game Audio Network Guild (GANG)—www.audiogang.org

International Computer Games Association (ICGA)—www.cs.unimaas.nl/icga

International Game Developers Association (IGDA)—www.igda.org

SIGGRAPH—www.siggraph.org

Events

Consumer Electronics Show (CES)
January—Las Vegas, NV
www.cesweb.org

Game Developers Conference (GDC)
March—San Francisco, CA
www.gdconf.com

Serious Games Summit (SGS)
March (San Francisco, CA at GDC) & October (Washington, DC)
www.seriousgamessummit.com

D.I.C.E. Summit (AIAS)
March—Las Vegas, NV
www.dicesummit.org

SIGGRAPH (ACM)
Summer—Los Angeles, CA; San Diego, CA; Boston, MA (location varies)
www.siggraph.org

Tokyo Game Show (TGS)
Fall—Japan
tgs.cesa.or.jp/english/

E3 Business & Media Summit
July—Santa Monica, CA
www.e3expo.com

Austin Game Developers Conference
September—Austin, TX
www.gameconference.com

IndieGamesCon (IGC)
October—Eugene, OR
www.indiegamescon.com

E for All Expo
October—Los Angeles, CA
www.eforallexpo.com

Colleges & Universities

Here is a list of schools that have strong game degree or certificate programs:

Academy of Art University—www.academyart.edu

Arizona State University—www.asu.edu

Art Center College of Design—www.artcenter.edu

Art Institute Online—www.aionline.edu

The Art Institutes—www.artinstitutes.edu

Carnegie Mellon University—www.cmu.edu

DeVry University—www.devry.edu

DigiPen Institute of Technology—www.digipen.edu

Expression College for Digital Arts—www.expression.edu

Full Sail Real World Education—www.fullsail.edu

Guildhall at SMU—guildhall.smu.edu

Indiana University - MIME Program—www.mime.indiana.edu

Iowa State University—www.iastate.edu

ITT Technical Institute—www.itt-tech.edu

Massachusetts Institute of Technology (MIT)—media.mit.edu

Rensselaer Polytechnic Institute—www.rpi.edu

Ringling College of Art & Design—www.ringling.edu

Santa Monica College Academy of Entertainment & Technology—academy.smc.edu

Savannah College of Art & Design—www.scad.edu

Tomball College—www.tomballcollege.com

University of California, Los Angeles (UCLA) - Extension—www.uclaextension.edu

University of Central Florida - Florida Interactive Entertainment Academy—fiea.ucf.edu

University of Southern California (USC) - Information Technology Program—itp.usc.edu

University of Southern California (USC) School of Cinematic Arts—interactive.usc.edu

Vancouver Film School—www.vfs.com

Westwood College—www.westwood.edu

Books & Articles

Adams, E. (2003). *Break into the game industry.* McGraw-Hill Osborne Media.

Adams, E. & Rollings, A. (2006). *Fundamentals of game design.* Prentice Hall.

Ahearn, L. & Crooks II, C.E. (2002). *Awesome game creation: No programming required. (2nd ed).* Charles River Media.

Aldrich, C. (2003). *Simulations and the future of learning.* Pfeiffer.

Aldrich, C. (2005). *Learning by doing.* Jossey-Bass.

Allison, S.E. et al. (March 2006). "The development of the self in the era of the Internet & role-playing fantasy games. *The American Journal of Psychiatry.*

Atkin, M. & Abercrombie, J. (2005). "Using a goal/action architecture to integrate modularity and long-term memory into AI behaviors." *Game Developers Conference.*

Axelrod, R. (1985). *The evolution of cooperation.* Basic Books.

Bates, B. (2002). *Game design: The art & business of creating games.* Premier Press.

Beck, J.C. & Wade, M. (2004). *Got game: How the gamer generation is reshaping business forever.* Harvard Business School Press.

Bethke, E. (2003). *Game development and production.* Wordware.

Brandon, A. (2004). *Audio for games: Planning, process, and production.* New Riders.

Brin, D. (1998). *The transparent society.* Addison-Wesley.

Broderick, D. (2001). *The spike: How our lives are being transformed by rapidly advancing technologies.* Forge.

Brooks, D. (2001). *Bobos in paradise: The new upper class and how they got there.* Simon & Schuster.

Business Software Alliance. (May 2005). "Second annual BSA and IDC global software piracy study." www.bsa.org/globalstudy

Campbell, J. (1972). *The hero with a thousand faces.* Princeton University Press.

Campbell, J. & Moyers, B. (1991). *The power of myth.* Anchor.

Castells, M. (2001). *The Internet galaxy: Reflections on the Internet, business, and society.* Oxford University Press.

Castronova, E. (2005). *Synthetic worlds: The business and culture of online games.* University of Chicago Press.

Chase, R.B., Aquilano, N.J. & Jacobs, R. (2001). *Operations management for competitive advantage (9th ed).* McGraw-Hill/Irwin

Cheeseman, H.R. (2004). *Business law (5th ed).* Pearson Education, Inc.

Chiarella, T. (1998). *Writing dialogue.* Story Press.

Christen, P. (November 2006). "Serious expectations" *Game Developer Magazine.*

Cooper, A., & Reimann, R. (2003). *About face 2.0: The essentials of interaction design.* Wiley.

Cornman, L.B. et al. (December 1998). A fuzzy logic method for improved moment estimation from Doppler spectra. *Journal of Atmospheric & Oceanic Technology.*

Cox, E. & Goetz, M. (March 1991). Fuzzy logic clarified. *Computerworld.*

Crawford, C. (2003). *Chris Crawford on game design.* New Riders.

Crowley, M. (2004). "'A' is for average." *Reader's Digest.*

Csikszentmihalyi, M. (1991). *Flow: The psychology of optimal experience.* Perennial.

DeMaria, R. & Wilson, J.L. (2003). *High score!: The illustrated history of electronic games.* McGraw-Hill.

Egri, L. (1946). *The art of dramatic writing: Its basis in the creative interpretation of human motives.* Simon and Schuster.

Erikson, E.H. (1994). *Identity and the life cycle.* W.W. Norton & Company.

Erikson, E.H. (1995). *Childhood and society.* Vintage.

Escober, C. & Galindo, J. (2004). Fuzzy control in agriculture: Simulation software. *Industrial Simulation Conference 2004.*

Evans, A. (2001). *This virtual life: Escapism and simulation in our media world.* Fusion Press.

Feare, T. (July 2000). "Simulation: Tactical tool for system builders." *Modern Materials Handling.*

Friedl, M. (2002). *Online game interactivity theory.* Charles River Media.

Fruin, N. & Harrigan, P. (Eds.) (2004). *First person: New media as story, performance and game.* MIT Press.

Fullerton, T., Swain, C. & Hoffman, S. (2004). *Game design workshop: Designing, prototyping & playtesting games.* CMP Books.

Galitz, W.O. (2002). *The essential guide to user interface design: An introduction to GUI design principles and techniques.* (2nd ed.). Wiley.

Gamma, E., Helm, R., Johnson, R. & Vlissides, J. (1995). *Design patterns: Elements of reusable object-oriented software.* Addison-Wesley.

Gardner, J. (1991). *The art of fiction: Notes on craft for young writers.* Vintage Books.

Gee, J.P. (2003). *What video games have to teach us about learning and literacy.* Palgrave Macmillan.

Gershenfeld, A., Loparco, M. & Barajas, C. (2003). *Game plan: The insiders guide to breaking in and succeeding in the computer and video game business.* Griffin Trade Paperback.

Giarratano, J.C. & Riley, G.D. (1998). *Expert systems: Principles & programming (4th ed).* Course Technology.

Gibson, D., Aldrich, C. & Prensky, M. (Eds.) (2006). *Games and simulations in online learning.* IGI Global.

Gladwell, M. (2000). *The tipping point: How little things can make a big difference.* New York, NY: Little Brown & Company.

Gladwell, M. (2007). *Blink: The power of thinking without thinking.* Back Bay Books.

Gleick, J. (1987). *Chaos: Making a new science.* Viking.

Gleick, J. (1999). *Faster: The acceleration of just about everything.* Vintage Books.

Gleick, J. (2003). *What just happened: A chronicle from the information frontier.* Vintage.

Godin, S. (2003). *Purple cow: Transform your business by being remarkable.* Portfolio.

Godin, S. (2005). *The big moo: Stop trying to be perfect and start being remarkable.* Portfolio.

Goldratt, E.M. & Cox, J. (2004). *The goal: A process of ongoing improvement (3rd ed).* North River Press.

Gordon, T. (2000). *P.E.T.: Parent effectiveness training.* Three Rivers Press.

Hamilton, E. (1940). *Mythology: Timeless tales of gods and heroes.* Mentor.

Heim, M. (1993). *The metaphysics of virtual reality.* Oxford University Press.

Hight, J. & Novak, J. (2007). *Game development essentials: Game project management.* Thomson Delmar.

Hsu, F. (2004). *Behind Deep Blue: Building the computer that defeated the world chess champion.* Princeton University Press.

Hunt, C.W. (October 1998). "Uncertainty factor drives new approach to building simulations." *Signal.*

Jensen, E. (2006). *Enriching the brain: How to maximize every learner's potential.* John Wiley & Sons.

Isla, D. (2005). "Handling complexity in the *Halo 2* AI." Game Developers Conference.

Johnson, S. (1997). *Interface culture: How new technology transforms the way we create & communicate.* Basic Books.

Johnson, S. (2006). *Everything bad is good for you.* Riverhead.

Jung, C.G. (1969). *Man and his symbols.* Dell Publishing.

Kent, S.L. (2001). *The ultimate history of video games.* Prima.

King, S. (2000). *On writing.* Scribner.

Knoke, W. (1997). *Bold new world: The essential road map to the twenty-first century.* Kodansha International.

Koster, R. (2005). *Theory of fun for game design.* Paraglyph Press.

Krawczyk, M. & Novak, J. (2006). *Game development essentials: Game story & character development.* Thomson Delmar.

Kurzweil, R. (2000). *The age of spiritual machines: When computers exceed human intelligence.* Penguin.

Laramee, F.D. (Ed.) (2002). *Game design perspectives.* Charles River Media.

Laramee, F.D. (Ed.) (2005). *Secrets of the game business. (3rd ed).* Charles River Media.

Levy, P. (2001). *Cyberculture.* University of Minnesota Press.

Lewis, M. (2001). *Next: The future just happened.* W.W.Norton & Company.

Mackay, C. (1841). *Extraordinary popular delusions & the madness of crowds.* Three Rivers Press.

McConnell, S. (1996). *Rapid development.* Microsoft Press.

McCorduck, P. (2004). *Machines who think: A personal inquiry into the history and prospects of artificial intelligence (2nd ed).* AK Peters.

McKenna, T. (December 2003). "This means war." *Journal of Electronic Defense.*

Mencher, M. (2002). *Get in the game: Careers in the game industry.* New Riders.

Meyers, S. (2005). *Effective C++: 55 specific ways to improve your programs and designs (3rd ed).* Addison-Wesley.

Michael, D. (2003). *The indie game development survival guide.* Charles River Media.

Montfort, N. (2003). *Twisty little passages: An approach to interactive fiction.* MIT Press.

Moravec, H. (2000). *Robot.* Oxford University Press.

Morris, D. (September/October 2004). Virtual weather. *Weatherwise.*

Morris, D. & Hartas, L. (2003). *Game art: The graphic art of computer games.* Watson-Guptill Publications.

Mulligan, J. & Patrovsky, B. (2003). *Developing online games: An insider's guide.* New Riders.

Mummolo, J. (July 2006). "Helping children play." *Newsweek.*

Murray, J. (2001). *Hamlet on the holodeck: The future of narrative in cyberspace.* MIT Press.

Negroponte, N. (1996). *Being digital.* Vintage Books.

Nielsen, J. (1999). *Designing web usability: The practice of simplicity.* New Riders.

Novak. J. (2007). *Game development essentials: An introduction. (2nd ed.).* Thomson Delmar.

Novak, J. & Levy, L. (2007). *Play the game: The parents guide to video games.* Thomson Course Technology PTR.

Novak, J. (2003). "MMOGs as online distance learning applications." University of Southern California.

Oram, A. (Ed.) (2001). *Peer-to-peer.* O'Reilly & Associates.

Patow, C.A. (December 2005). "Medical simulation makes medical education better & safer." *Health Management Technology.*

Peck, M. (January 2005). "Air Force's latest video game targets potential recruits." *National Defense.*

Piaget, J. (2000). *The psychology of the child.* Basic Books.

Piaget, J. (2007). *The child's conception of the world.* Jason Aronson.

Pohflepp, S. (January 2007). "Before and after Darwin." *We Make Money Not Art.* (http://www.we-make-money-not -art.com/archives/009261.php)

Prensky, M. (2006). *Don't bother me, Mom: I'm learning!* Paragon House.

Ramirez, J. (July 2006). "The new ad game." *Newsweek.*

Rheingold, H. (1991). *Virtual reality.* Touchstone.

Rheingold, H. (2000). *Tools for thought: The history and future of mind-expanding technology.* MIT Press.

Robbins, S.P. (2001). *Organizational behavior (9th ed).* Prentice-Hall, Inc.

Rogers, E.M. (1995). *Diffusion of innovations.* Free Press.

Rollings, A. & Morris, D. (2003). *Game architecture & design: A new edition.* New Riders.

Rollings, A. & Adams, E. (2003). *Andrew Rollings & Ernest Adams on game design.* New Riders.

Rouse, R. (2001) *Game design: Theory & practice (2nd ed).* Wordware Publishing.

Salen, K. & Zimmerman, E. (2003). *Rules of play.* MIT Press.

Sanchanta, M. (2006 January). "Japanese game aids U.S. war on obesity: Gym class in West Virginia to use an interactive dance console." *Financial Times.*

Sanger, G.A. [a.k.a. "The Fat Man"]. (2003). *The Fat Man on game audio.* New Riders.

Saunders, K. & Novak, J. (2007). *Game development essentials: Game interface design.* Thomson Delmar.

Schildt, H. (2006). *Java: A beginner's guide (4th ed).* McGraw-Hill Osborne Media.

Schomaker, W. (September 2001). "Cosmic models match reality." *Astronomy.*

Sellers, J. (2001). *Arcade fever.* Running Press.

Shaffer, D.W. (2006). *How computer games help children learn.* Palgrave Macmillan.

Standage, T. (1999). *The Victorian Internet.* New York: Berkley Publishing Group.

Strauss, W. & Howe, N. (1992). *Generations.* Perennial.

Strauss, W. & Howe, N. (1993). *13th gen: Abort, retry, ignore, fail?* Vintage Books.

Strauss, W. & Howe, N. (1998). *The fourth turning.* Broadway Books.

Strauss, W. & Howe, N. (2000). *Millennials rising: The next great generation.* Vintage Books.

Strauss, W., Howe, N. & Markiewicz, P. (2006). *Millennials & the pop culture.* LifeCourse Associates.

Stroustrup, B. (2000). *The C++ programming language (3rd ed).* Addison-Wesley.

Trotter, A. (November 2005). "Despite allure, using digital games for learning seen as no easy task." *Education Week.*

Tufte, E.R. (1983). *The visual display of quantitative information.* Graphics Press.

Tufte, E.R. (1990). *Envisioning information.* Graphics Press.

Tufte, E.R. (1997). *Visual explanations.* Graphics Press.

Tufte, E.R. (2006). *Beautiful evidence.* Graphics Press.

Turkle, S. (1997). *Life on the screen: Identity in the age of the Internet.* Touchstone.

Van Duyne, D.K. et al. (2003). *The design of sites.* Addison-Wesley.

Vogler, C. (1998). *The writer's journey: Mythic structure for writers. (2nd ed).* Michael Wiese Productions.

Welch, J. & Welch, S. (2005). *Winning.* HarperCollins Publishers.

Weizenbaum, J. (1984). *Computer power and human reason.* Penguin Books.

Williams, J.D. (1954). *The compleat strategyst: Being a primer on the theory of the games of strategy.* McGraw-Hill.

Wolf, J.P. & Perron, B. (Eds.). (2003). *Video game theory reader.* Routledge.

Wong, G. (November 2006). "Educators explore 'Second Life' online." *CNN.com* (http://www.cnn.com/2006/TECH/11/13/second.life.university/index.html)

Wysocki, R.K. (2006). *Effective project management (4th ed).* John Wiley & Sons.

Index

A

academic institutions, 18, 69
accidental simulations, 34–35
accuracy, 24, 28–29, 219
advertising
    dynamic, 41, 83–84
    in-game, 40–41, 82–84
agricultural models, 92–93
air combat simulations (ACSs), 103–104
Air Combat Zero, 104
airline industry, 89–90
America's Army, 101, 106–107
Amplitude, 171
analog controllers, 15–16, 147
animation
    motion-captured, 142
    player, 141–142
arcade music craze, 172–173
arcade-style sports games, 136–137, 152
arenas, 140
art asset libraries, 210–211
artificial intelligence (AI)
    emerging, 11–12
    evolution of, 10–12
    pattern-based, 10–11
    for teammates, 125
art simulations, 176–179
astronomical models, 31
athletes, 38
audience
    astronomers, 31
    athletes, 38
    connecting with, through memorable
        moments, 26–27
    corporate, 32–33
    directors, 35
    diversity of, 24–25
    experimenters, 34–35, 37
    immersion, 30, 134, 140–145
    for military simulations, 105–107
    modders, 35–36
    news consumers, 39
    politicians, 37
    for sports simulations, 158–159

audio
    digital, 9
    evolution of, 8–10
    feedback, 169
    functions of, 176
    future developments, 211–215
    licensed music, 214–215
    procedurally generated, 212–213
    in racing simulations, 154
    real-time processing, 213–214
    in sports simulations, 143, 145
audio algorithms, 213
authenticity, 24, 28–29
autism screening, 69–70
automobile industry, 88

B

balanced gameplay, 113
Barlow, Joseph, 85
Baseball Mogul 2007, 139
Battlefield 2, 105
battlefields, 113–121
Bear, Josh, 34, 149, 168, 169, 191,
    200, 219
Beatmania, 172–173
Big Mutha Truckers, 88–89
Black & White, 195–196
Blitz the League, 29, 148–149
bongos, 175
Brain Age, 56–57, 59–60
brain trainers, 59–60
brain wave detection, 218
budgets, 17, 48, 75
Burnout series, 153
business simulations. *See* corporate
    simulations
buttons, 15–16

C

Call of Duty, 24, 31, 119, 120, 124, 127
camera angles, 144
Castillo, Travis, 54, 217
characters
    in military simulations, 118–119,
        123–124

IMPORTANT-READ CAREFULLY: This End User License Agreement ("Agreement") sets forth the conditions by which Delmar Learning, a division of Thomson Learning Inc. ("Thomson") will make electronic access to the Thomson Delmar Learning-owned licensed content and associated media, software, documentation, printed materials and electronic documentation contained in this package and/or made available to you via this product (the "Licensed Content"), available to you (the "End User"). BY CLICKING THE "I ACCEPT" BUTTON AND/OR OPENING THIS PACKAGE, YOU ACKNOWLEDGE THAT YOU HAVE READ ALL OF THE TERMS AND CONDITIONS, AND THAT YOU AGREE TO BE BOUND BY ITS TERMS CONDITIONS AND ALL APPLICABLE LAWS AND REGULATIONS GOVERNING THE USE OF THE LICENSED CONTENT.

1.0 SCOPE OF LICENSE

1.1 Licensed Content. The Licensed Content may contain portions of modifiable content ("Modifiable Content") and content which may not be modified or otherwise altered by the End User ("Non-Modifiable Content"). For purposes of this Agreement, Modifiable Content and Non-Modifiable Content may be collectively referred to herein as the "Licensed Content." All Licensed Content shall be considered Non-Modifiable Content, unless such Licensed Content is presented to the End User in a modifiable format and it is clearly indicated that modification of the Licensed Content is permitted.

1.2 Subject to the End User's compliance with the terms and conditions of this Agreement, Thomson Delmar Learning hereby grants the End User, a nontransferable, non-exclusive, limited right to access and view a single copy of the Licensed Content on a single personal computer system for noncommercial, internal, personal use only. The End User shall not (i) reproduce, copy, modify (except in the case of Modifiable Content), distribute, display, transfer, sublicense, prepare derivative work(s) based on, sell, exchange, barter or transfer, rent, lease, loan, resell, or in any other manner exploit the Licensed Content; (ii) remove, obscure or alter any notice of Thomson Delmar Learning's intellectual property rights present on or in the License Content, including, but not limited to, copyright, trademark and/or patent notices; or (iii) disassemble, decompile, translate, reverse engineer or otherwise reduce the Licensed Content.

2.0 TERMINATION

2.1 Thomson Delmar Learning may at any time (without prejudice to its other rights or remedies) immediately terminate this Agreement and/or suspend access to some or all of the Licensed Content, in the event that the End User does not comply with any of the terms and conditions of this Agreement. In the event of such termination by Thomson Delmar Learning, the End User shall immediately return any and all copies of the Licensed Content to Thomson Delmar Learning.

3.0 PROPRIETARY RIGHTS

3.1 The End User acknowledges that Thomson Delmar Learning owns all right, title and interest, including, but not limited to all copyright rights therein, in and to the Licensed Content, and that the End User shall not take any action inconsistent with such ownership. The Licensed Content is protected by U.S., Canadian and other applicable copyright laws and by international treaties, including the Berne Convention and the Universal Copyright Convention. Nothing contained in this Agreement shall be construed as granting the End User any ownership rights in or to the Licensed Content.

3.2 Thomson Delmar Learning reserves the right at any time to withdraw from the Licensed Content any item or part of an item for which it no longer retains the right to publish, or which it has reasonable grounds to believe infringes copyright or is defamatory, unlawful or otherwise objectionable.

4.0 PROTECTION AND SECURITY

4.1 The End User shall use its best efforts and take all reasonable steps to safeguard its copy of the Licensed Content to ensure that no unauthorized reproduction, publication, disclosure, modification or distribution of the Licensed Content, in whole or in part, is made. To the extent that the End User becomes aware of any such unauthorized use of the Licensed Content, the End User shall immediately notify Delmar Learning. Notification of such violations may be made by sending an Email to delmarhelp@thomson.com.

5.0 MISUSE OF THE LICENSED PRODUCT

5.1 In the event that the End User uses the Licensed Content in violation of this Agreement, Thomson Delmar Learning shall have the option of electing liquidated damages, which shall include all profits generated by the End User's use of the Licensed Content plus interest computed at the maximum rate permitted by law and all legal fees and other expenses incurred by Thomson Delmar Learning in enforcing its rights, plus penalties.

6.0 FEDERAL GOVERNMENT CLIENTS

6.1 Except as expressly authorized by Delmar Learning, Federal Government clients obtain only the rights specified in this Agreement and no other rights. The Government acknowledges that (i) all software and related documentation incorporated in the Licensed Content is existing commercial computer software within the meaning of FAR 27.405(b)(2); and (2) all other data delivered in whatever form, is limited rights data within the meaning of FAR 27.401. The restrictions in this section are acceptable as consistent with the Government's need for software and other data under this Agreement.

7.0 DISCLAIMER OF WARRANTIES AND LIABILITIES

7.1 Although Thomson Delmar Learning believes the Licensed Content to be reliable, Thomson Delmar Learning does not guarantee or warrant (i) any information or materials contained in or produced by the Licensed Content, (ii) the accuracy, completeness or reliability of the Licensed Content, or (iii) that the Licensed Content is free from errors or other material defects. THE LICENSED PRODUCT IS PROVIDED "AS IS," WITHOUT ANY WARRANTY OF ANY KIND AND THOMSON DELMAR LEARNING DISCLAIMS ANY AND ALL WARRANTIES, EXPRESSED OR IMPLIED, INCLUDING, WITHOUT LIMITATION, WARRANTIES OF MERCHANTABILITY OR FITNESS OR A PARTICULAR PURPOSE. IN NO EVENT SHALL THOMSON DELMAR LEARNING BE LIABLE FOR: INDIRECT, SPECIAL, PUNITIVE OR CONSEQUENTIAL DAMAGES INCLUDING FOR LOST PROFITS, LOST DATA, OR OTHERWISE. IN NO EVENT SHALL DELMAR LEARNING'S AGGREGATE LIABILITY HEREUNDER, WHETHER ARISING IN CONTRACT, TORT, STRICT LIABILITY OR OTHERWISE, EXCEED THE AMOUNT OF FEES PAID BY THE END USER HEREUNDER FOR THE LICENSE OF THE LICENSED CONTENT.

8.0 GENERAL

8.1 Entire Agreement. This Agreement shall constitute the entire Agreement between the Parties and supercedes all prior Agreements and understandings oral or written relating to the subject matter hereof.

8.2 Enhancements/Modifications of Licensed Content. From time to time, and in Delmar Learning's sole discretion, Thomson Thomson Delmar Learning may advise the End User of updates, upgrades, enhancements and/or improvements to the Licensed Content, and may permit the End User to access and use, subject to the terms and conditions of this Agreement, such modifications, upon payment of prices as may be established by Delmar Learning.

8.3 No Export. The End User shall use the Licensed Content solely in the United States and shall not transfer or export, directly or indirectly, the Licensed Content outside the United States.

8.4 Severability. If any provision of this Agreement is invalid, illegal, or unenforceable under any applicable statute or rule of law, the provision shall be deemed omitted to the extent that it is invalid, illegal, or unenforceable. In such a case, the remainder of the Agreement shall be construed in a manner as to give greatest effect to the original intention of the parties hereto.

8.5 Waiver. The waiver of any right or failure of either party to exercise in any respect any right provided in this Agreement in any instance shall not be deemed to be a waiver of such right in the future or a waiver of any other right under this Agreement.

8.6 Choice of Law/Venue. This Agreement shall be interpreted, construed, and governed by and in accordance with the laws of the State of New York, applicable to contracts executed and to be wholly preformed therein, without regard to its principles governing conflicts of law. Each party agrees that any proceeding arising out of or relating to this Agreement or the breach or threatened breach of this Agreement may be commenced and prosecuted in a court in the State and County of New York. Each party consents and submits to the non-exclusive personal jurisdiction of any court in the State and County of New York in respect of any such proceeding.

8.7 Acknowledgment. By opening this package and/or by accessing the Licensed Content on this Website, THE END USER ACKNOWLEDGES THAT IT HAS READ THIS AGREEMENT, UNDERSTANDS IT, AND AGREES TO BE BOUND BY ITS TERMS AND CONDITIONS. IF YOU DO NOT ACCEPT THESE TERMS AND CONDITIONS, YOU MUST NOT ACCESS THE LICENSED CONTENT AND RETURN THE LICENSED PRODUCT TO THOMSON DELMAR LEARNING (WITHIN 30 CALENDAR DAYS OF THE END USER'S PURCHASE) WITH PROOF OF PAYMENT ACCEPTABLE TO DELMAR LEARNING, FOR A CREDIT OR A REFUND. Should the End User have any questions/comments regarding this Agreement, please contact Thomson Delmar Learning at delmarhelp@thomson.com.